CHEDDAR
THROUGH TIME

Andrew Pickering
& Nicola Foster

AMBERLEY PUBLISHING

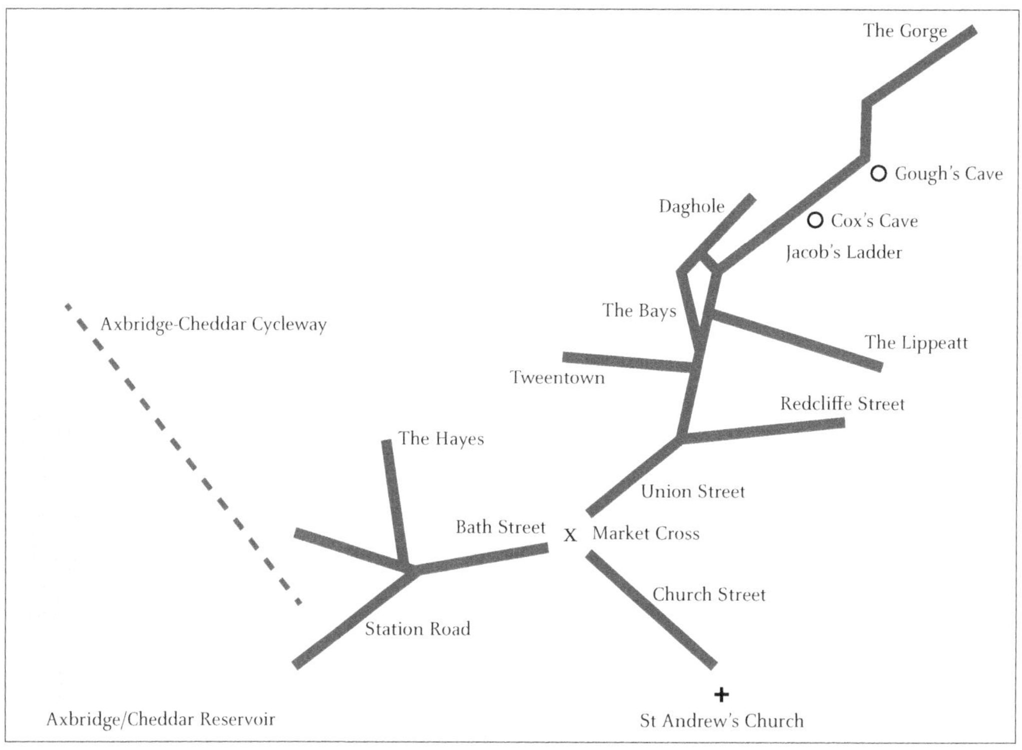

First published 2011

Amberley Publishing
The Hill, Stroud
Gloucestershire, GL5 4EP

www.amberley-books.com

ISBN 978 1 4456 0053 6

British Library Cataloguing in Publication Data.
A catalogue record for this book is available from the British Library.

Typeset in 9.5pt on 12pt Celeste.
Typesetting by Amberley Publishing.
Printed in the UK.

Introduction

'For most people Cheddar means the three C's: Caves, Cliffs and Cheese.
To these might be added Church and Cross.'
Coysh A. W., Mason E. J., Waite V. (1954) *The Mendips*, Robert Hale, p. 169

At the start of the twentieth century, the period from which many of the photographs in this collection date, Cheddar had a population of around 2,000. Well placed between the limestone hills to the north and the marshes to the south, the village had several industries including quarrying, paper-making and the manufacturing of shirts. Paper-making at Cheddar, exploiting pure Mendip spring water, dated from 1765. The railway, now dismantled, was hugely important for carrying raw materials, goods and produce in and out of the village. Electricity was provided by a gasometer, which provided the lighting for the famous caves close by. The chief crops in the area were wheat, oats, barley, beans, peas, potatoes and fine strawberries. Plenty of Somerset cider has long been available in the vicinity of Cheddar. The sparkling, 'champagne', cider made by the Sealeys at nearby Rodney Stoke was dubbed 'the Wine of Wessex'. It was produced using traditional apple varieties, including Kingston Blacks, White Jerseys, and Tom Tanners, as well as Herbert Harry Sealey's own graft – 'Stoke Reds'. By the end of the twentieth century, the major players in the cider industry, such as the Shepton Mallet-based company Showerings, had absorbed most of the independent producers, including Sealeys, and most of the apple juice for their cider was imported from France. However, in recent years companies such as Thatchers have revived an interest in beverages derived from locally grown English apple varieties.

By the middle of the twentieth century, the initiatives of two local entrepreneurial families over the last half century – the Goughs and the Coxes – had reconfigured Cheddar's social and economic landscape:

'They still make cheese at Cheddar, but it is not now their sole occupation, for, alas, the town now specialises in tourist-luring and souvenir-selling, and the narrow road to the gorge is bristling with cafes, bric-a-brac shops, touters, and notices, and so chock-a-block with vehicles of every description, and sightseers of every type, that to reach the gorge at all is a physical struggle.'
Ruth Manning-Sanders (1949), *The West of England*, Batsford, p. 133.

However, the Cheddar tourist is not an invention of modern times. The earliest sightseeing reference for Cheddar dates from 1130 when Henry, the Archdeacon of Huntington, described its caves, long before the discovery of the extent of Gough's and Cox's caverns, as 'under the ground which were like great halls or rooms'. Subsequent visitors included Daniel Defoe, who wrote a detailed commentary on the communal cheese-making process.

These days, now that the railway has gone, tourists are most likely to start their excursion in the gorge itself, having parked in one of the parking bays in the vicinity of Gough's or Cox's caves. The narrow road has been widened and, although it can still be a very busy place, it is well worth taking the time to visit both the gorge and the fascinating village that lies at its foot. In addition to its cliffs, caves and cheese, Cheddar has its industrial and agricultural heritage and a rich social history, not least in relation to its many churches and schools.

This collection of archive and modern photographs introduces many of the village's most interesting sites, some long celebrated as major tourist attractions, others less well known but of great interest to inquisitive visitors and locals alike. Starting in the gorge above Gough's Cave and ending at the Axbridge Reservoir, this book can be used as a practical guide through Cheddar's busy highways and haunted byways.

Acknowledgements

Andrew Pickering: text and contemporary photographs. Nicola Foster: picture research and contemporary photographs.

The compiling of this book would not have been possible without the great generosity of a number of past and present residents of Cheddar who were willing to loan us their remarkable collections of photographs and associated memorabilia, and to share their extensive knowledge of the life of the village over the last 150 years. In particular, the authors extend their thanks to Hugh Alsop, Vera Bancroft, Mark Bailey, Mr Brice, Anne Carney, Irene Gray, Audrey Hill, Terri King, Brooke McCarthy, Richard O'Conner, Brian Savill, Hazel Southall, Chris Simms, Gill Scard, Jackie Skidmore and Rex Thomas. Thanks also to the Bath Arms, Cheddar Bridge Touring Park, Cheddar First School, Cheddar Gorge Cheese Company, Cheddar Fire Brigade, Cheddar Post Office, Gough's Caves, Fairlands Middle School, Kings of Wessex Community School, St Andrew's Church, Cheddar Brownies and the Strawberry Special (Draycott).

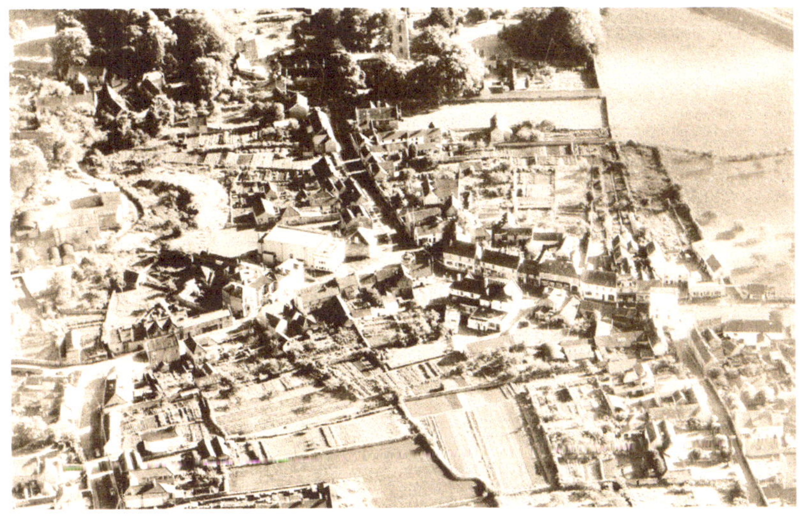

Aerial Views of Cheddar, Then and Now

The large white building in the earlier of the two photographs is the Regal Cinema, which was built in 1939. From the Market Cross in front of it, the heart of the village of Cheddar, radiate Union Street to the left (east), Bath Street to the right (west), and Church Street beyond (south). St Andrew's church can be seen towards the top of the picture. There is plenty of evidence of cultivation on allotments in open spaces now largely built over. In the foreground of the colour photograph can be seen Cheddar's community school – the Kings of Wessex School – which occupies the site of what was formerly Manor Farm. Beyond the modern buildings stand the ruins of a fourteenth century chapel and archaeologists discovered the remains of a Saxon 'palace' in the space between, now defined by concrete markers. Running along the bottom edge of the photograph is the old railway line, the Strawberry Line, now used as a cycle way linking Cheddar and Axbridge. Cheddar Gorge begins in the right-hand corner of the picture and the observation tower at the top of Jacob's Ladder can be seen on the edge of the photograph.

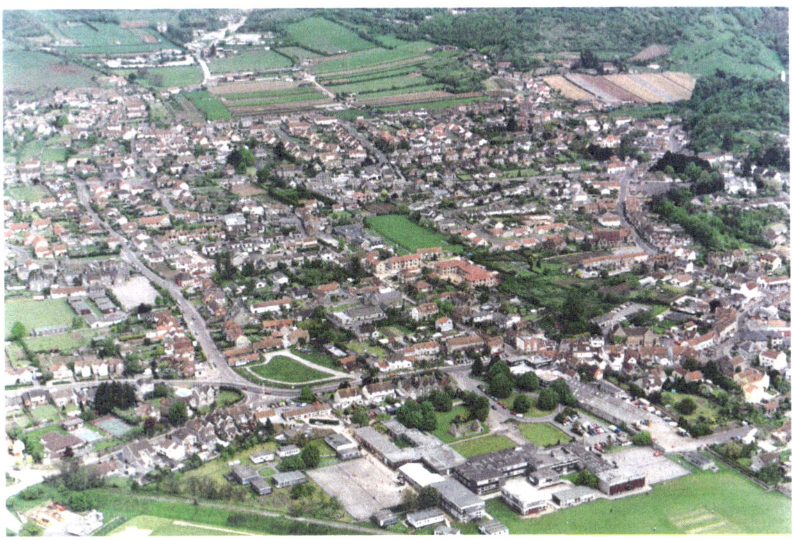

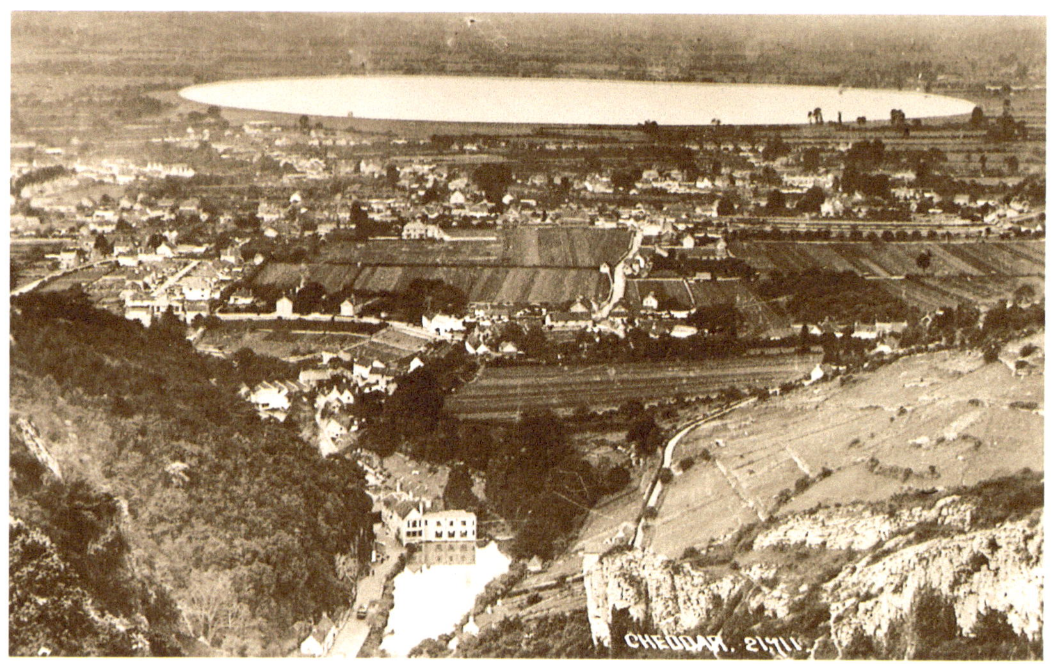

Views of Cheddar from the North Rim of the Gorge

The earlier of the two images shows empty spaces in the middle distance, which are now largely filled with residential building. In the foreground stands the Cliff Hotel (Cox's Mill Hotel) below its own manmade lake, which provided power in the days when it operated as a corn mill. In the early eighteenth century, the River Yeo, fed by nine springs in the gorge, powered twelve mills; by the end of the eighteenth century this had reduced to four corn mills and three paper mills. The great Cheddar reservoir, then as now, dominates the landscape from this high vantage point.

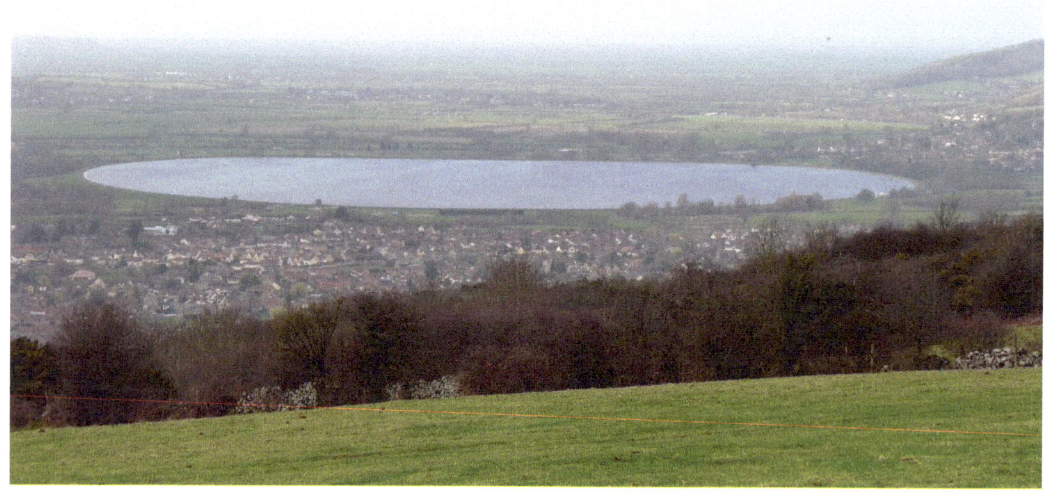

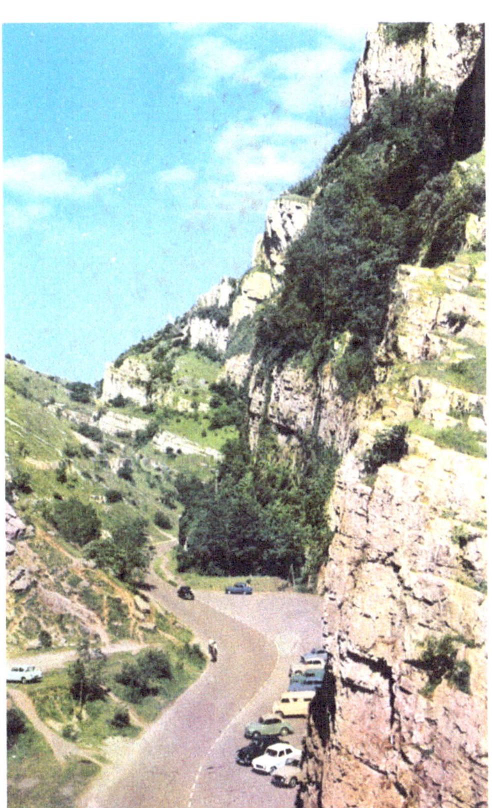

The Cliffs of Cheddar Gorge

The cliffs of Cheddar Gorge are as striking from above as below. They attract thousands of tourists from all over the world each year but comparatively few manage to climb one of the surrounding hills to gain views such as these.

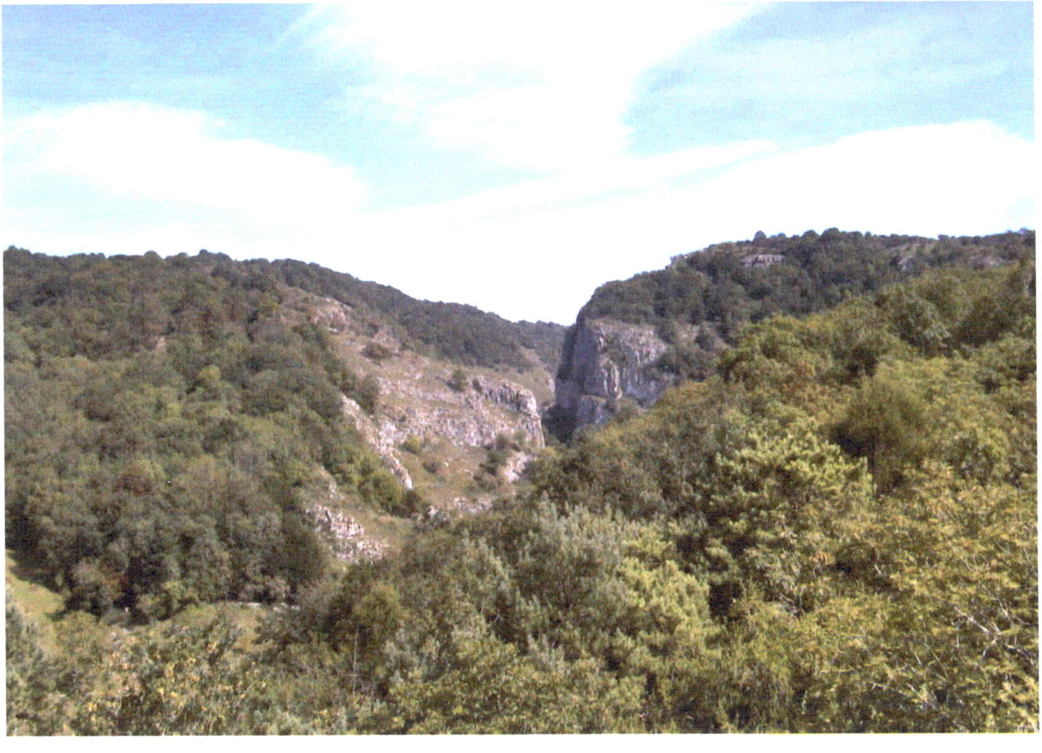

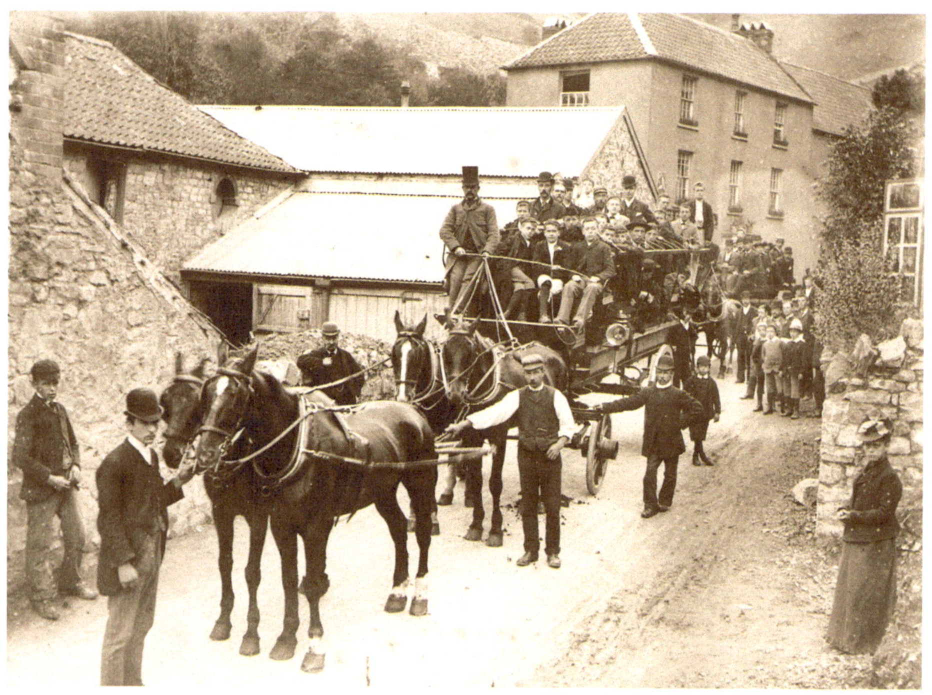

Travel to Cheddar

A hundred years ago, most visitors to Cheddar would have arrived by train and disembarked at Cheddar Station a couple of miles to the south-west of the gorge. From here the short journey to the famous caves would be on foot or, as in the picture shown, in some form of horse-drawn conveyance. These days, now that the railway is closed, most visitors arrive by car or coach and start their visit from one of the many roadside parking bays located along both sides of the gorge directly to the north of the village.

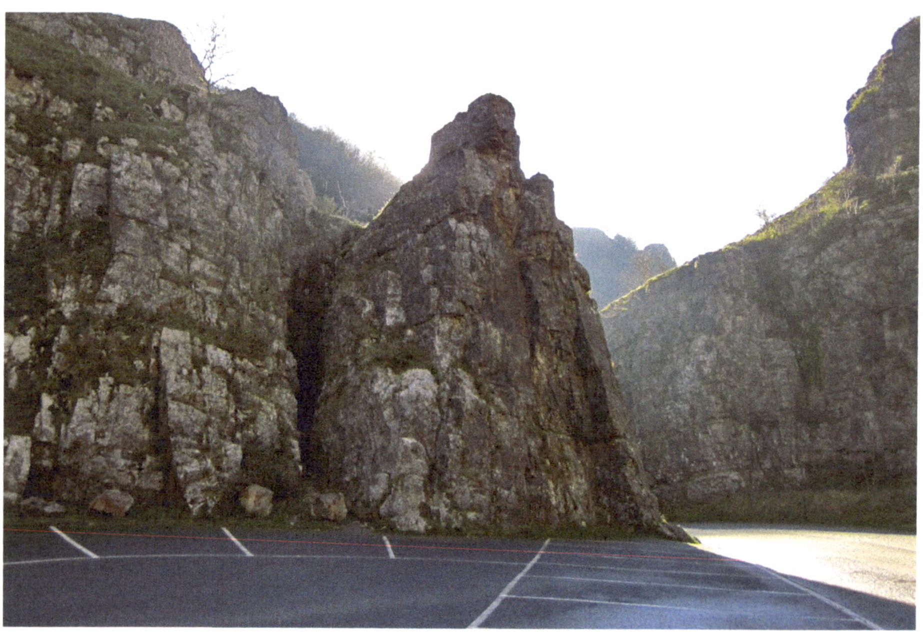

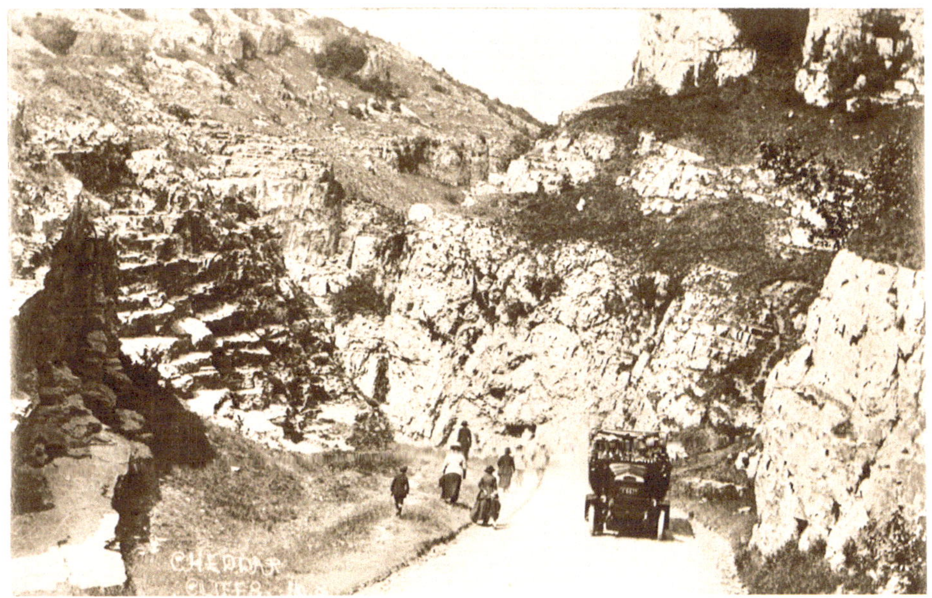

Holiday Traffic

In the picture above, a charabanc – the precursor of the modern coach – carries sightseers past a group of people taking a stroll along the gorge. The views they enjoyed are much the same as those shared by modern visitors. In the 1950s, one visitor observed 'In summer it is easier to walk than take a car, for the approach roads are often congested with holiday traffic; in any case the cliffs rise so abruptly that it is quite impossible to see them properly from a saloon car.' (Coysh A. W., Mason E. J., Waite V. (1954) *The Mendips*, Robert Hale, p. 5)

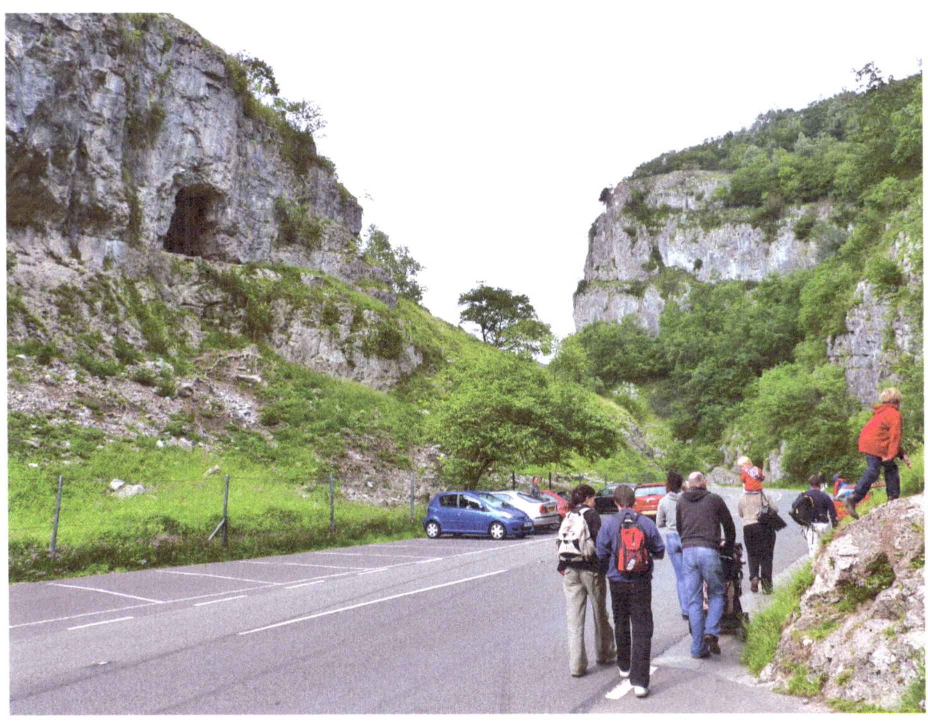

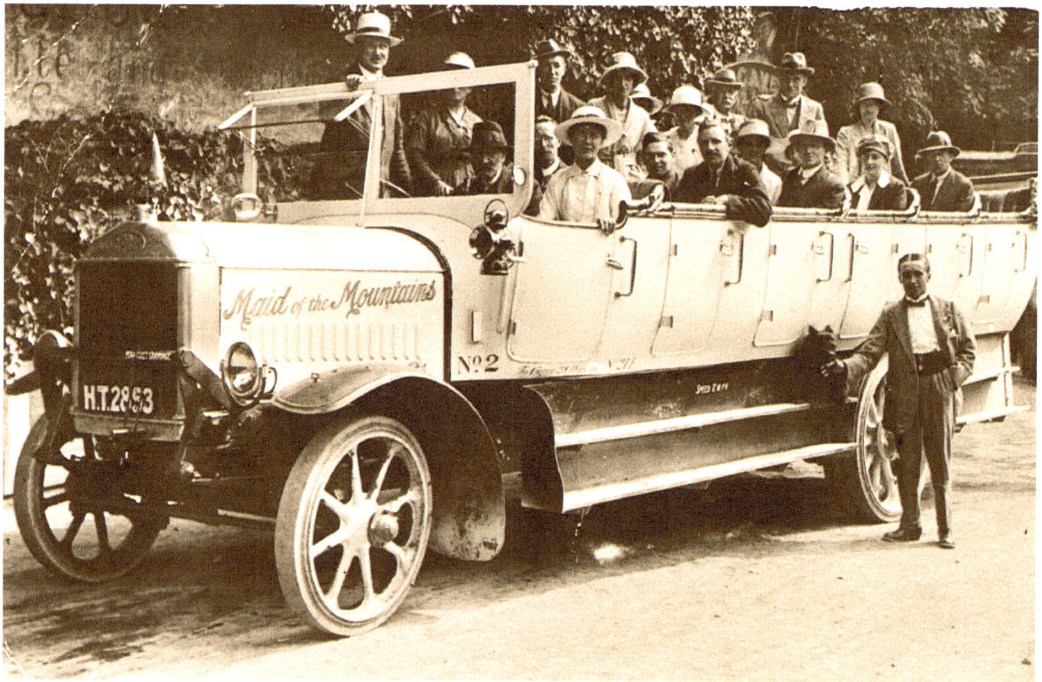

Open-Top Tours

The open-top tour of Cheddar Gorge is now generations old. The modern double-decker replaces the Maid of the Mountains charabanc used between the World Wars. It can be presumed it acquired its name in about 1930 when a film of the same name was made in the gorge.

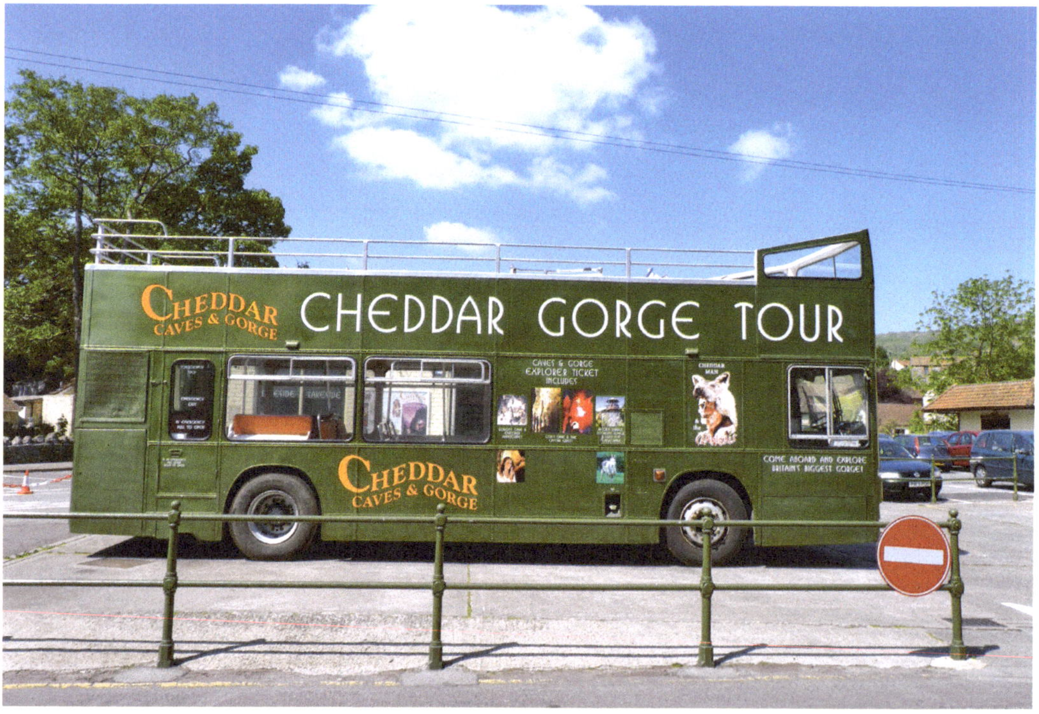

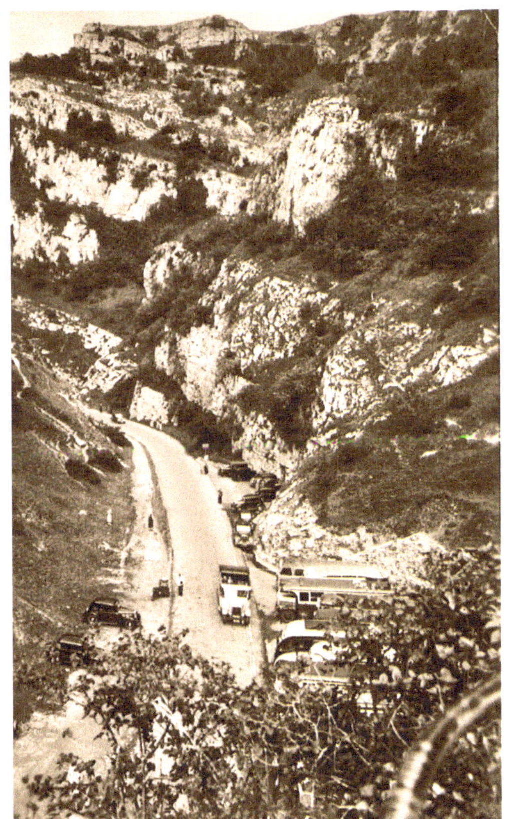

Charabancs and Coaches

By the middle of the twentieth century the first coaches were arriving in Cheddar Gorge. In the picture above, a lone charabanc carries visitors down the road, passing several coaches on its left. The spot from where the early photograph was taken is now a popular destination for those keen on climbing and abseiling. In the modern photograph, a more modern mode of holiday transport, the 'dormobile', fills half a coach bay.

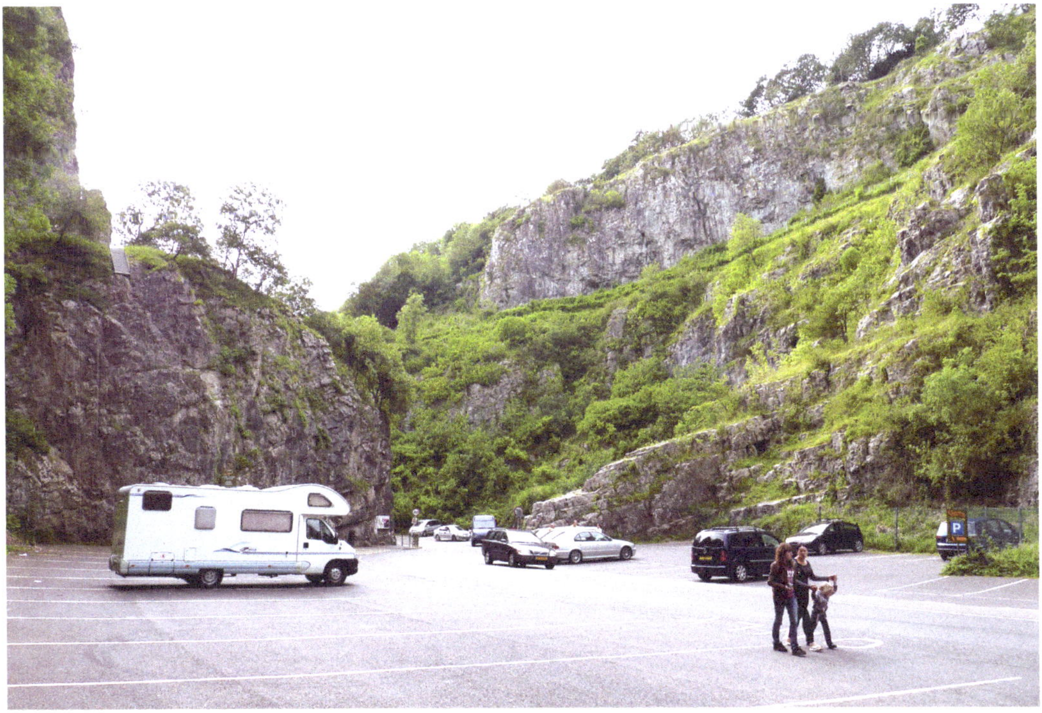

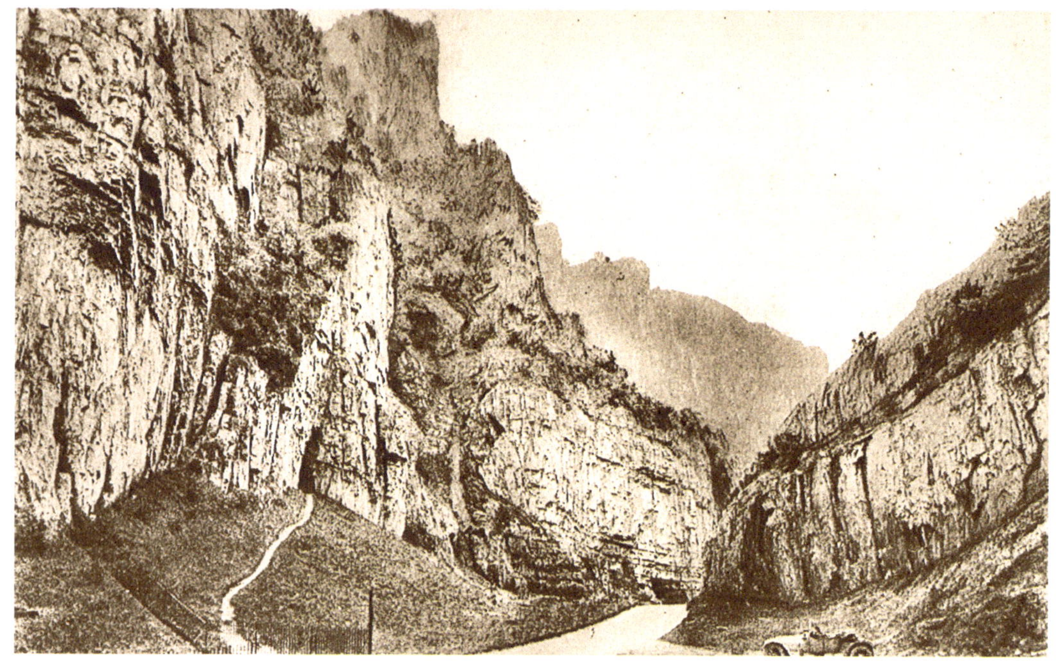

The Gorge: Beautiful but Potentially Hazardous

In 1939, two visitors, Mrs Kate Scott of Corsham in Wiltshire and five-year-old Arthur John White of Combe Down near Bath, were killed by the fall of over half a ton of rocks, probably loosened by a combination of ivy groawth and heavy rainfall. This tragedy occurred despite the fact that then, as now, the owners of the gorge routinely cut back and burned the scrub growing on the cliffs.

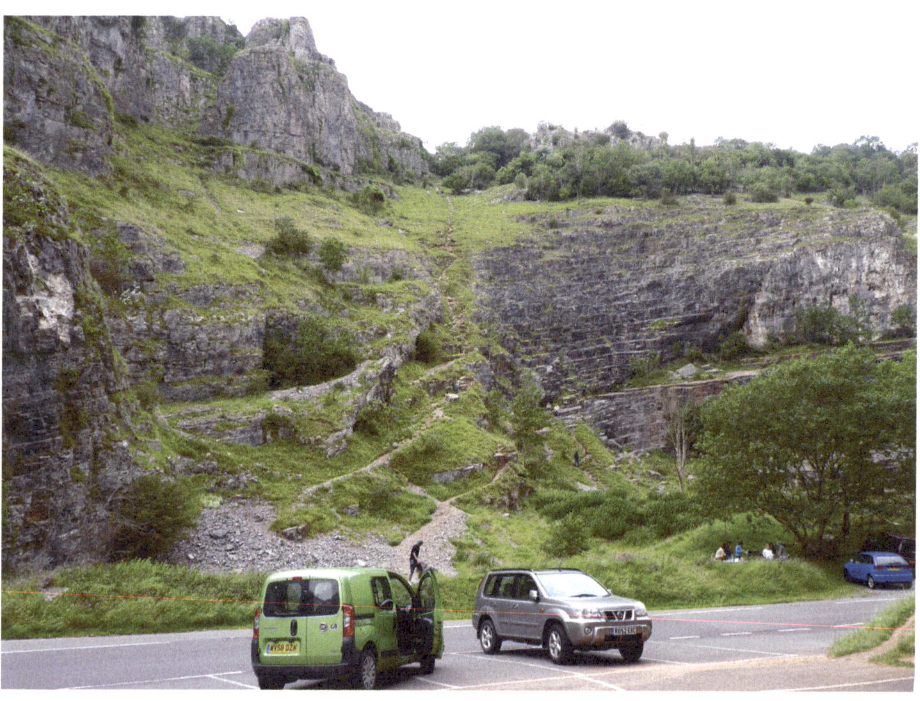

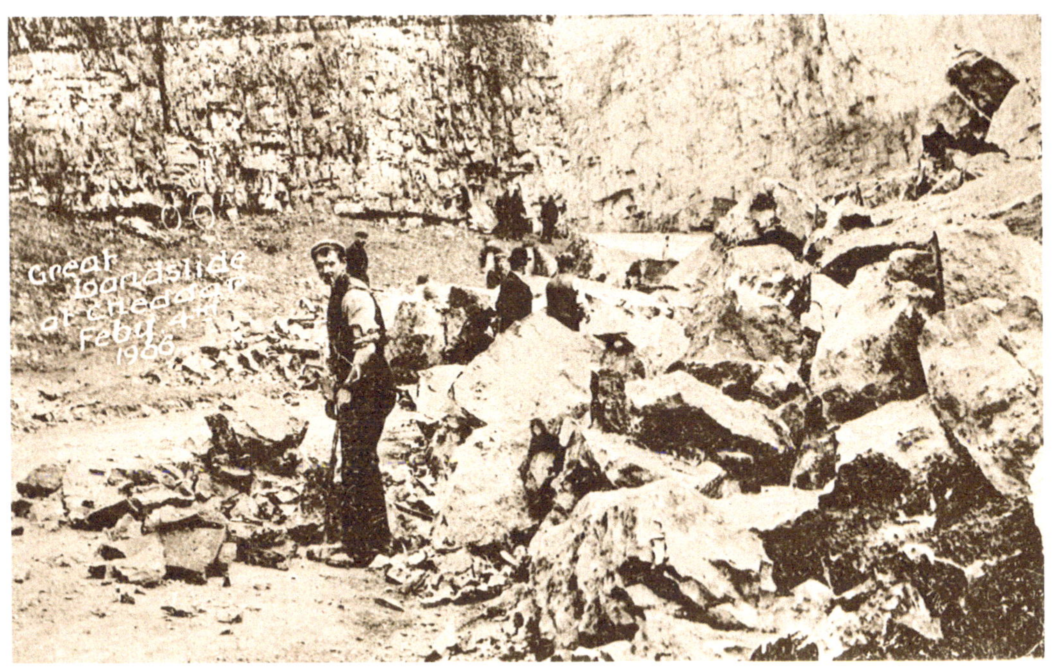

Winter-Time Rock Falls

Winter-time rock falls are a natural feature of Cheddar Gorge, but the falls and landslips were all the more likely when the cliff faces in the gorge were quarried. The rock fall in the picture is one that occurred in February 1906. Although such a major event is unlikely to affect modern visitors, traffic signs warn the motorist of the potential for boulders lying in the road.

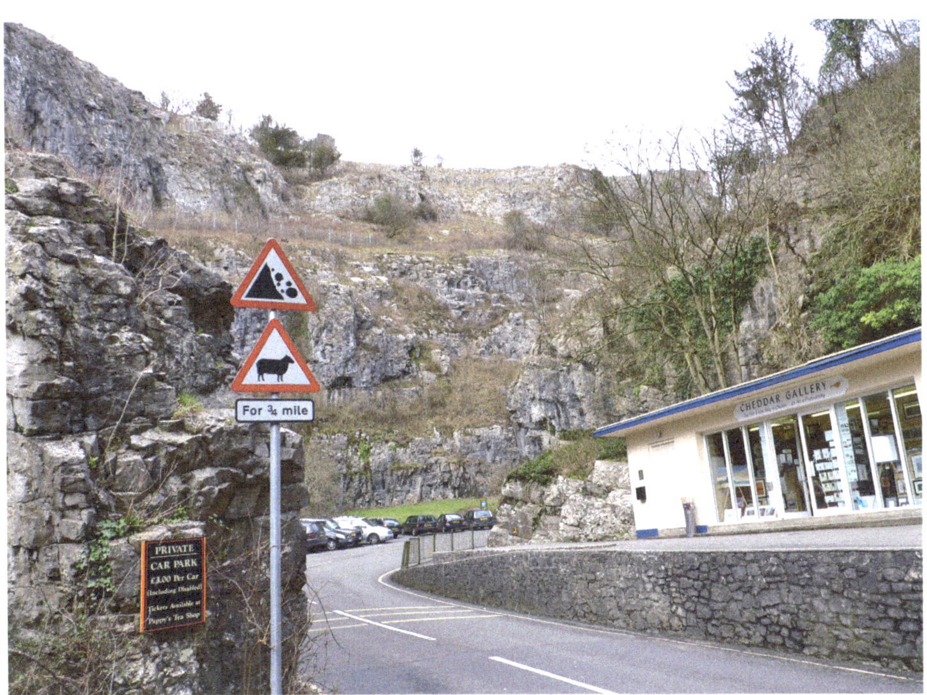

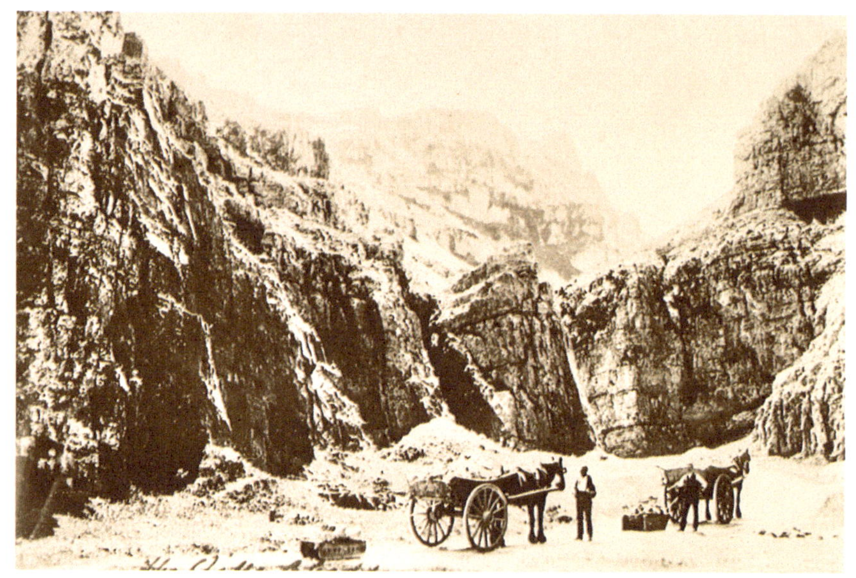

Batts Combe and Callow Rock

Quarrying took place in Cheddar Gorge for generations, but in more recent times it is an activity confined to two large quarries near to the village but away from the Gorge itself – Batts Combe and Callow Rock. Founded by two brothers – George and Fred Ford – in 1926, Batts Combe quarry was producing 4,000 tonnes of limestone a day by 2005. Everything quarried was sold to a single company – until September 2010, the Corus Group, which has since been absorbed into the giant multi-national Tata Steel Europe. Cheddar Gorge can be seen beyond the quarry in the modern photograph.

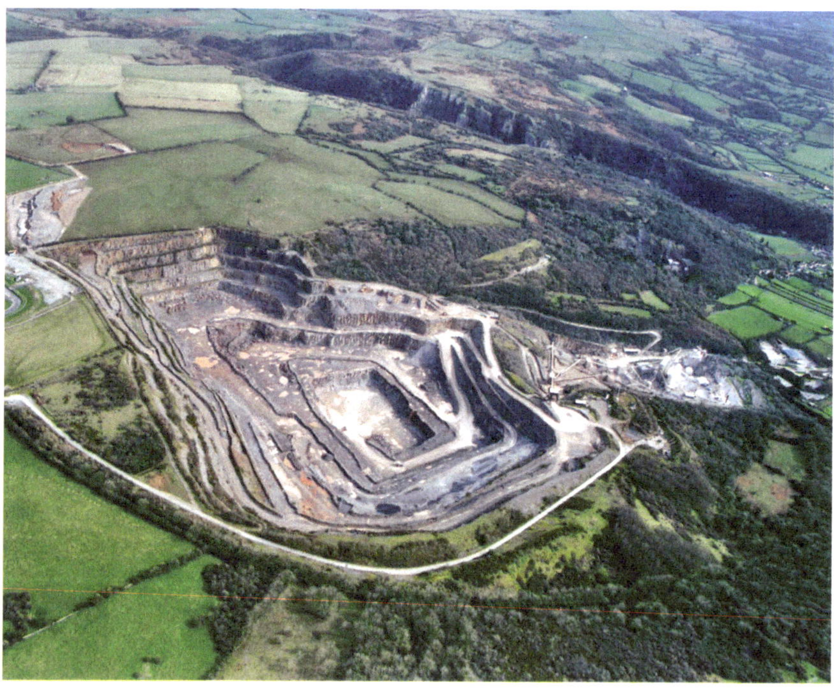

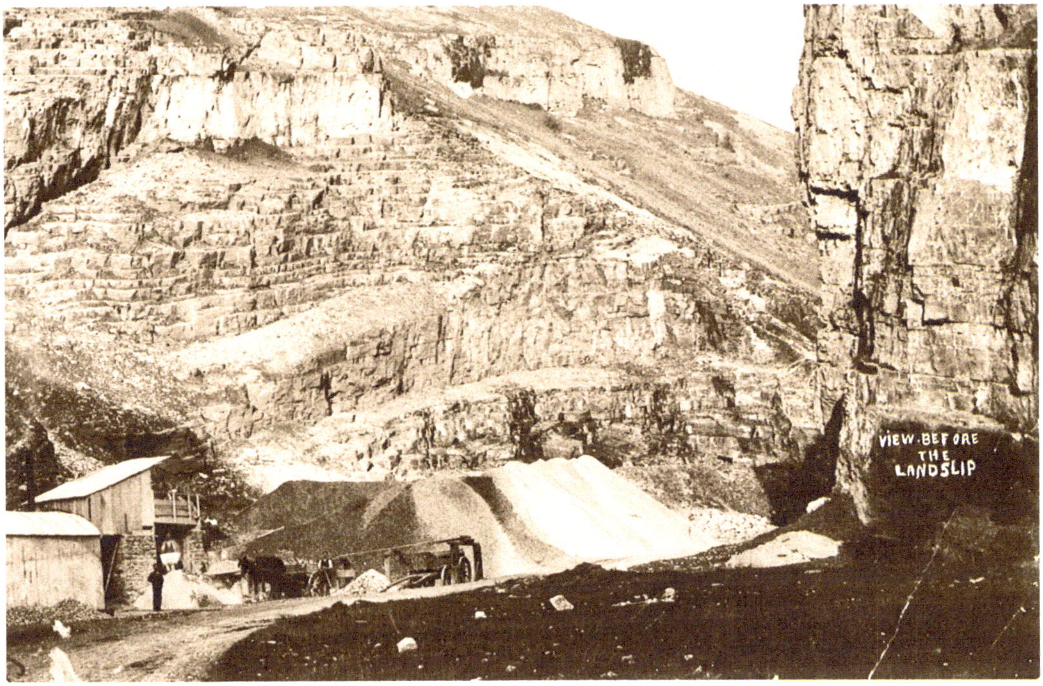

Quarry-Scarred Cliffs

Quarrying in the gorge came to an end after several great 'landslips' at the turn of the nineteenth and twentieth centuries. However, the quarrying of stone in the past is abundantly evident in scarred cliffs along the narrow gorge and the occasional recesses providing convenient places for off-road parking. The colour photograph records a destructive landslip in Batts Combe quarry in 1968.

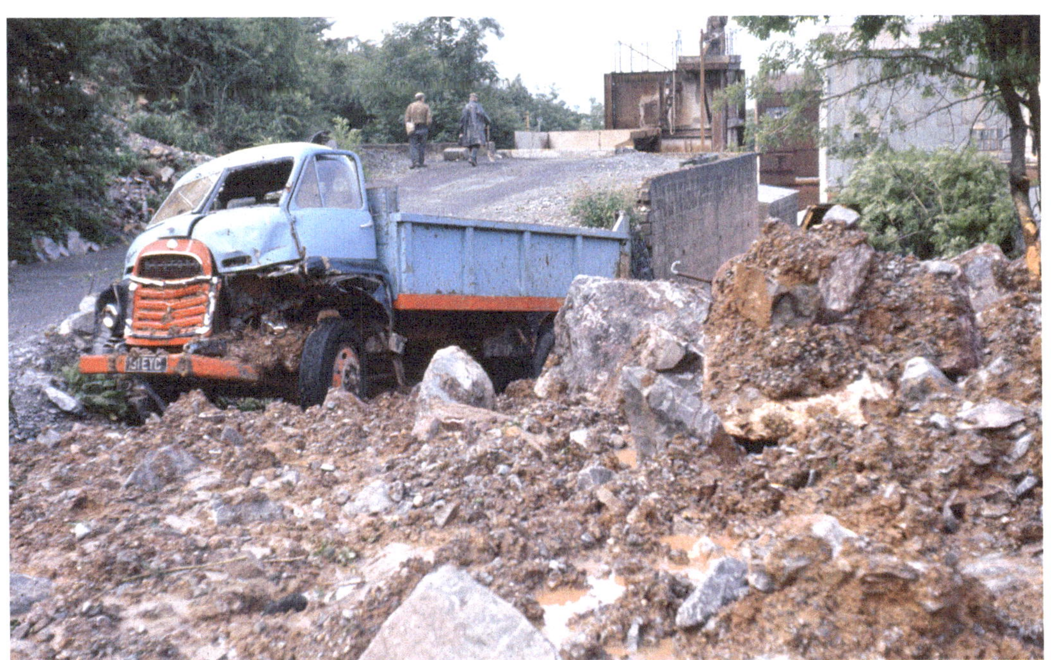

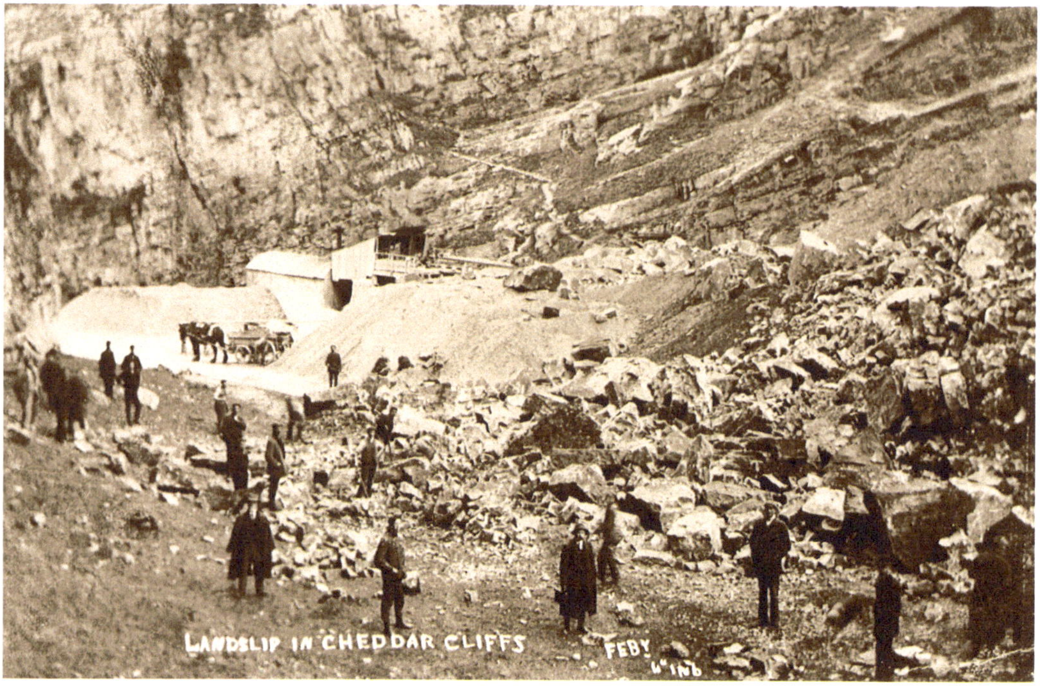

Landslips

These two photographs of quarry landslips show how history sometimes repeats itself. Clearly the quarrymen and other workers had a major task ahead of them in reopening access through the gorge after the major landslip of 1908. The more recent photograph is another picture taken at the time of the 1968 quarry slip.

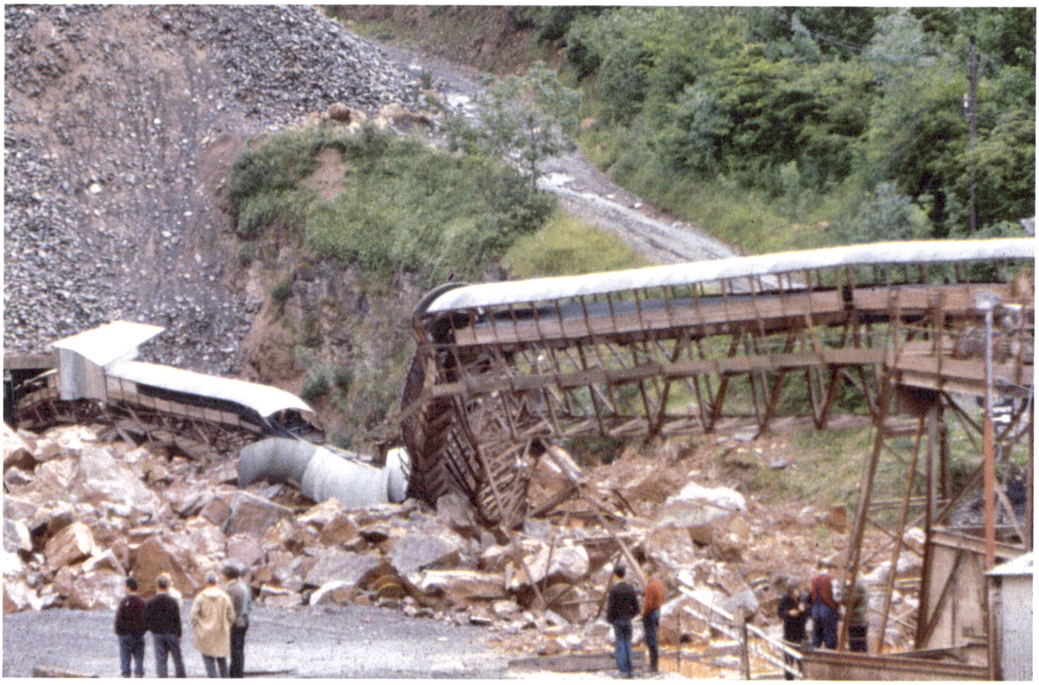

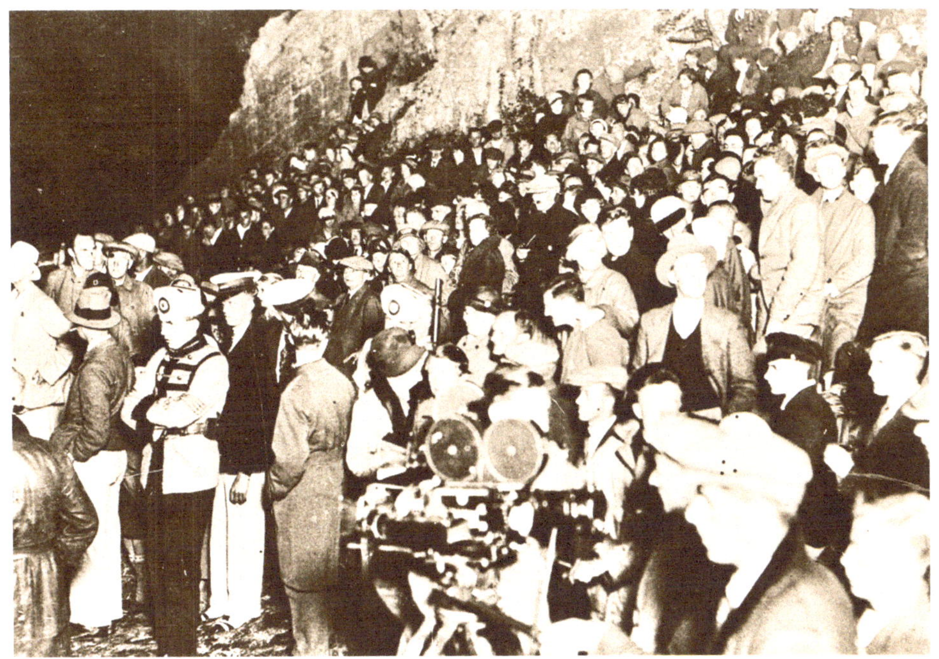

The Maid of the Mountains

In the early 1930s Cheddar became the setting for a major movie. Released in September 1932, *The Maid of the Mountains* was a black-and-white film version of the popular three-act musical comedy, based on the book by Frederick Lonsdale and first put on stage in 1916. In 1995, scenes from the film, based on archive photographs, were reproduced by local people in the Cheddar Pageant.

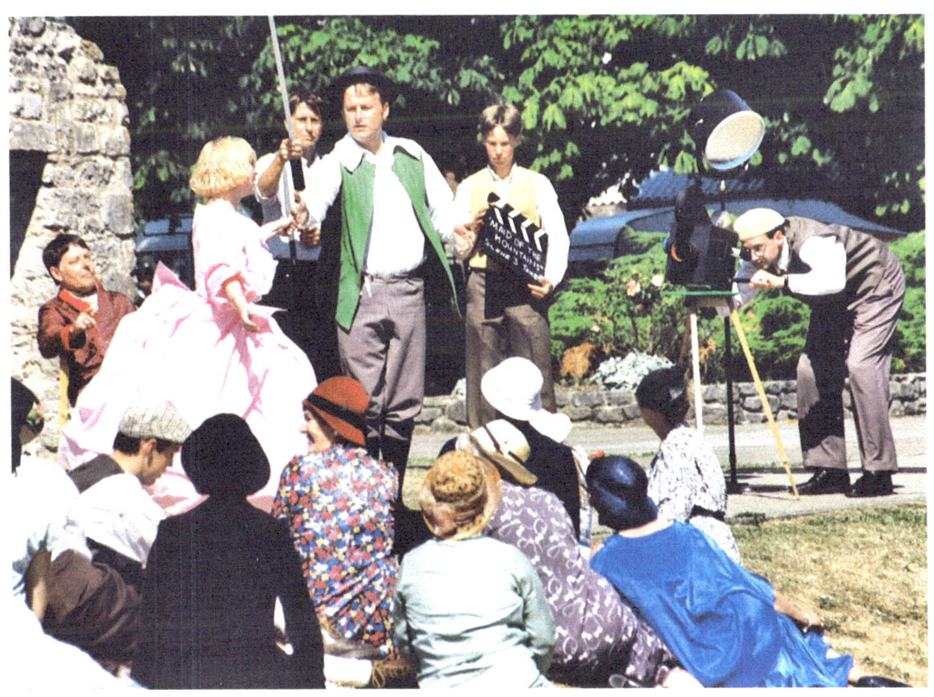

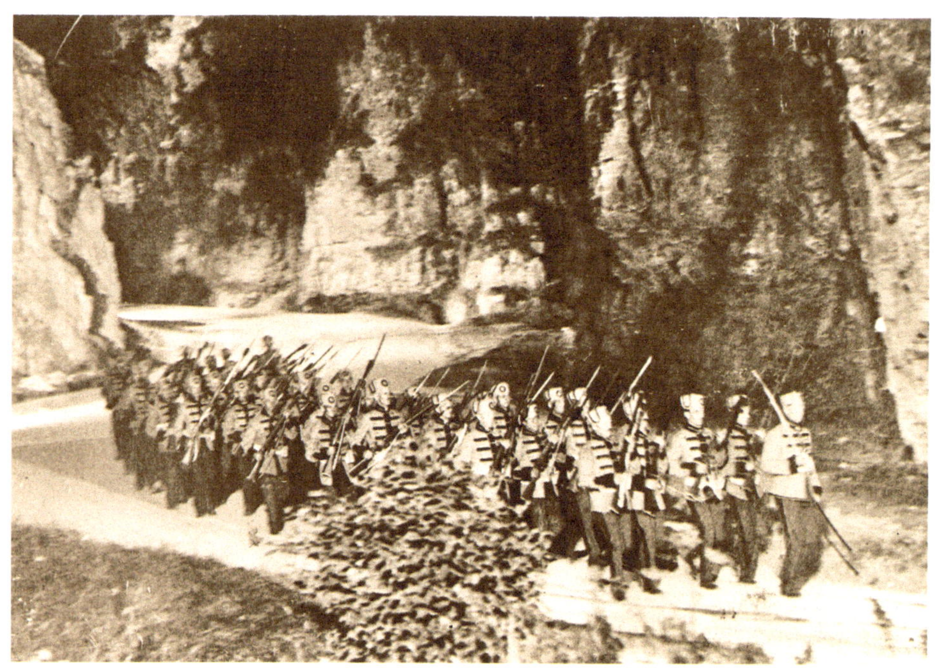

The 1995 Cheddar Pageant

Cheddar Gorge provided the perfect backdrop for the story's romantic Italianate mountain setting. The director was Lupino Lane, represented in the Cheddar pageant by the man in the foreground in the colour photograph. The 1995 Cheddar Pageant, itself already a part of Cheddar's rich social history, took place on 22 July and the two performances that day entertained and informed well over a thousand locals and visitors. The cast itself numbered 200 and another 100 constituted the backstage crew.

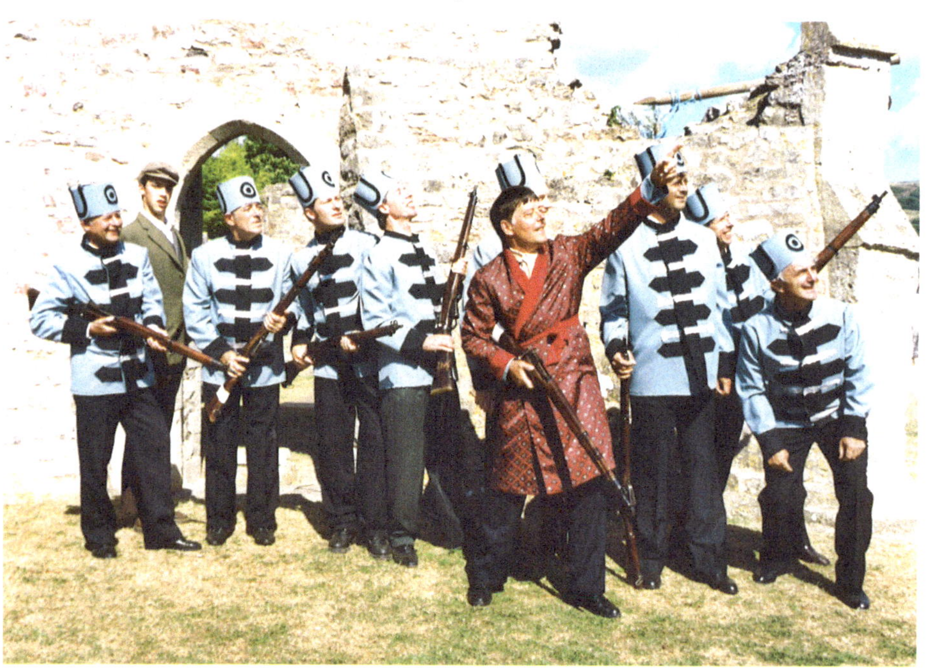

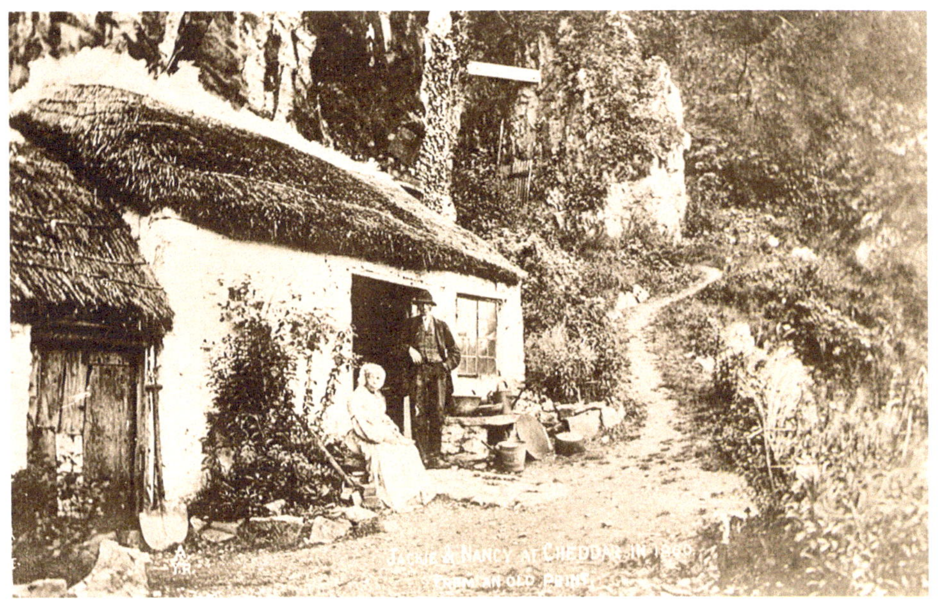

Sundowner's Cottage

The quaint Tiny Tea Room is the first building on the right on the descent along the gorge into Cheddar. It is reputed to be an exceptionally rare example of a 'sundowner's cottage'. Allegedly this simple building was built in a single night, between dusk and dawn, and thus, according to tradition, its builder was permitted to live rent free upon the premises thereafter. The fact that the cottage has not yet been listed as a building of special significance by English Heritage casts doubt on this attractive legend. The ramshackle cottage that once stood nearby, a little further up the gorge, looks rather more like a genuine 'sundowner', and this might explain the legend now associated with the café.

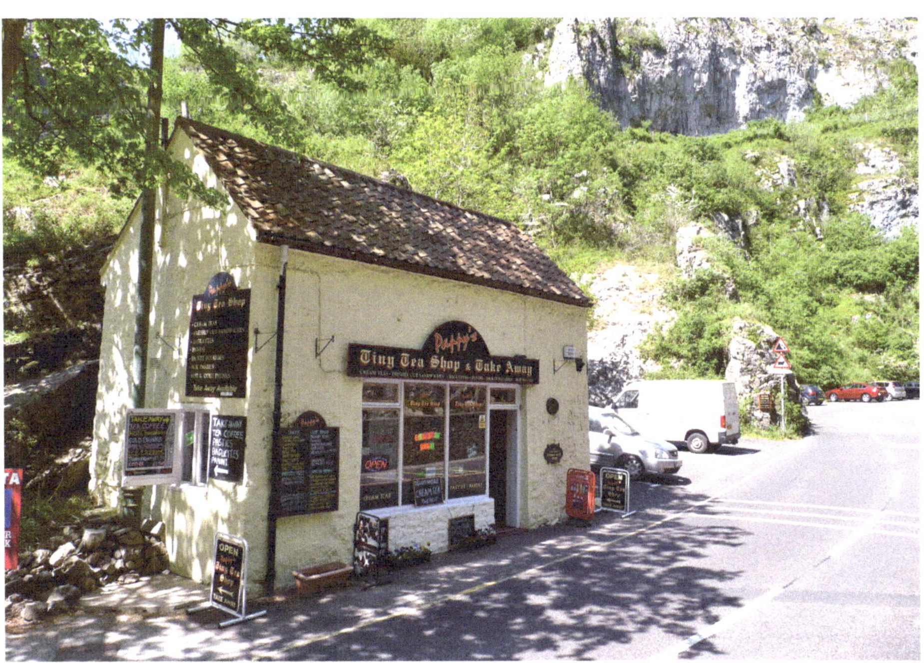

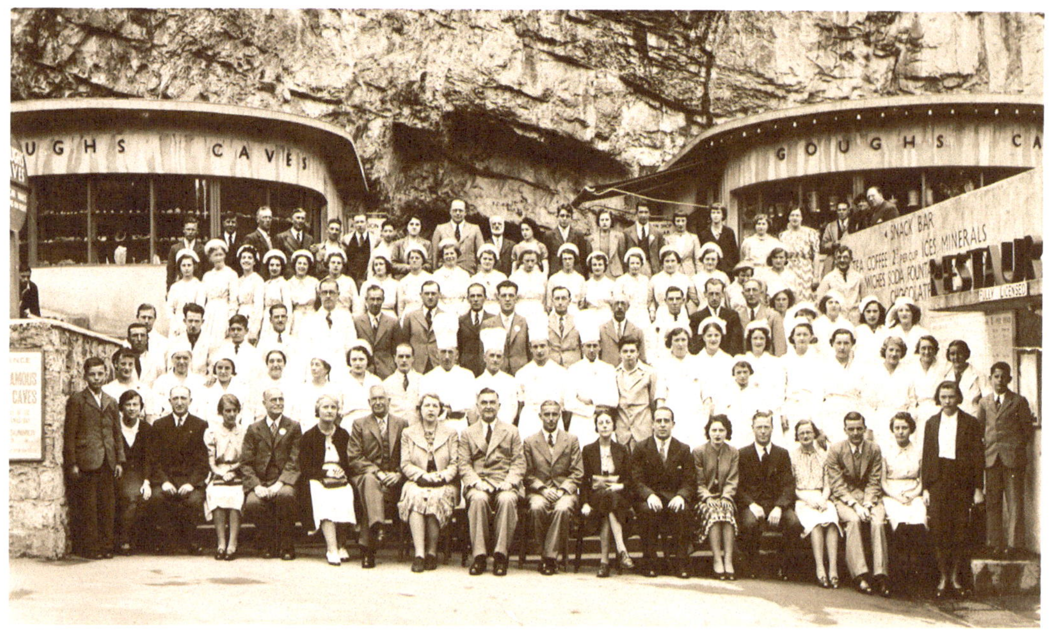

Gough's Cave

Opposite the Tiny Tea Room is the entrance to the main tourist attraction in Cheddar Gorge: Gough's Cave. Regarded as Britain's most beautiful limestone cave, among its many special features it has the largest colony of horseshoe bats in the United Kingdom. The older image, probably taken in the mid-1930s, shows the ninety-four staff of the visitor centre beside the entrance to the caves. The linear design of the newer buildings replaces the elegant curves of the distinctive art deco style of the earlier structure. This early all-concrete building had been completed in 1934 and the architect, Sir Geoffrey Jellicoe, won an award for his design, which included a glass-bottomed fish pond and fountain forming the roof and ceiling of the restaurant. This is now a terrace for outdoor eating.

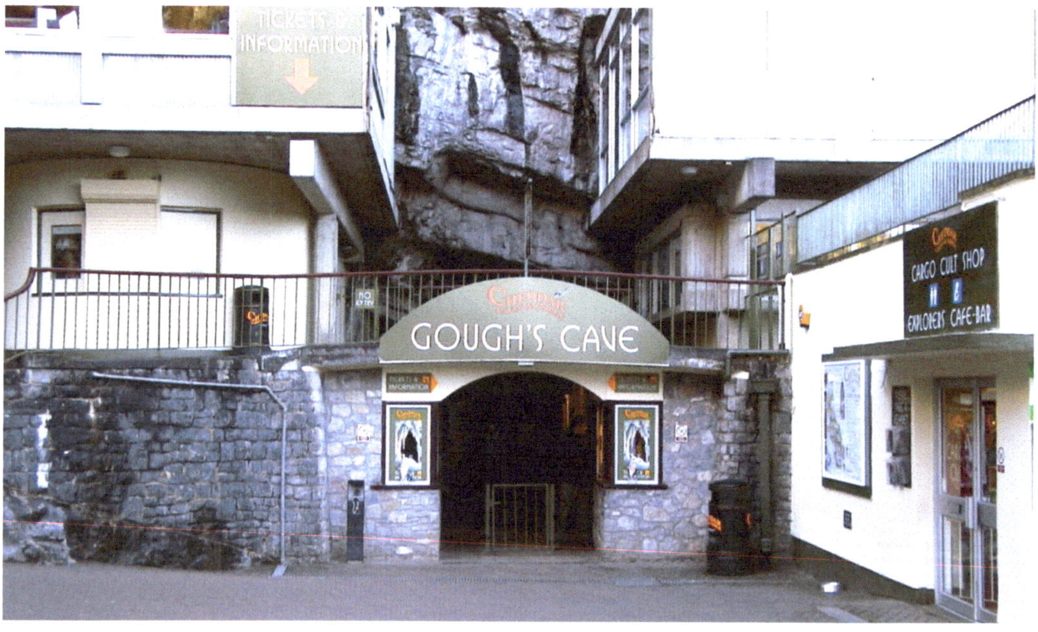

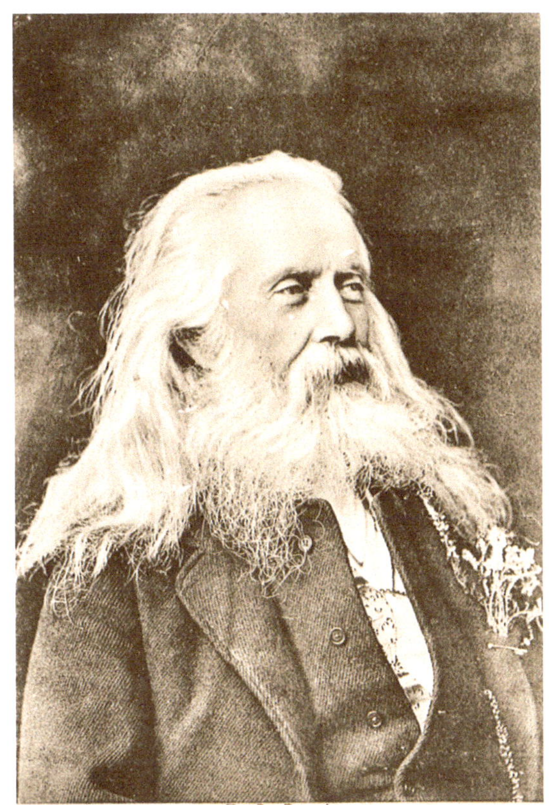

Richard Cox Gough

Richard Cox Gough (1827–1902) discovered and opened up the cave system, through the unexcavated entrance formerly called Sand Hole, between 1892 and 1898. By the time of his death in 1902 the caves had become a major tourist attraction and, like the great man himself in this studio photograph, from 1899 they were 'illuminated by electricity'. In 1929, the admission charge was one shilling. Gough had settled in Cheddar around 1870 after a career as a sea captain. In 1995, David Gough met the actor playing his great-grandfather's role in the Cheddar Pageant. Richard Gough's memorial stone can be found inside St Andrew's church.

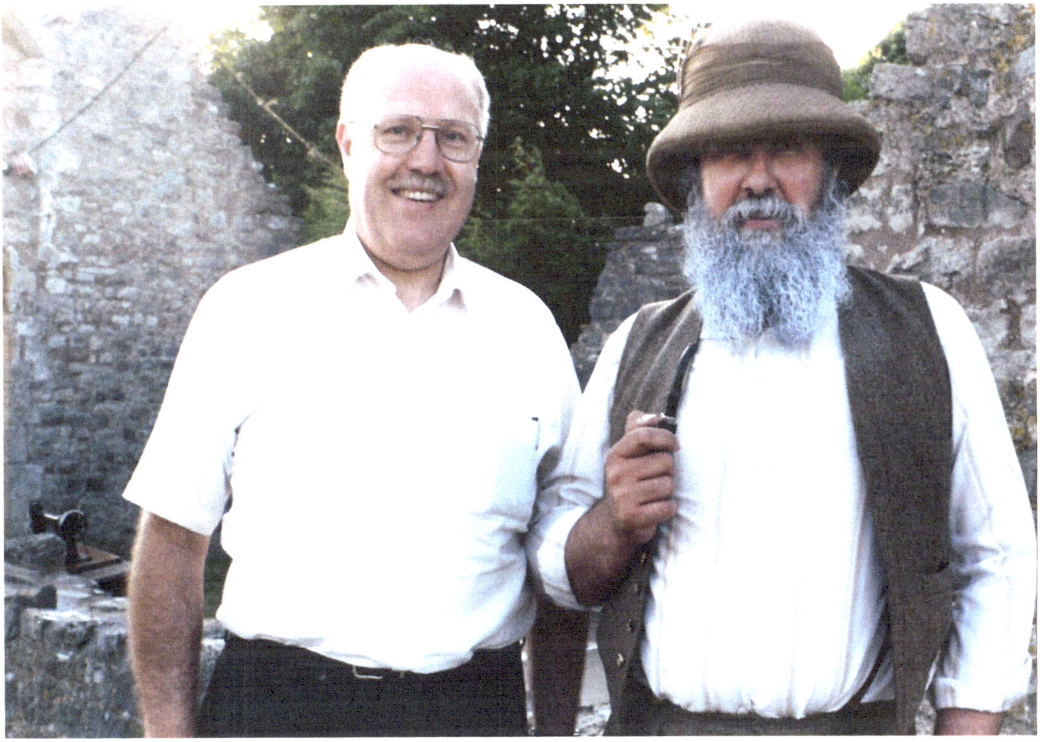

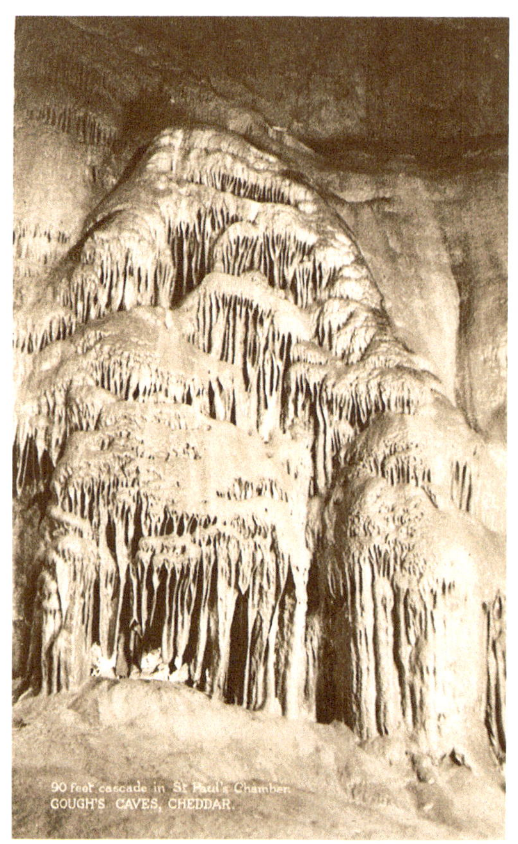

Gough's Cave, Unchanged

Thankfully, the fascinating geological formations within the caverns have been protected and such wonders as the 90-foot cascade in St Paul's Chamber in the Gough's Cave complex remains unchanged in the short interval of time since this photograph was taken in the early twentieth century. Dissolved limestone accounts for the remarkable stalactites and stalagmites in the Cheddar cave systems. The relatively late discovery of these caves saved them from the damage suffered at nearby Wookey due to the activities of early souvenir hunters, including the famous seventeenth-century man of letters, Alexander Pope, who amassed a substantial collection of its 'sparry concretions' for his grotto in Twickenham.

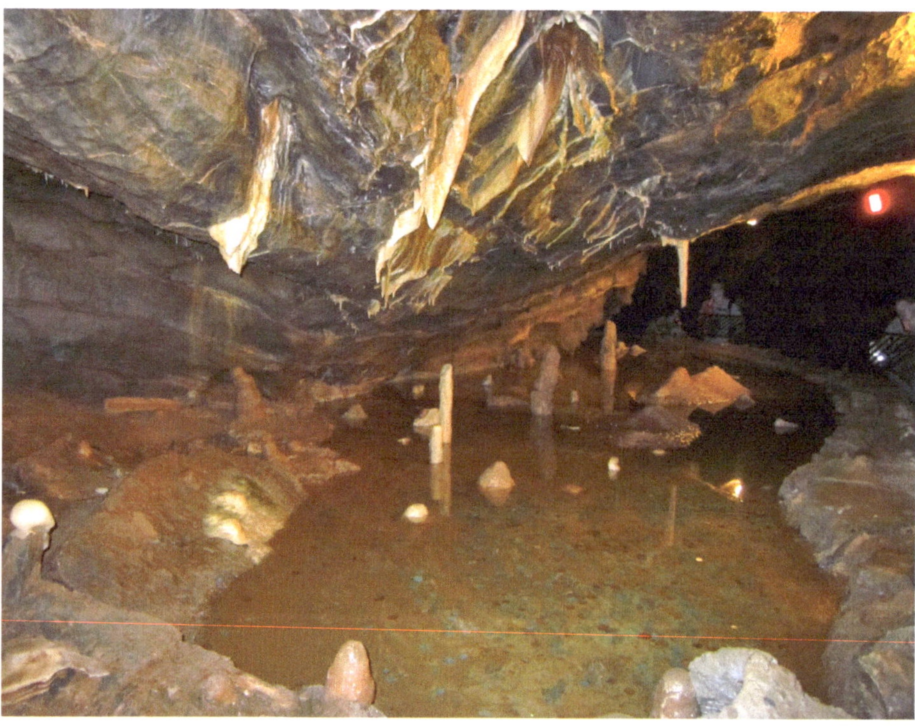

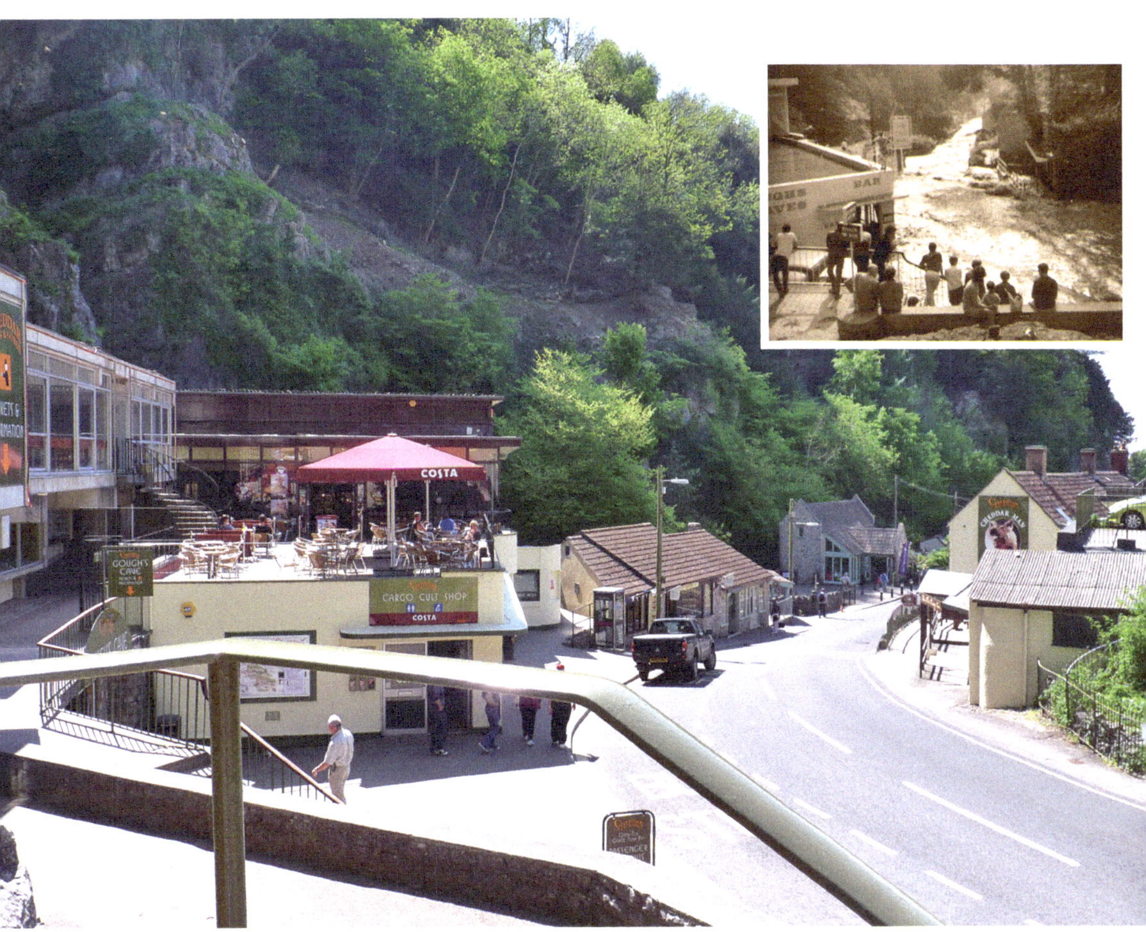

Trapped at the Cave Man

Typically, Gough's Cave is flooded once or twice a year. In 1968, the flood waters poured through the entrance of the caves for three days. At the time, Richard O'Connor was working as a barman with a friend, Peter Pilkington, in the 'Cave Man' restaurant to the right of the entrance. He recalls the drama of the night of 10 July 1968: 'The Cave Man was bounded on one side by a river, on another by the sheer overhanging cliff and by the road, which was now a raging torrent of mud, boulders and water. We were trapped. I was in the downstairs bar when the steel door finally gave way. I managed to fling myself through the kitchens and I reached the back stairs just as the water arrived. We spent that night in darkness, apart from the lightning hitting the cliffs... Downstairs was flooded to a depth of several feet, and there was a constant crash of rocks falling off the cliff onto the roof... My overriding memory of the night was the noise of the boulders grinding around downstairs, the rocks bouncing off the roof, and of course the constant thunder. It was not a happy night.'

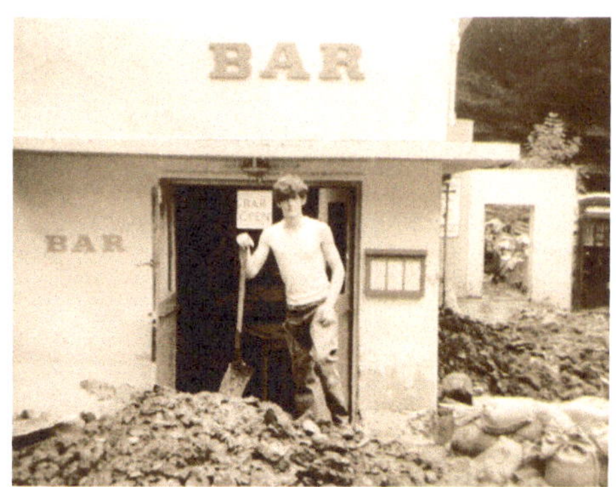

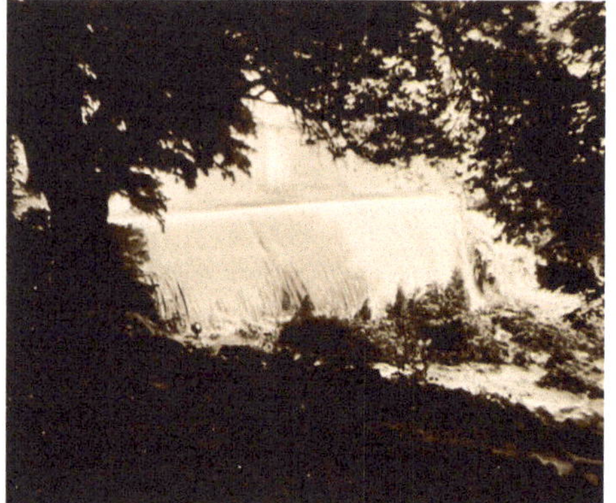

Devastation

The following day Richard witnessed the full extent of the damage: 'By morning, the rain had stopped...We managed to escape by making our way up, over the entrance to the cave and down to the village by clambering over the hillside on the far side of the torrent. When the cascade had subsided a bit from the cave mouth, Peter and I roped ourselves together and entered the caves, as there was some concern that people may have been trapped inside. Fortunately, everyone got out in time. We then explored up the Gorge. The devastation was incredible. Huge boulders blocked the road and great swathes of road were entirely missing. As the Cave Man had acted as a buffer for the rest of the village, it sustained the worst damage, but the sheer volume of flooding was incredible.' The photograph shows Peter Pilkington, who ran the bar, starting to clear up after the flood. The wall behind him has clearly been damaged by boulders. Note his 'Bar Open' sign. This is now the entrance to the cave gift shop, and the 'Explorer's Café and Bar' is located on the floor above.

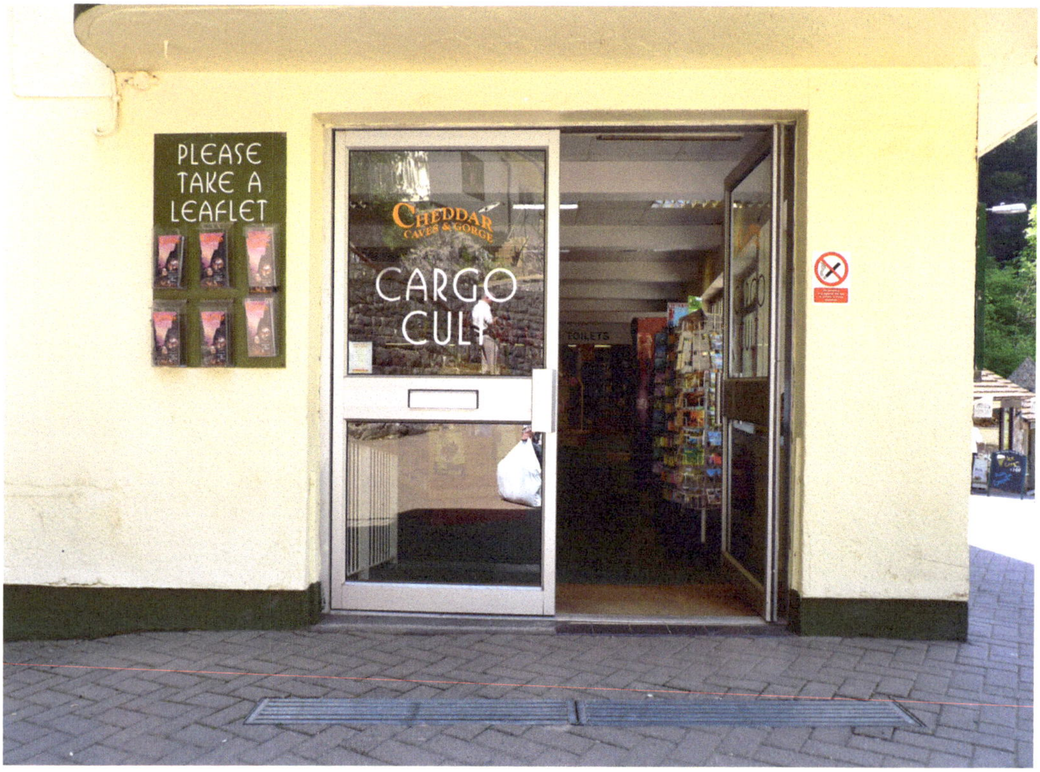

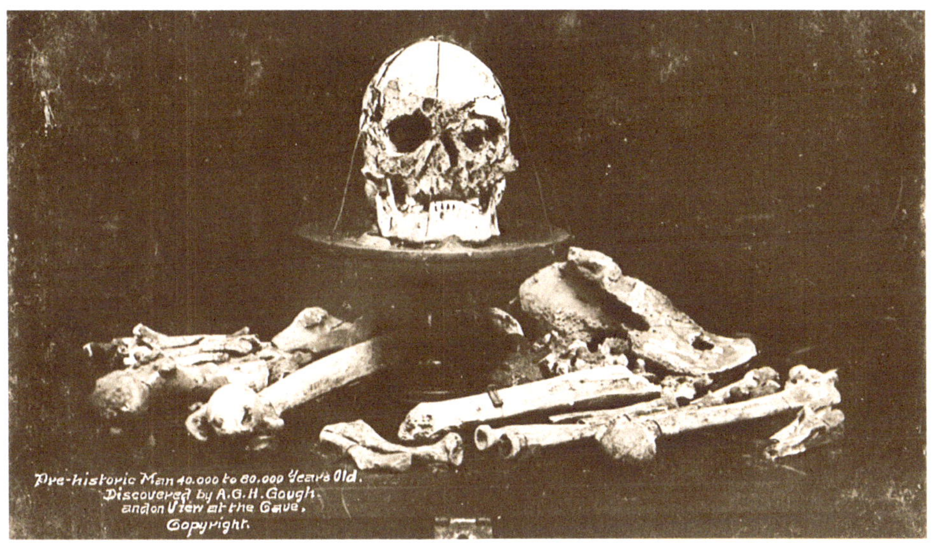

Cheddar Man

The bones of Cheddar Man were examined by the curator of Taunton Museum, H. St George Gray, the assistant of two great early archaeologists – General Pitt Rivers – and Arthur Bulleid. The postcard dates these remains, found in the entrance of Gough's Cave in 1902 by Richard Cox Gough's son, William, to between 40 and 80,000 years BP (Before Present). Archaeologists now believe the individual died about 9,000 years ago. DNA analysis of the bones in the late 1990s revealed that they belonged to a distant direct ancestor of a Cheddar school history teacher, Adrian Targett. Cheddar Man is now the focus of the small museum of archaeological material that was recently opened opposite Gough's Cave, having previously been located next to its entrance. Evidence of cut marks on human bones found in the vicinity has led to much lurid speculation regarding acts of prehistoric cannibalism.

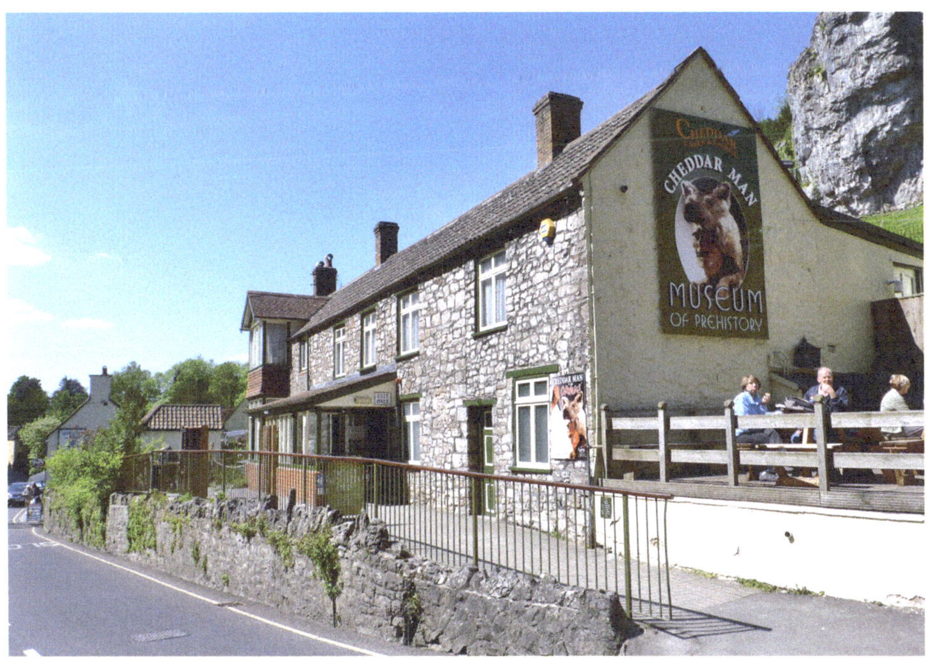

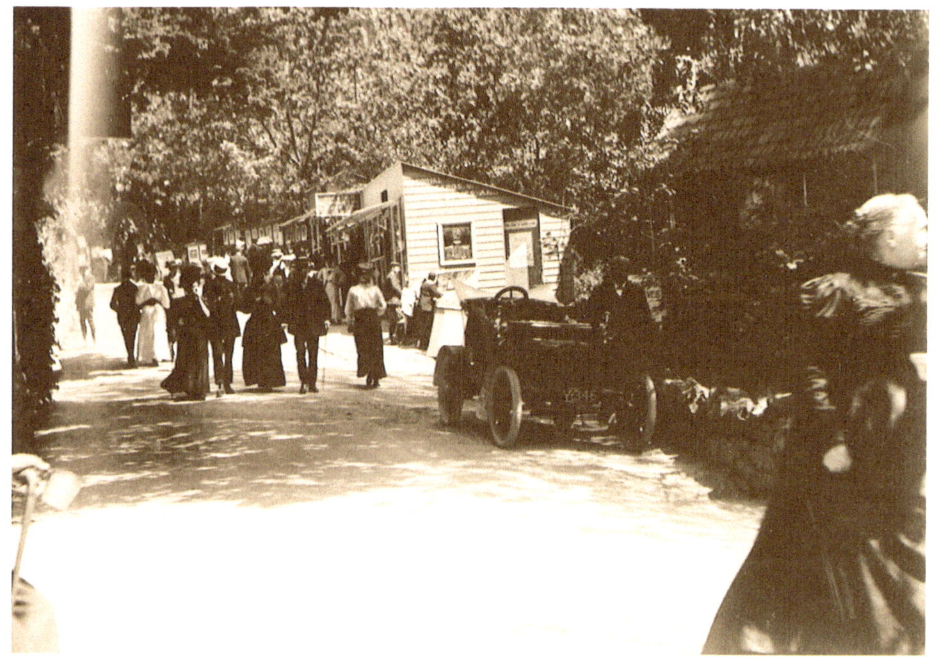

Tourism and Small Businesses

Tourists then and now wander up and down The Cliffs a little beyond the entrance to Gough's Cave. In the early twentieth century picture, the original arched entrance, very similar to the one that stands at the entrance to Jacob's Ladder, can just be seen in the distance where the buildings end. The shack to the right advertises 'Pictorial Postcards of Gough's Caves and Cheddar Cliffs', some no doubt that have been reproduced in this collection.

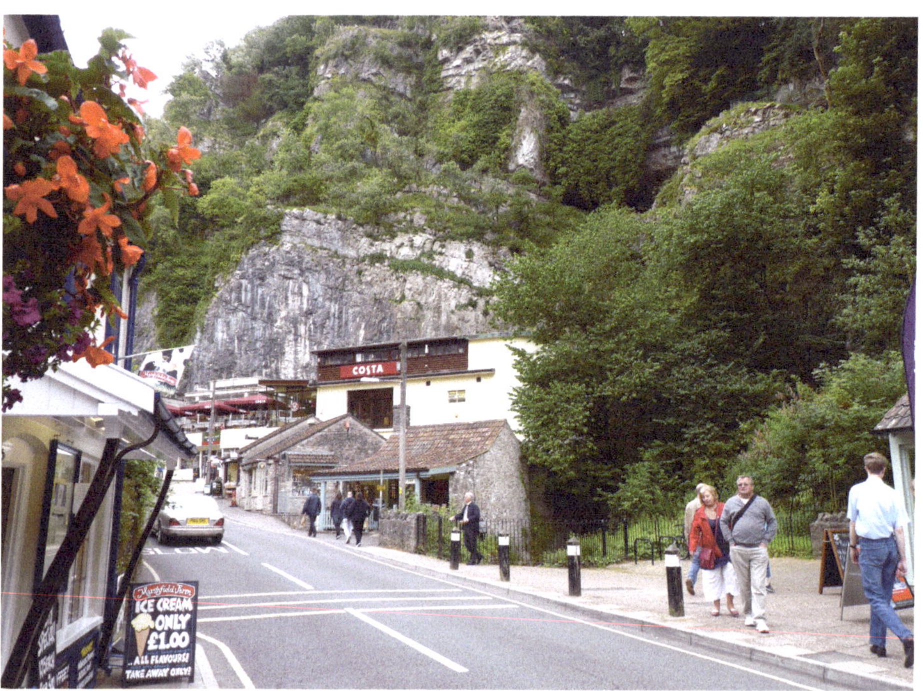

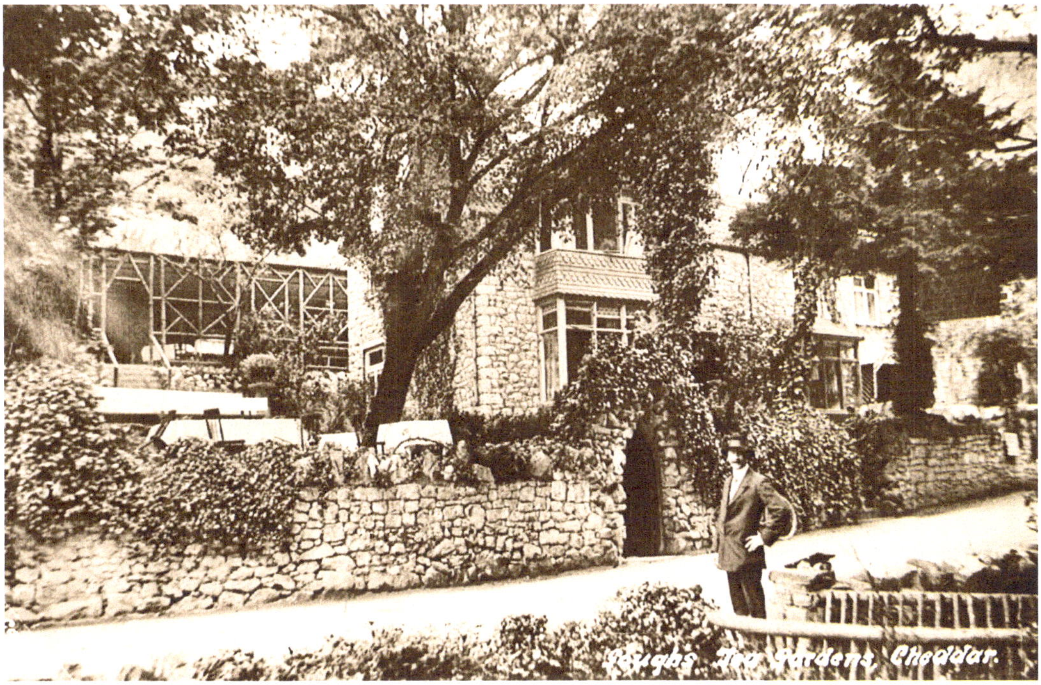

The Museum

The building that now houses the museum was formerly a restaurant with a 'tea garden' owned by the Gough family. Tourism in Cheddar has provided ample opportunities for small businesses for over 100 years. The 'head' of Lion Rock can be seen behind the building in the modern photograph.

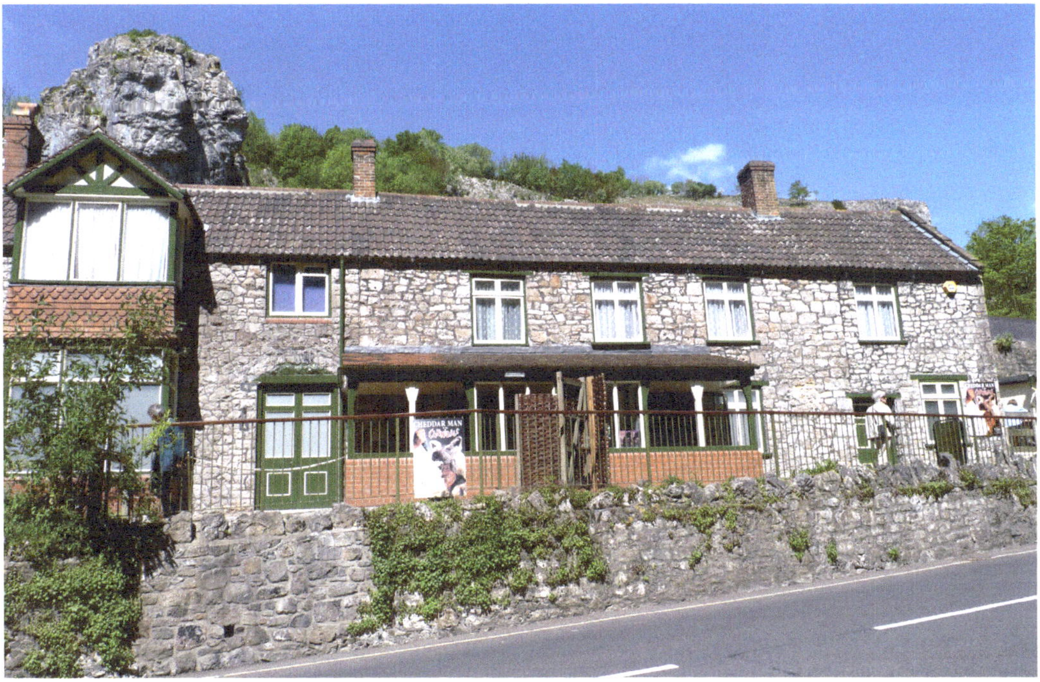

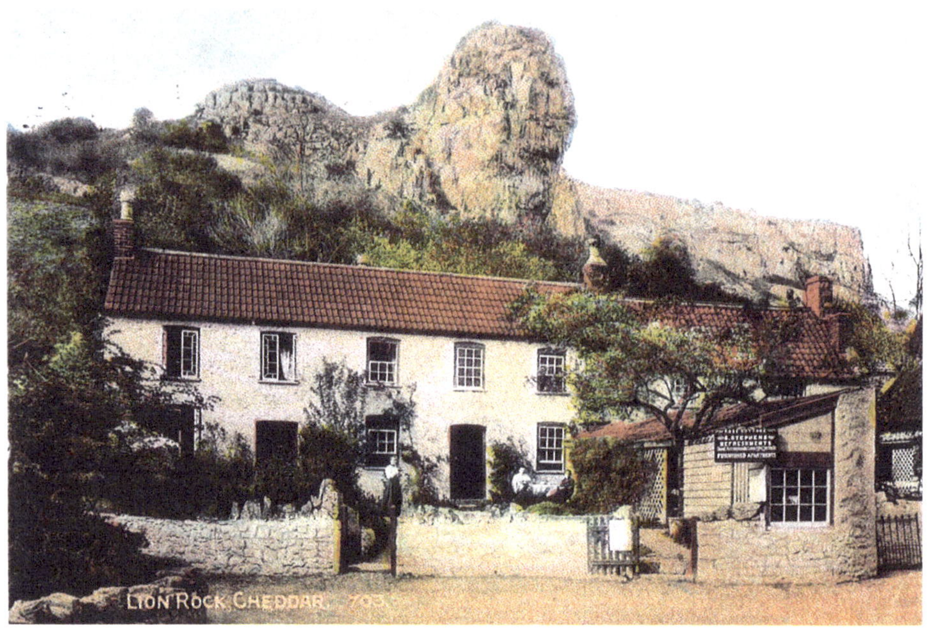

Lion Rock

Lion Rock is best seen in the winter before the lion's body is largely obscured by bushes. It is a striking outcrop overlooking the lower reaches of Cheddar Gorge, which really does look like a sitting lion! Richard Gough's home in the valley below was named Lion Rock House. Although some alteration to the roofline, along with an additional structure and retail outlet in the foreground, has appeared, the buildings in this view remain largely unchanged. Although its business has changed since its days as a restaurant and bed and breakfast establishment, when it was run by a member of the Gough family, Rose Cottage retains its charming name.

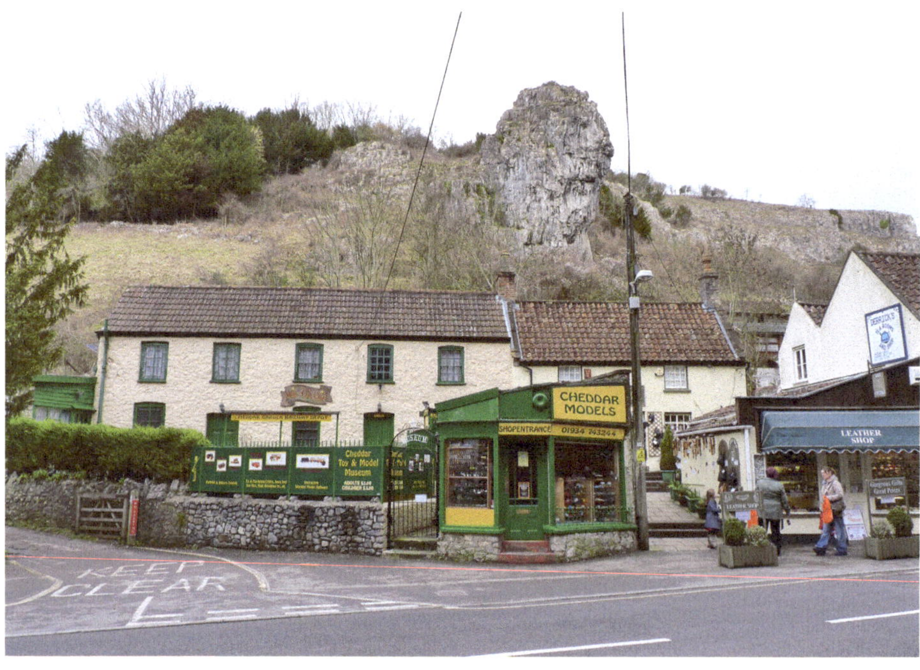

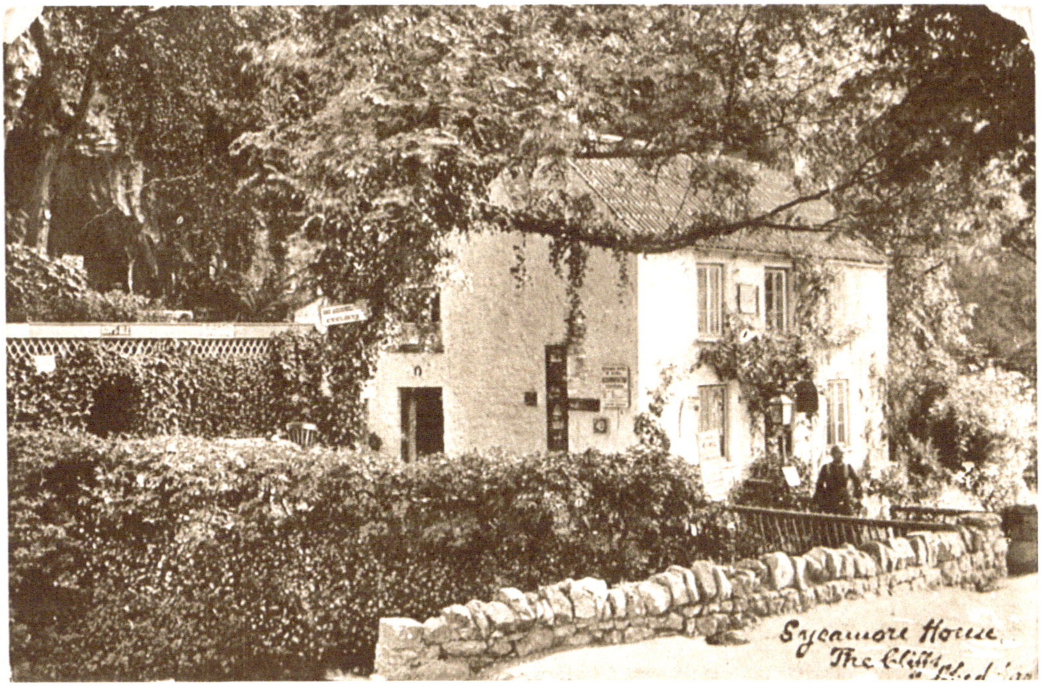

Sycamore House

On the other side of the road, Sycamore House once stood on the site of the attractive and deceptively old-looking National Trust shop, formerly the tourist information centre. With its quaint bridge across the stream, it was a popular subject for Cheddar Gorge souvenir postcards. Due to damage caused by a rock fall, Sycamore House was demolished in 1959.

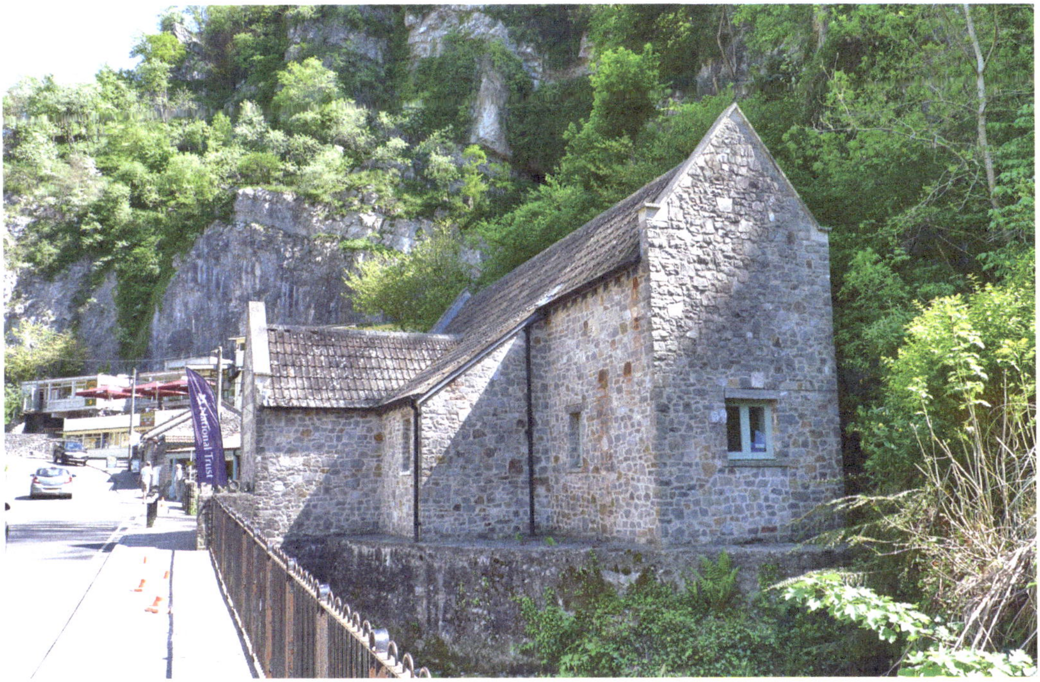

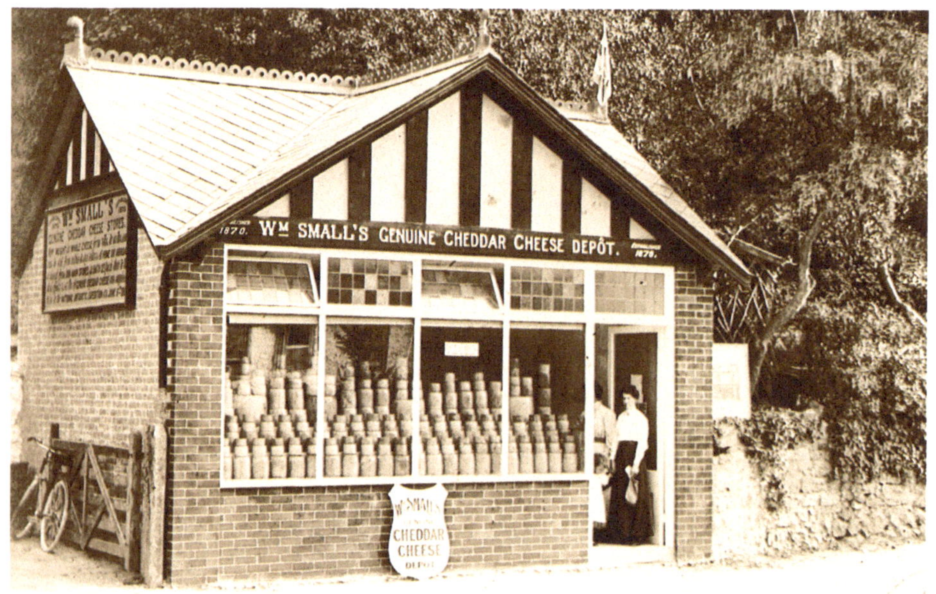

Cheddar's Cheese

Even more famous than its caves is Cheddar's cheese. Mr. Small's cheesemongery, next door to the National Trust shop, remains a distinctive and rather charming tourist attraction. The business was established in 1870. The earliest known reference to Cheddar cheese dates was made in about 1170 when Henry II purchased a substantial quantity of it. Once upon a time, the only 'genuine' Cheddar cheese was that produced within a 30-mile radius of Wells Cathedral.

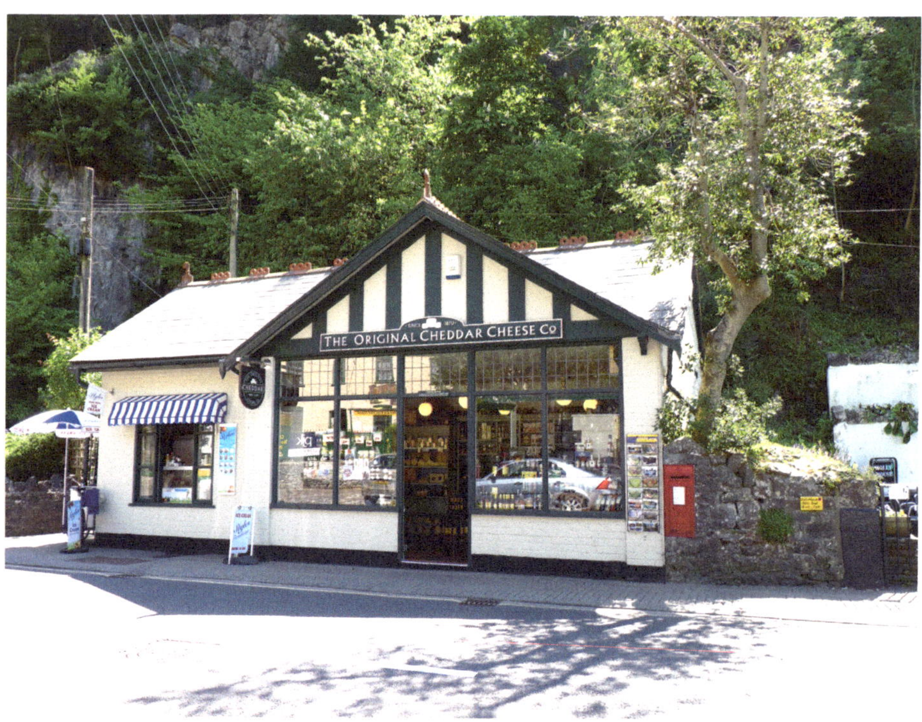

The Genuine Article

William Small became a master cheese taster in 1885, and his fine Cheddar cheese sold for seven pence per pound. The genuine Cheddar Cheese Store was the main purveyor of cheese in Cheddar when these premises were established in 1870. Half a century ago it was lamented that 'the genuine article seems now to be almost unobtainable by the ordinary consumer, who is fobbed off with a not very convincing imitation. [...] As in so many things we have retrogressed [...]; now there are very few, of the younger generation at least, who have ever tasted genuine Cheddar cheese, and as a sign of the times there is no longer that fascinating cheese shop in Cheddar which in the days of my youth sent delicious Cheddar cheeses of every size and weight all over England and all over the world.' (Coysh A. W., Mason E. J., Waite V. (1954) *The Mendips,* Robert Hale, p. 169). Thankfully, Cheddar cheese is once again being made in the village by the Cheddar Gorge Cheese Company.

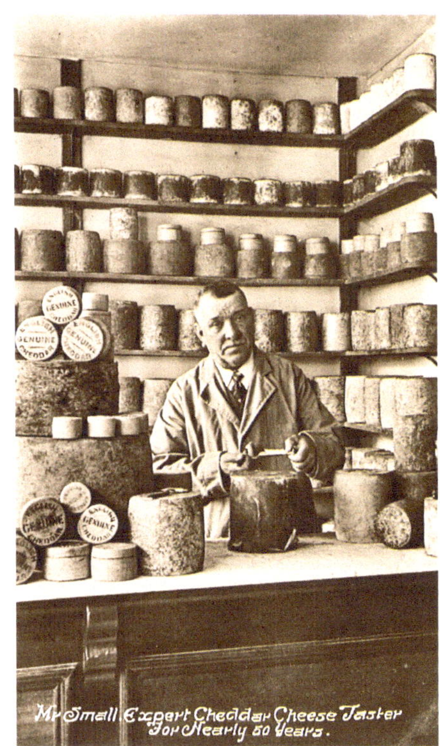

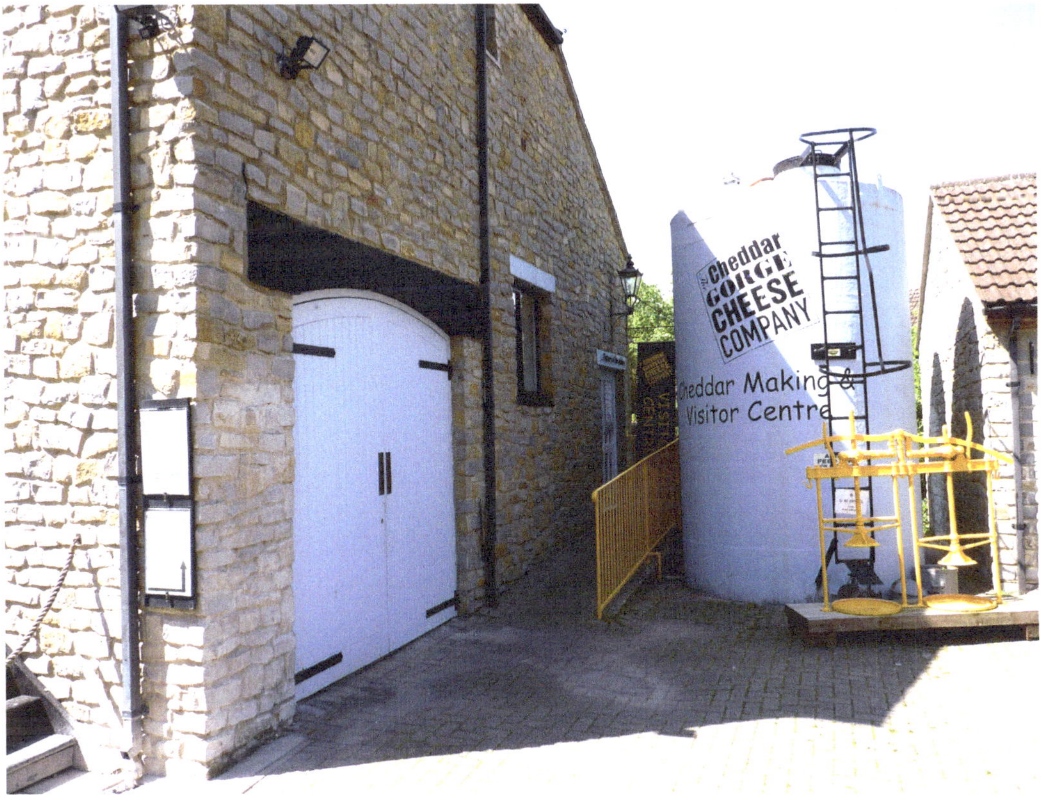

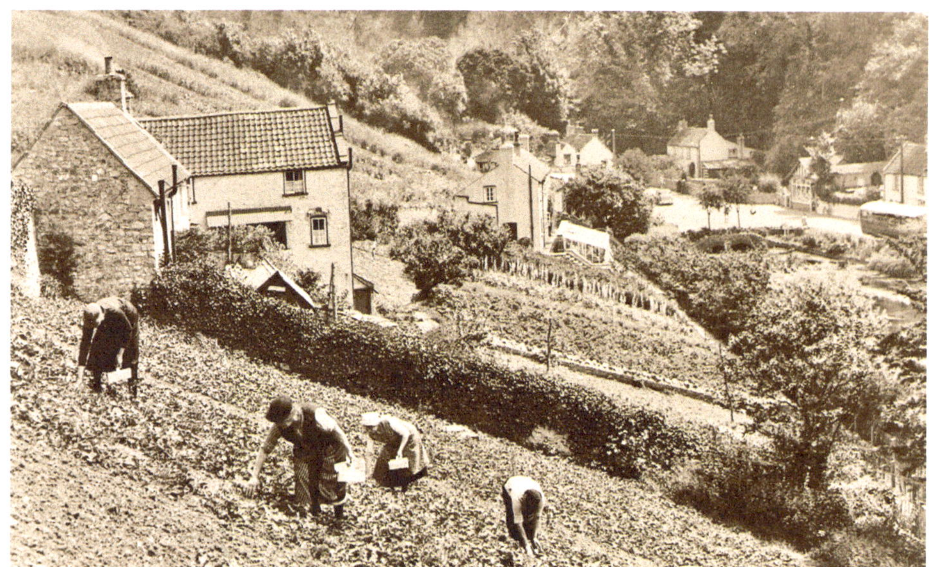

Strawberries

The growing and gathering of strawberries is a long-established business in the Cheddar Valley. They were first grown commercially by Samuel Spencer in 1901. In the photograph above strawberry pickers are at work on the slopes overlooking Cheddar. The rich red loam soil, combined with heavy rainfall and the shelter of the Mendip Hills – diminishing the chances of early or late frosts – has made the Cheddar Valley a perfect location for strawberry growing. In the middle years of the twentieth century, land was so valuable because of the strawberry business that it was hard to come by for the purpose of building new houses. William Small's cheesemongery can be seen in the valley below.

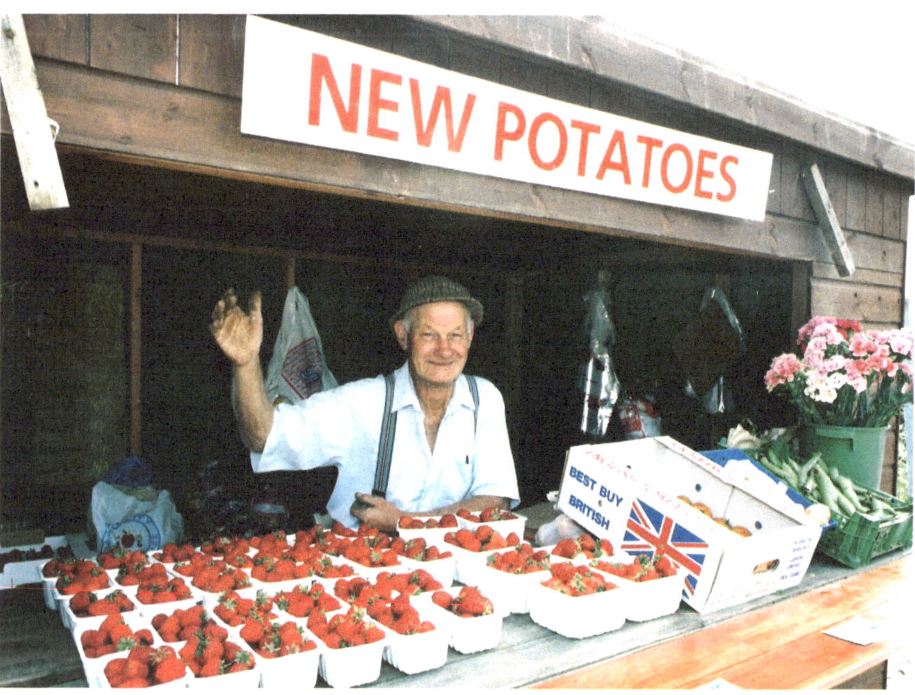

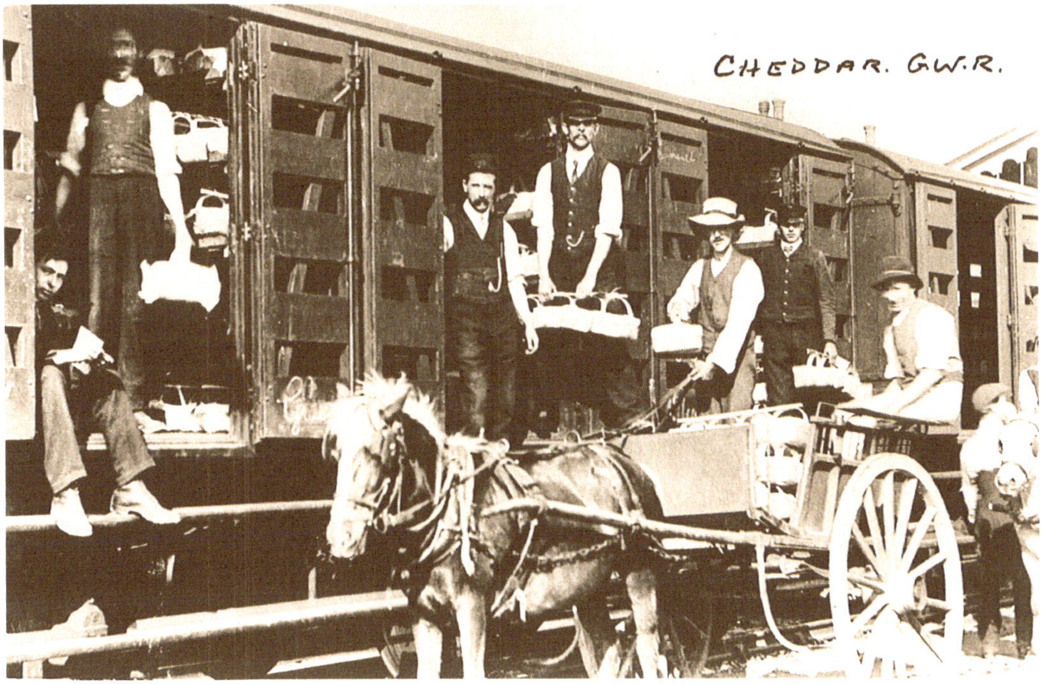

The Strawberry Line

The railway that once carried the strawberries from Cheddar was fondly known as 'the Strawberry Line'. Strawberries remain the pre-eminent crop of the extensive market gardens below the Gorge. The Royal Sovereigns grown by the Victorians have been replaced by the hardier Cambridge varieties, and they are now grown in vast cloches to protect the delicate fruit from the elements.

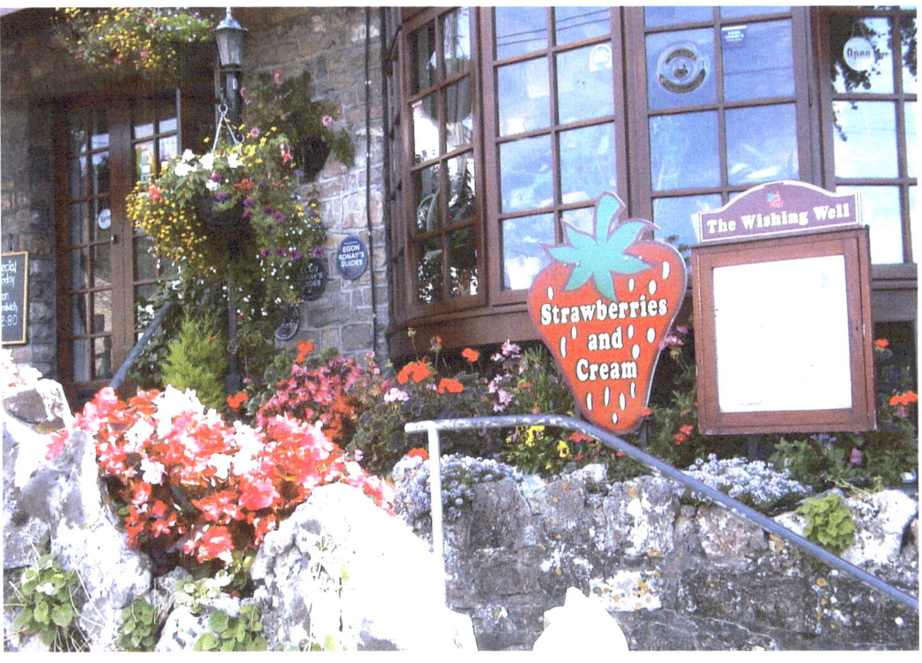

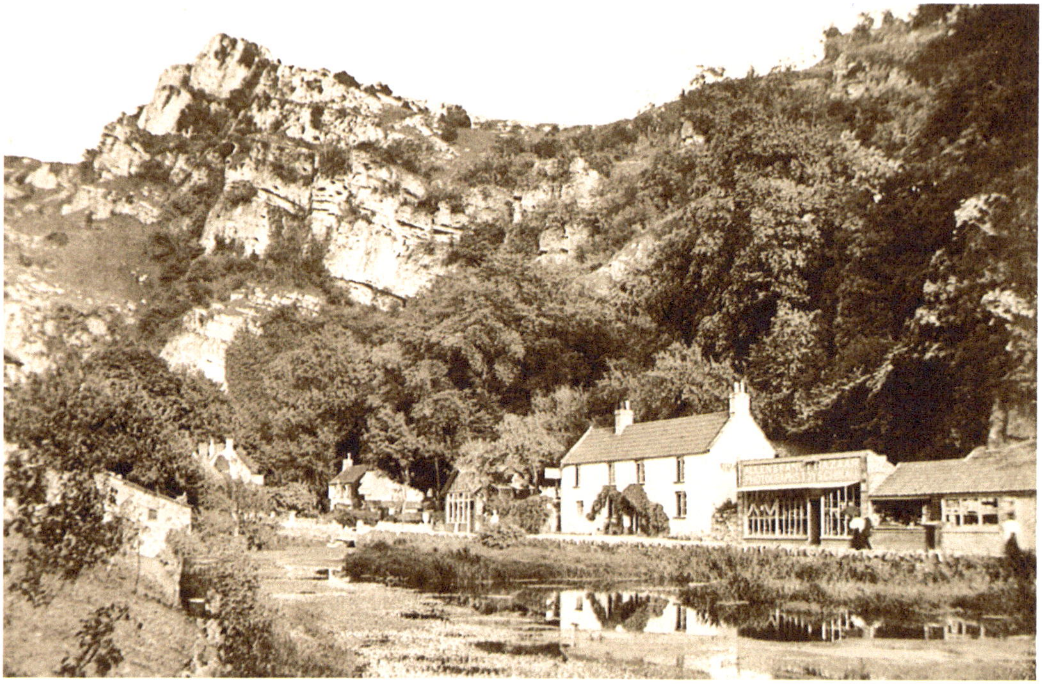

Holly House

Moving further down the gorge towards the centre of the village, Holly House, now the Holly House Tea Rooms and Take Away, has a dramatic cliff-side location and retains much of its white-washed charm. The early photograph is taken from the other side of the header lake, once providing the power for Cox's Mill.

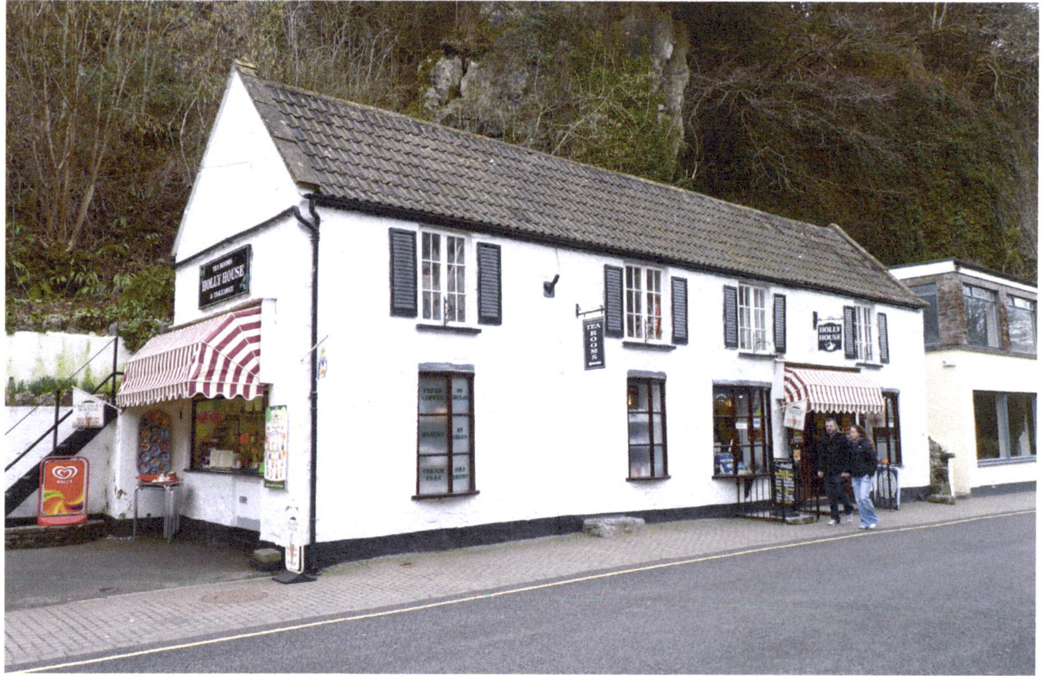

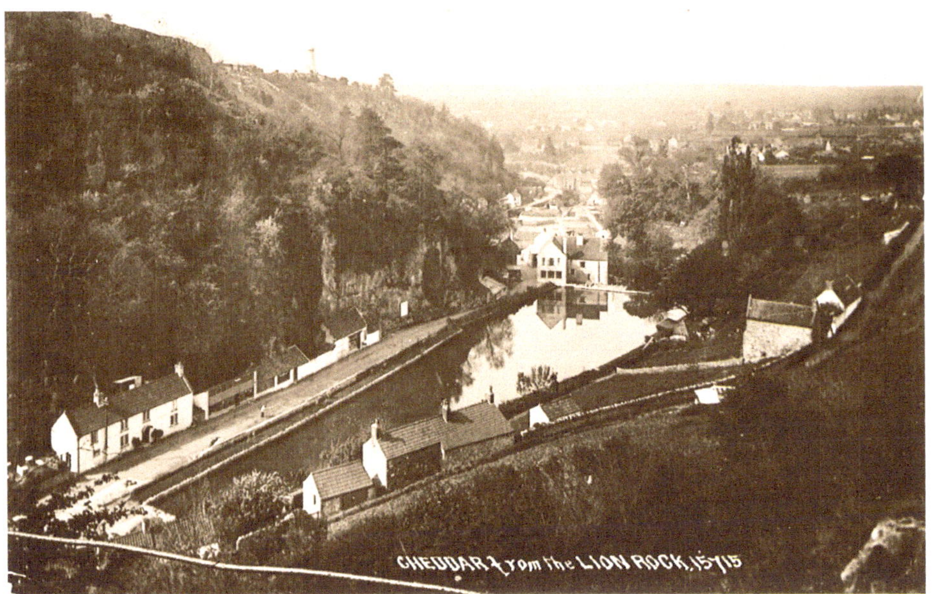

Cox's Mill

Cox's Mill, now Cox's Mill Hotel, is best viewed from the north edge of its header lake. It was, for many years, a corn mill owned by the family that gave its name to the cave system they opened up in the adjacent cliff face. In the older photograph, from the higher vantage point of Lion Rock, Holly House is on the left-hand side, and on the cliff top above the mill can be seen the top of Jacob's Ladder and the observation tower. In 1958, a rising pop star, Cliff Richard, aged eighteen and England's answer to Elvis Presley, stayed at the hotel when, appositely, it was known as the Cliff Hotel.

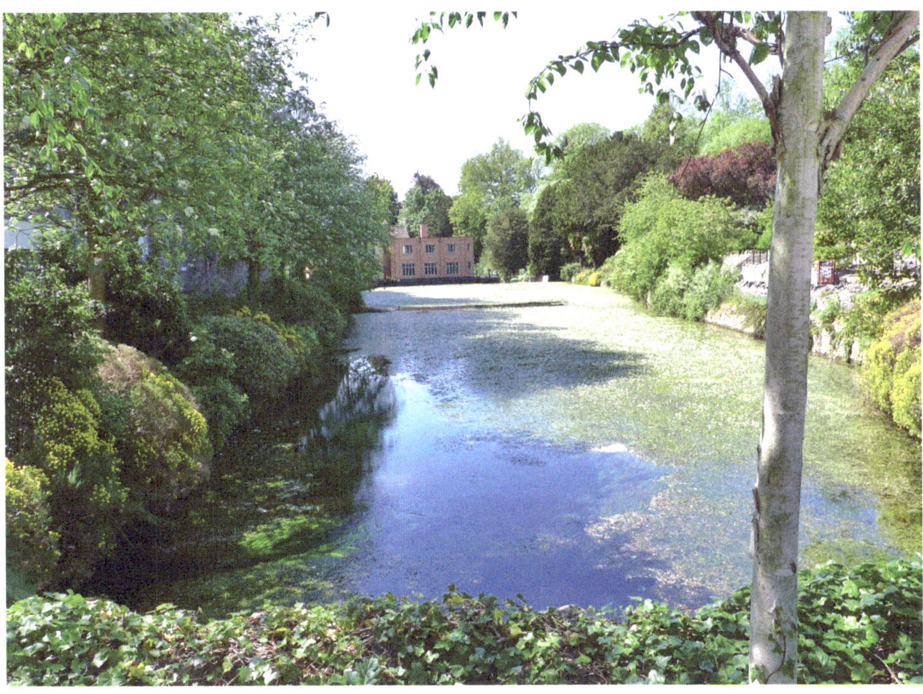

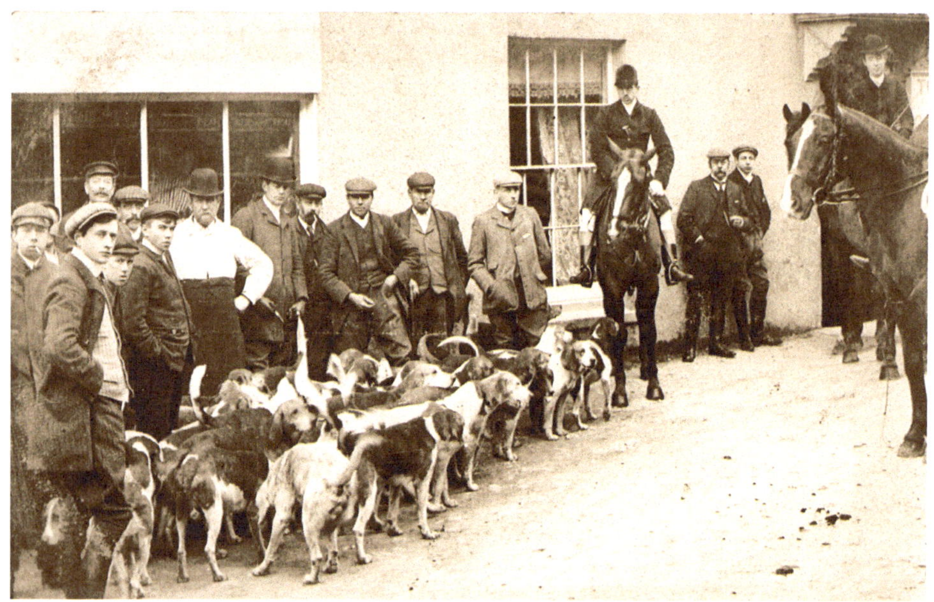

Paranormal Apparitions

Cox's Mill Hotel has been the subject of recent paranormal speculation regarding evidence of a range of alleged hauntings. In 2007, a hotel guest was greatly disturbed by the vision of a ghostly woman in the hotel's main function room, who appeared to be placing the corpse of a baby into a fireplace. Further spectral appearances prompted the South West Paranormal Group to investigate, using state-of-the-art equipment to record anomalies in a number of rooms in the hotel. Their findings have been recorded and published by author Mark Bailey. Still a focal point for locals and visitors alike, the early picture here suggests the hotel was the meeting place for the Mendip Hunt and Hounds in the days before their bloodsport was banned in the UK. Interestingly, one of the apparitions associated with the hotel is that of a man in the costume of a huntsman.

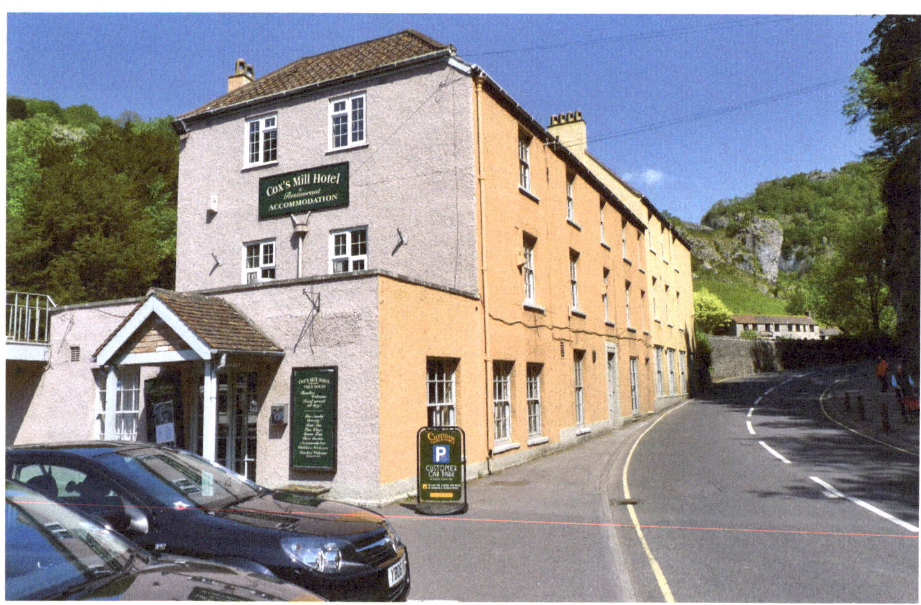

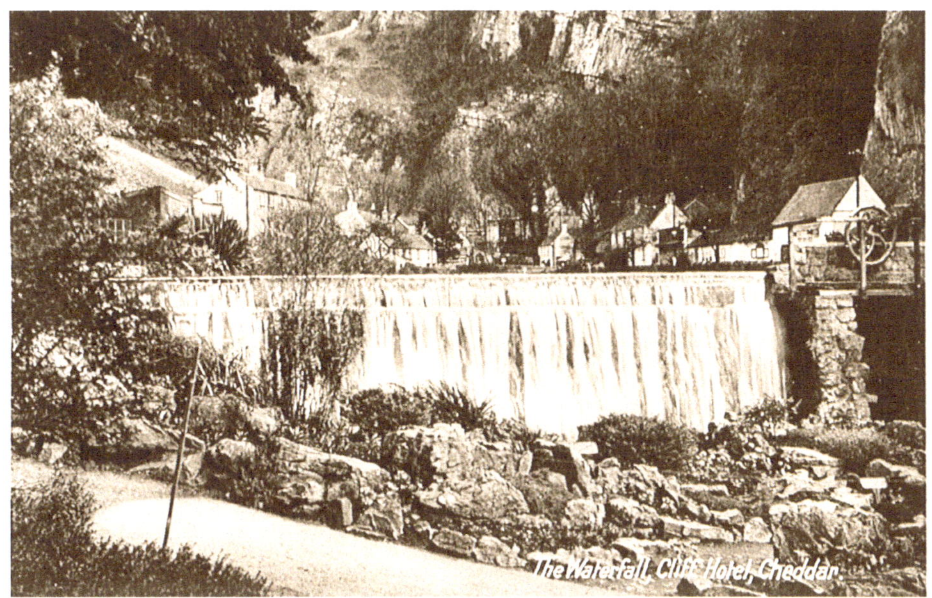

The Waterfall

The waterfall adjacent to and once serving Cox's Mill. Cox's Mill Hotel and Restaurant, for many years known as the Cliff Hotel, has long been a popular viewpoint for visitors to Cheddar. The expansion of the hotel building to the right of the recent picture has reduced the width of the waterfall, which appears to be an altogether less dramatic structure now than it was in earlier times. The Waterfall Restaurant is one of numerous eating places in the village.

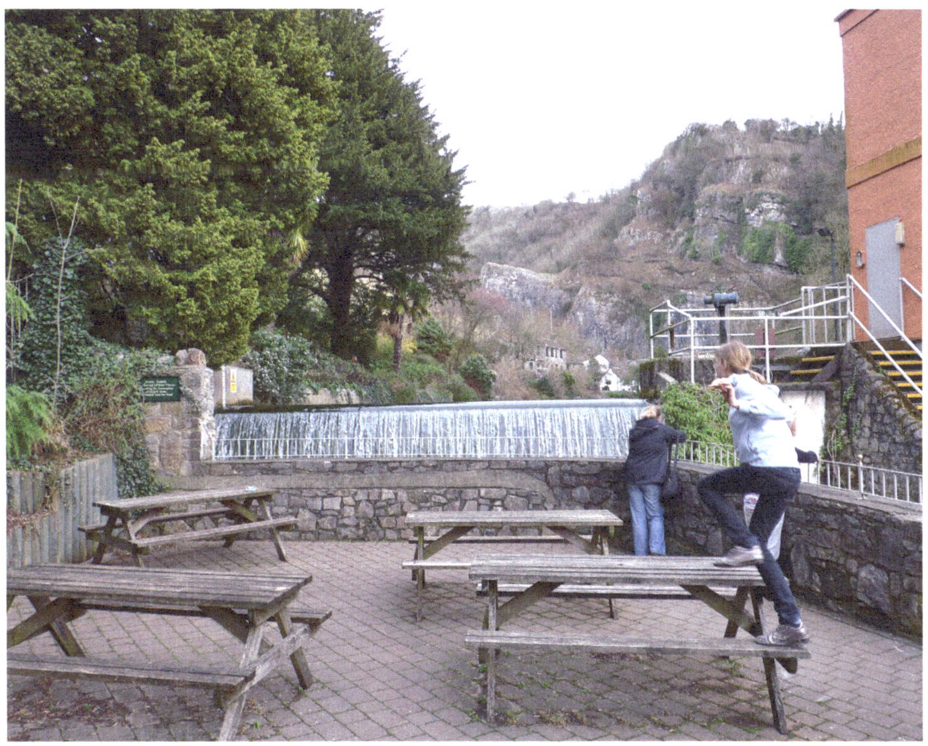

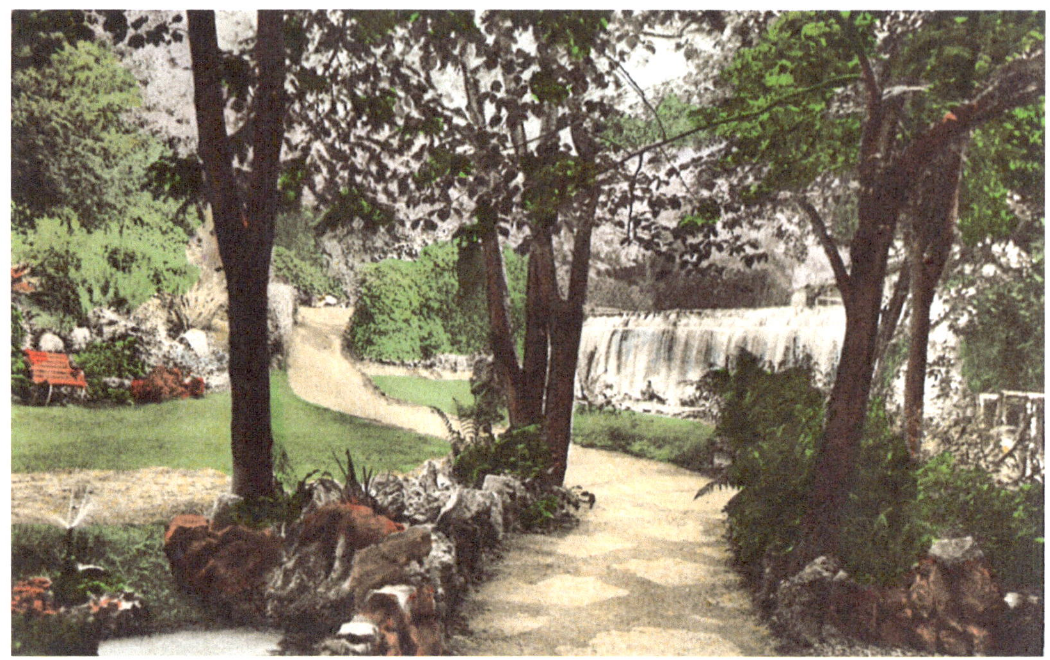

Cox's Mill Hotel Gardens

Much of the formerly elegant gardens of the Cliff Hotel, now Cox's Mill Hotel, has been paved, providing space for ubiquitous 'pub garden' picnic benches and tables, and additional parking for the hotel's customers. An impression of its former glory is gained from the pathway above the waterfall where the unkempt remains of its rockeries and decorative plantings can still be identified on the steep banks above the hotel and header lake.

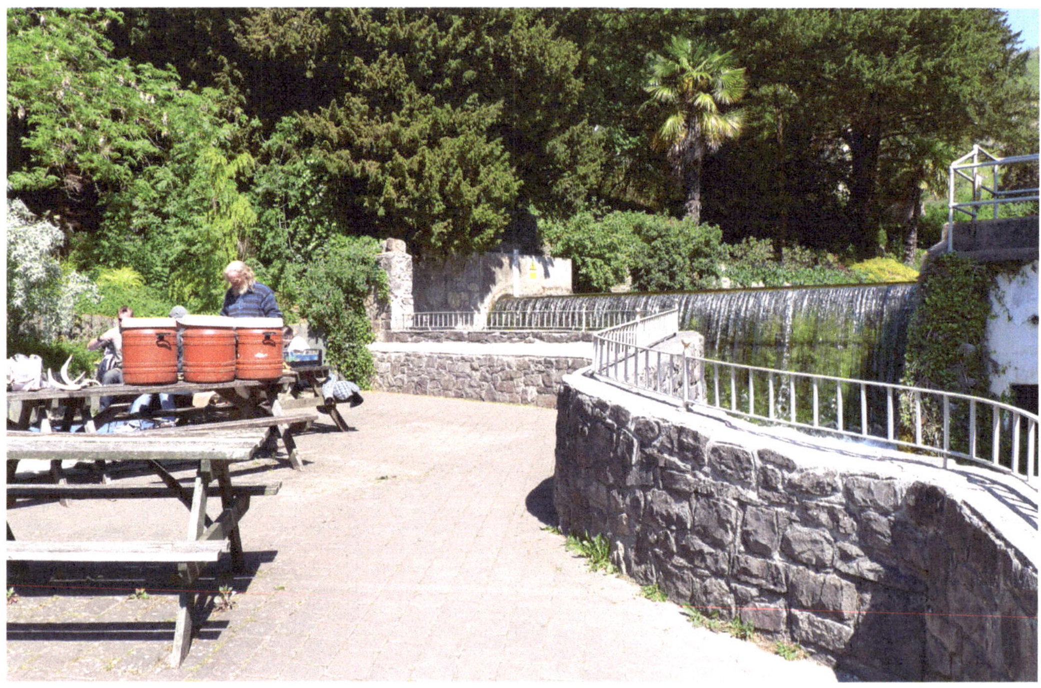

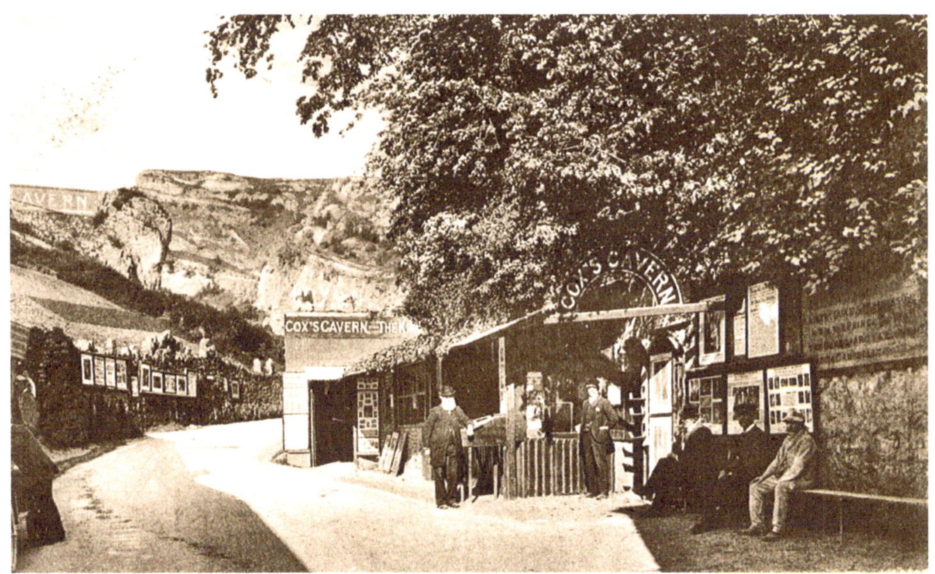

The Entrance to Cox's Cave

On the cliff face adjacent to Cox's Mill is the entrance to Cox's Cave. The old postcard shown here records a royal visit by 'the late King Edward VII' who died in 1910. It also remarks that of the 600 caves visited by one M. Martel of Paris, this was the one he most admired. A great banner, emblazoned with the word 'CAVERN' appears to be suspended on the back of the lion of Lion Rock. Ever since George Cox discovered the caverns that bear his name in 1837, Cheddar has thrived on tourism. Entrance to Cox's Cave was three shillings, one for those that belonged to a party of visitors. These days tickets – priced in pounds, not shillings – for all of the main attractions can be purchased at the central ticket office and shop at the foot of Jacob's Ladder. Cox's Cave was discovered by accident when George Cox was aiming to expand his mill premises in 1837. He made a suitable opening to the cavern by blasting the rock face with dynamite, in the process of which, much to the irritation of the hotelier, he blew in several hotel windows.

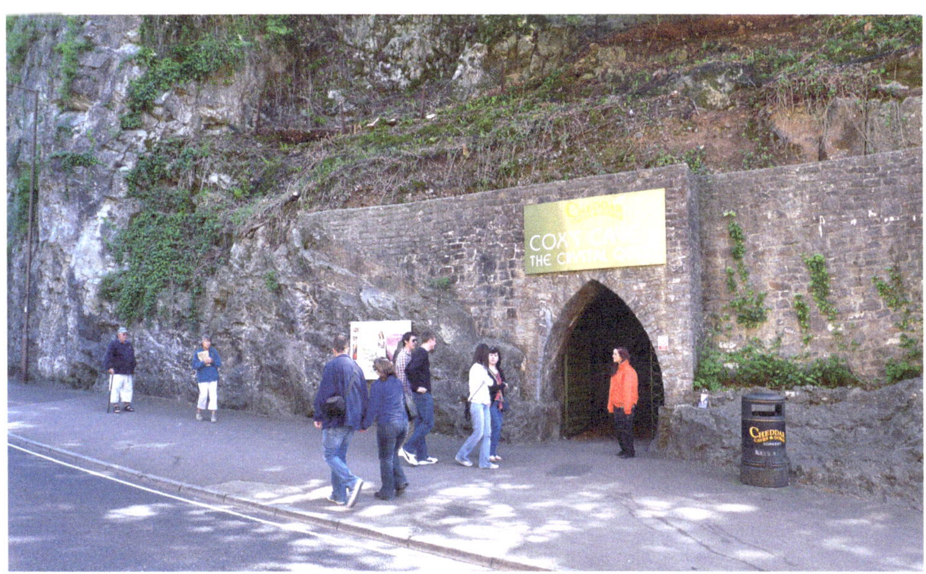

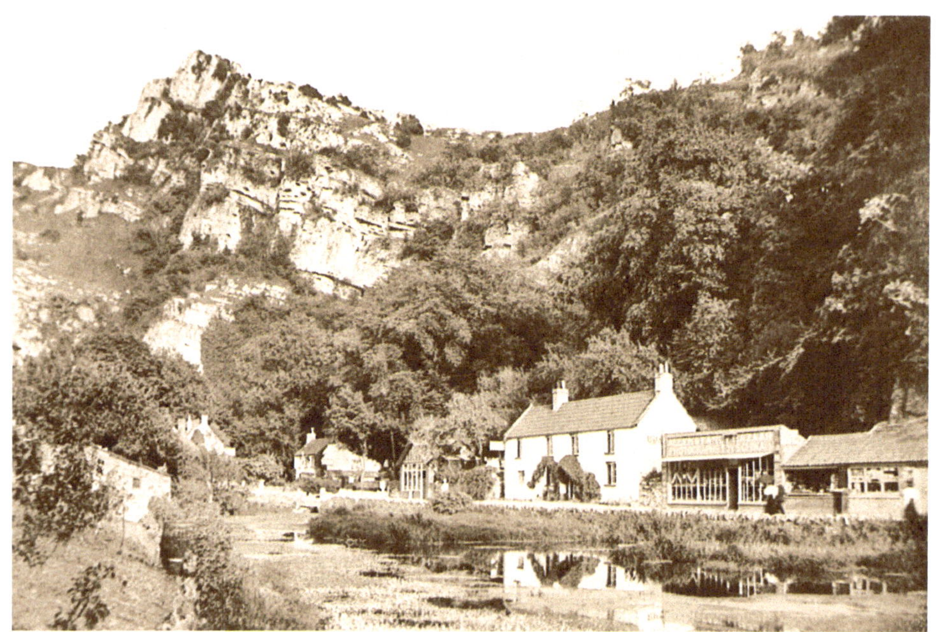

The Cliffs

In the summertime tourists flock to The Cliffs – the name of the B3135 road that runs through the gorge. One visitor, A. W. Coysh, in a book published back in 1954, commented, 'I like Cheddar best in the spring, before the crowds come. The little shops and cafés are freshly painted and have an expectant air, and the jackdaws chatter and scream as they carry building materials for their nests on the rock ledges.' (Coysh A. W., Mason E. J., Waite V. (1954) *The Mendips*, Robert Hale, p. 5) The archive photograph shows Allen's Fancy Bazaar (middle building), advertising photographs, toys and china, all of which are still readily available, together with leather goods, cheese and cider, in the village today.

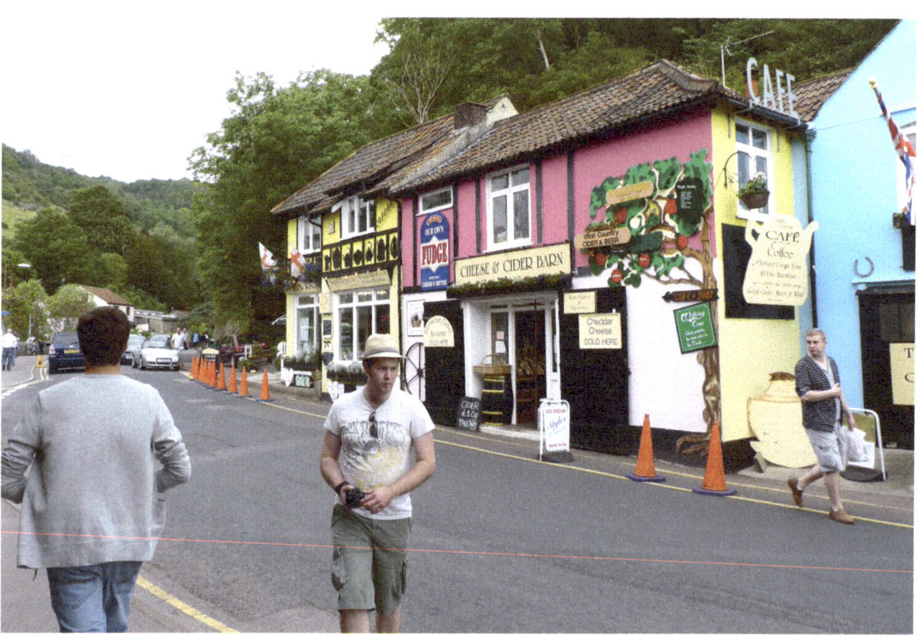

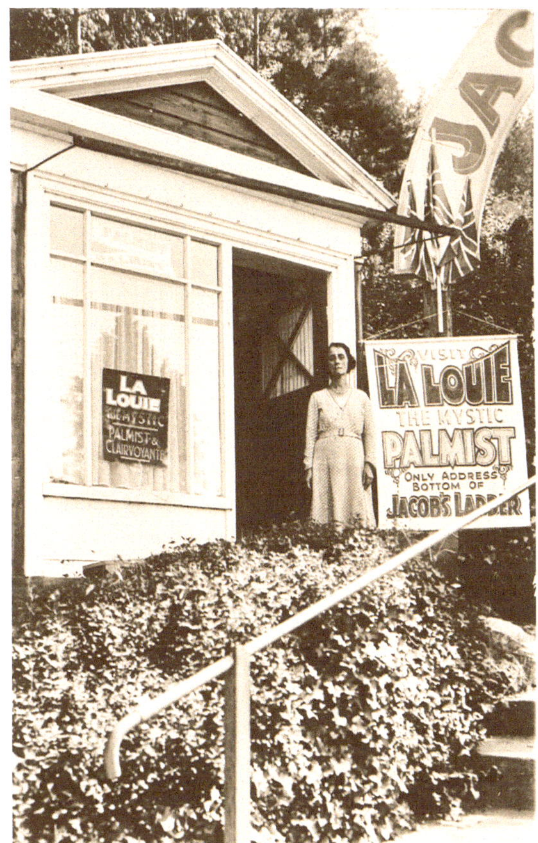

The Mystic Tower

La Louie, the palm reader, was renowned for accosting unsuspecting visitors on their way up to 'The Mystic Tower', also known as the White Tower, at the top of Jacob's Ladder. A creaky step alerted her to the presence of passers-by on their way up. These days the hut on the site of her premises is occupied by information officers and guides on busy days at the height of the tourist season.

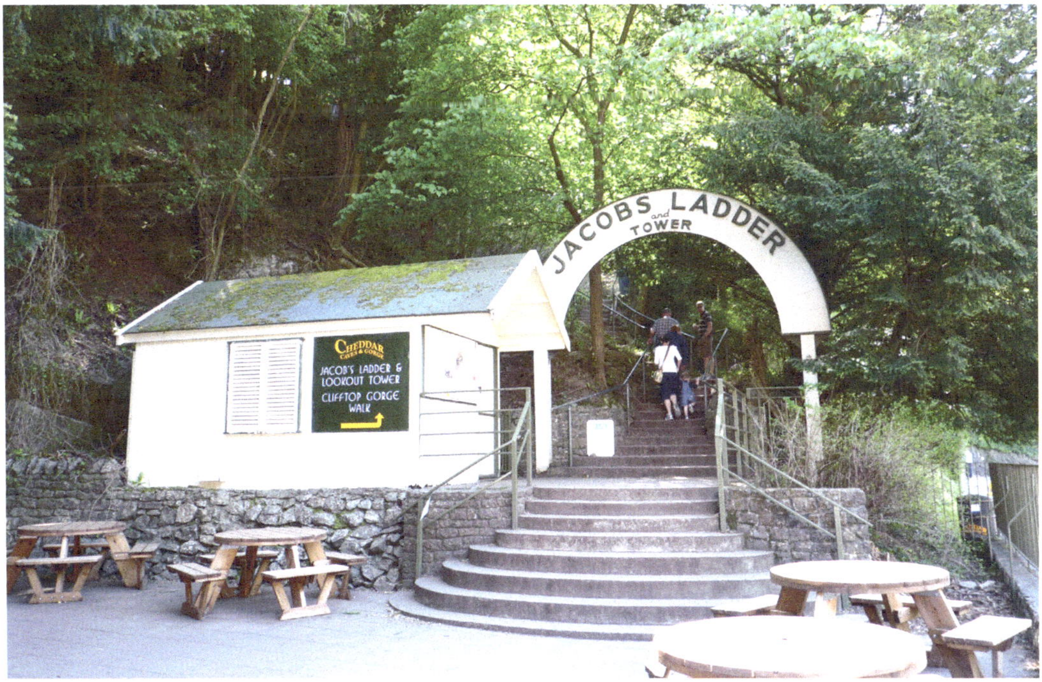

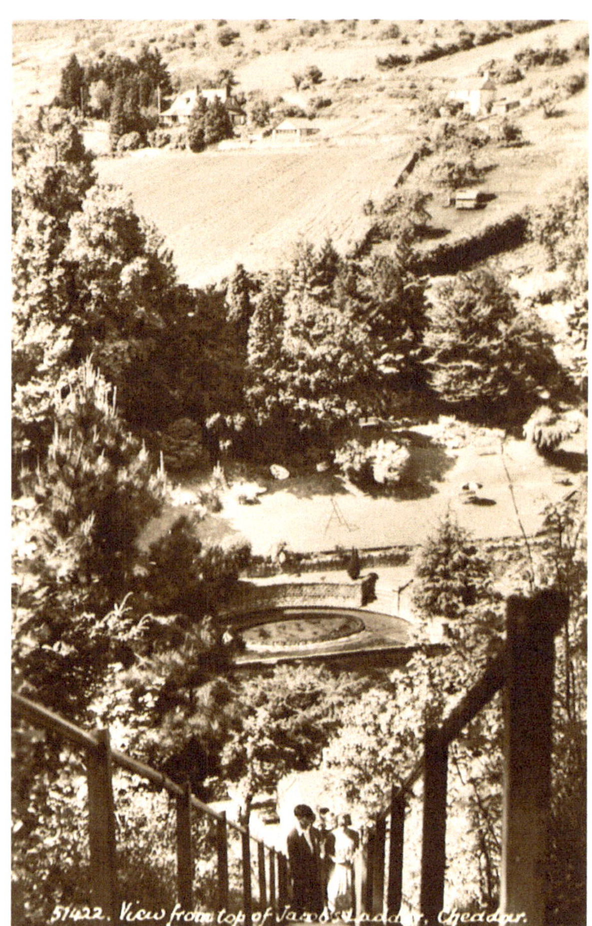

Jacob's Ladder

The 274 steps of Rowland Pavey's 'Jacob's Ladder' remain something of an endurance test for all but the fittest of visitors! At the time of their construction, towards the end of the first decade of the twentieth century, the intrepid tourist was rewarded with a pleasure garden known as 'Joyland', where hot meals could be purchased and diversions included a shooting gallery, a zipwire, and skittles. Of these entertainments only the view from the observation tower remains. In the background of the earlier picture can be seen fields on the hill slope opposite, cultivated for the growing of strawberries.

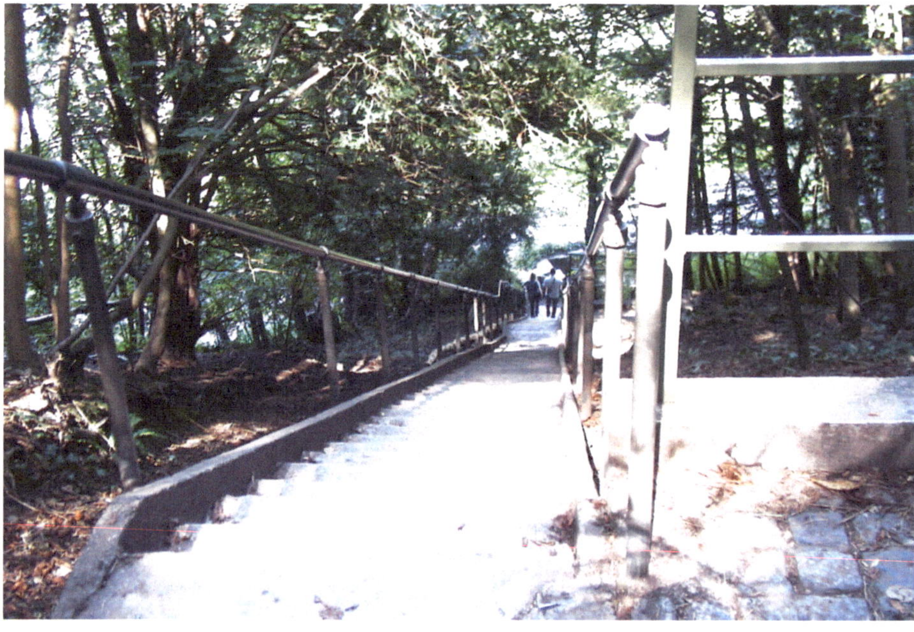

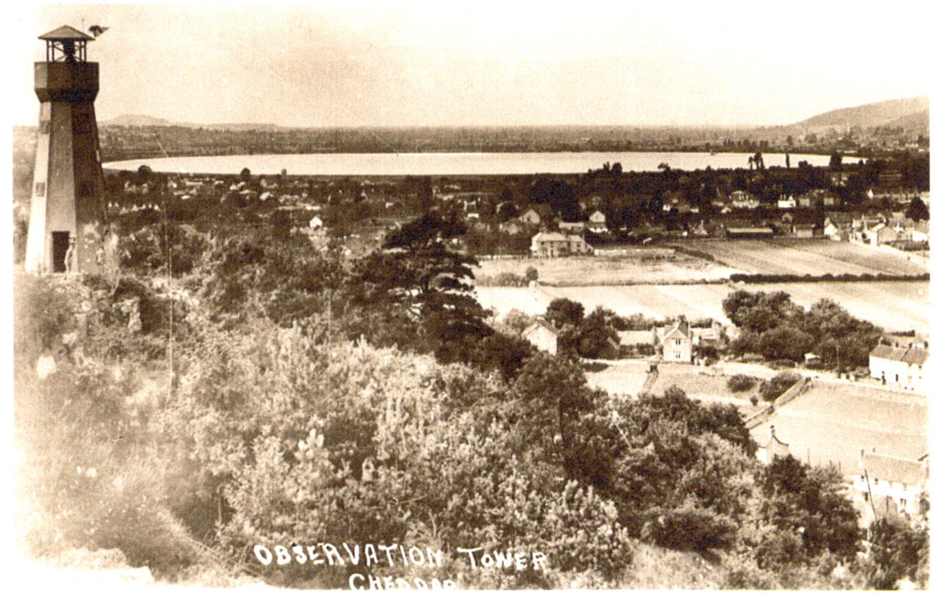

The Lookout Tower

High above Cheddar Gorge, the modern Lookout Tower was constructed of wrought iron in 1936. Its forty-eight steps lead to spectacular views on a clear day. It replaces the earlier wooden construction, the Mystic Tower, built in 1908 by Richard Gough's good friend, Rowland Pavey, water diviner and magician. His one attempt to fly across the gorge using his homemade wings of whalebone and whaleskin ended in an ignominious crash-landing in the cliff-side gorse bushes. He ended his days in a mental institution. The Mystic Tower once housed a camera obscura; it was destroyed in a gale in the 1930s.

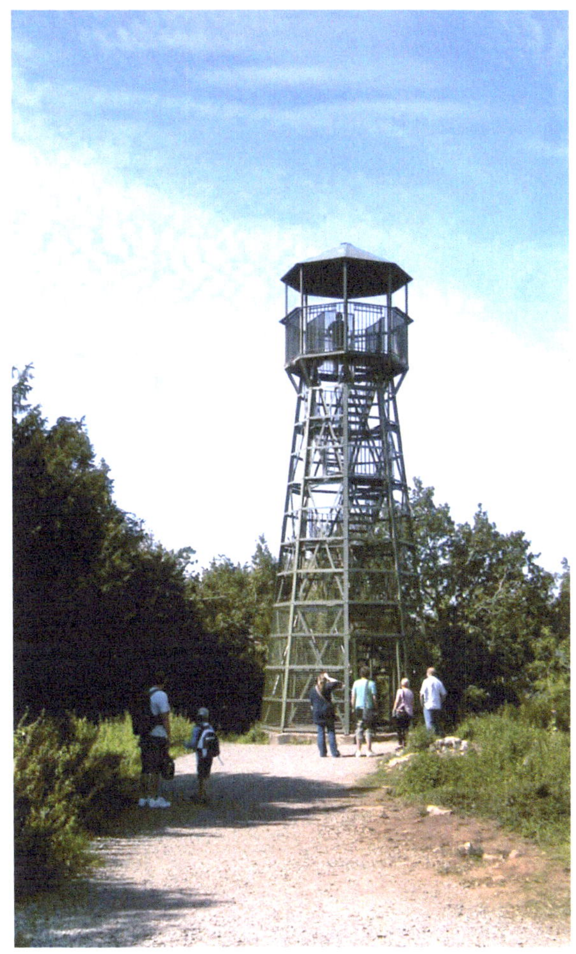

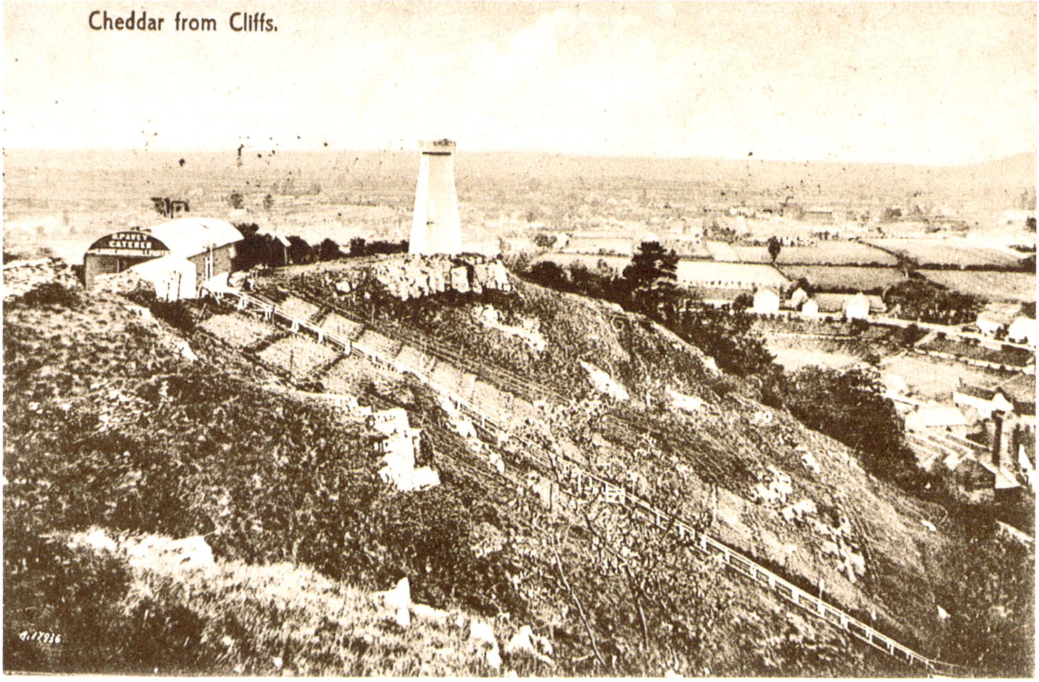

Cheddar from Cliffs.

Joyland

No trace remains of Pavey's utilitarian, shed-like catering outlet. The food was cooked down in the valley, presumably in the kitchens of Pavey's Hotel, and winched up to the hungry diners above. The recent photograph, taken from the top of the observation tower, shows Batts Combe quarry in the distance.

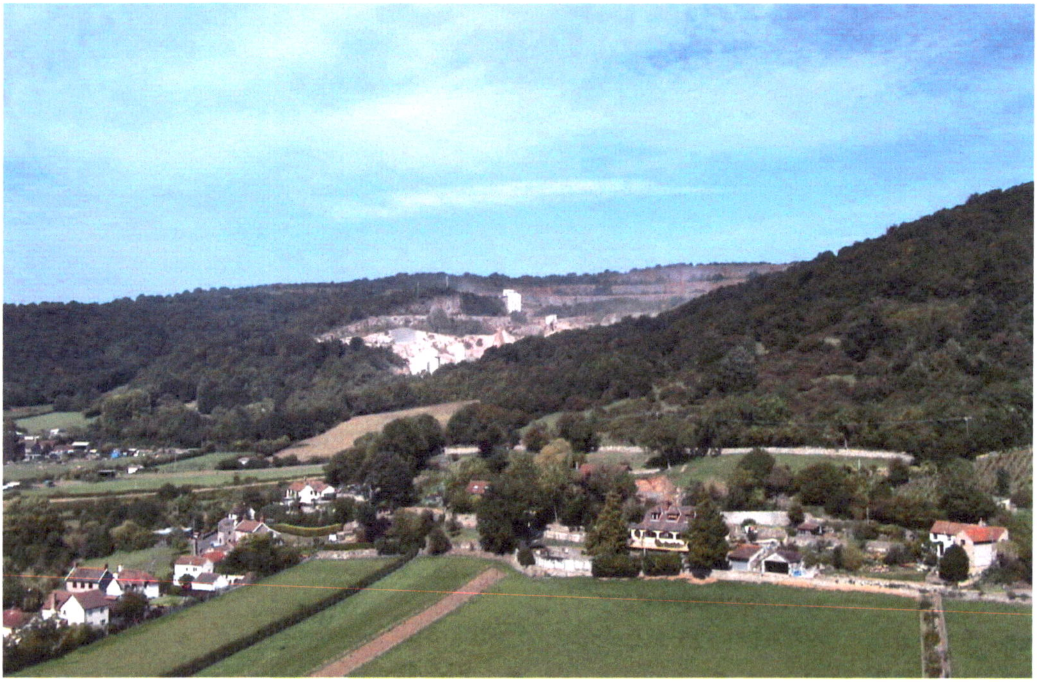

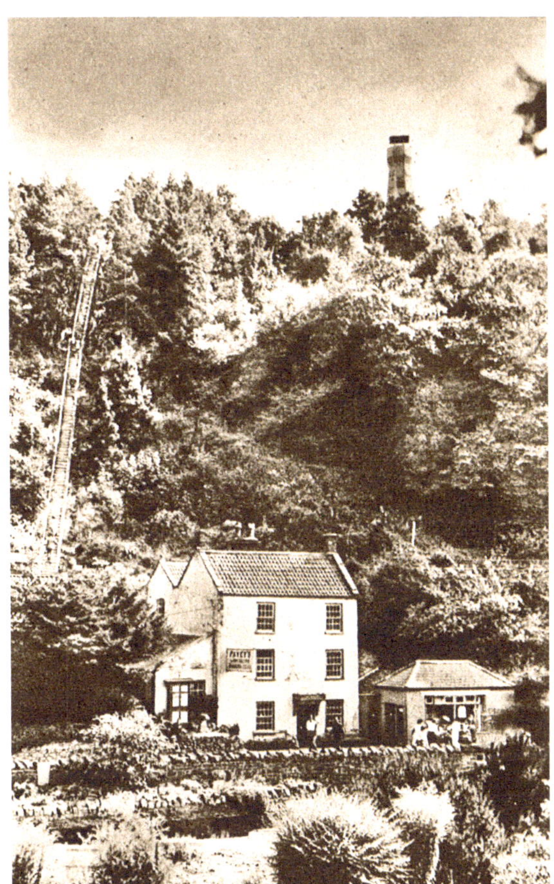

Pavey's Temperance Hotel

Pavey's Temperance Hotel stood near the foot of the eccentric local entrepreneur Rowland Pavey's Jacob's Ladder. The front of the original two-bay hotel structure was removed when the main road running up the gorge was widened. The back bay, visible in the modern photograph, now houses Old Rowland's Gift Shop, specialising in Christmas decorations.

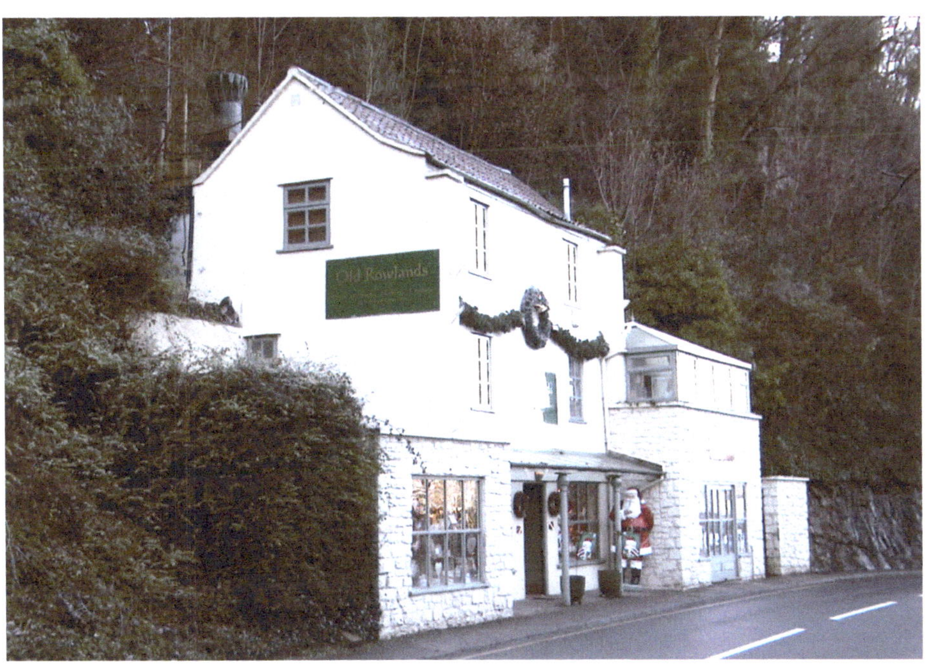

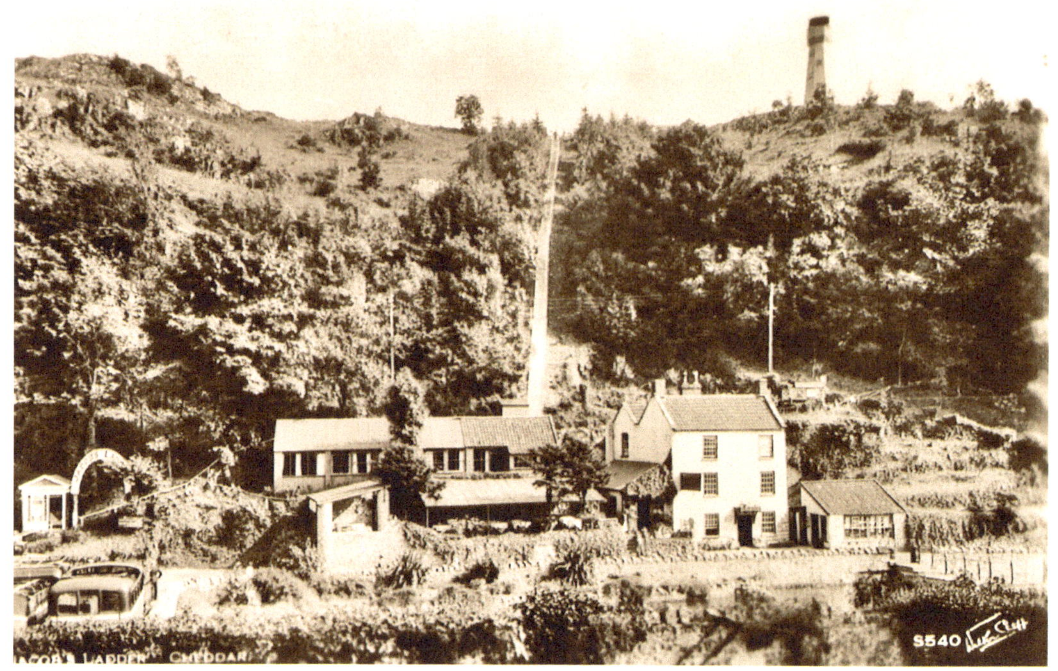

Pavey's Hotel and Jacob's Ladder

A view from across the valley shows Jacob's Ladder before it became largely obscured by trees and bushes. Rowland Pavey's Temperance Hotel in the foreground has lost its front bay in more recent times due to widening of the road. Both the Mystic Tower and Jacob's Ladder are clearly visible in the old photograph but trees completely obscure them from sight today. Pavey's tearooms, adjacent to the hotel, could sit 400 diners at a time.

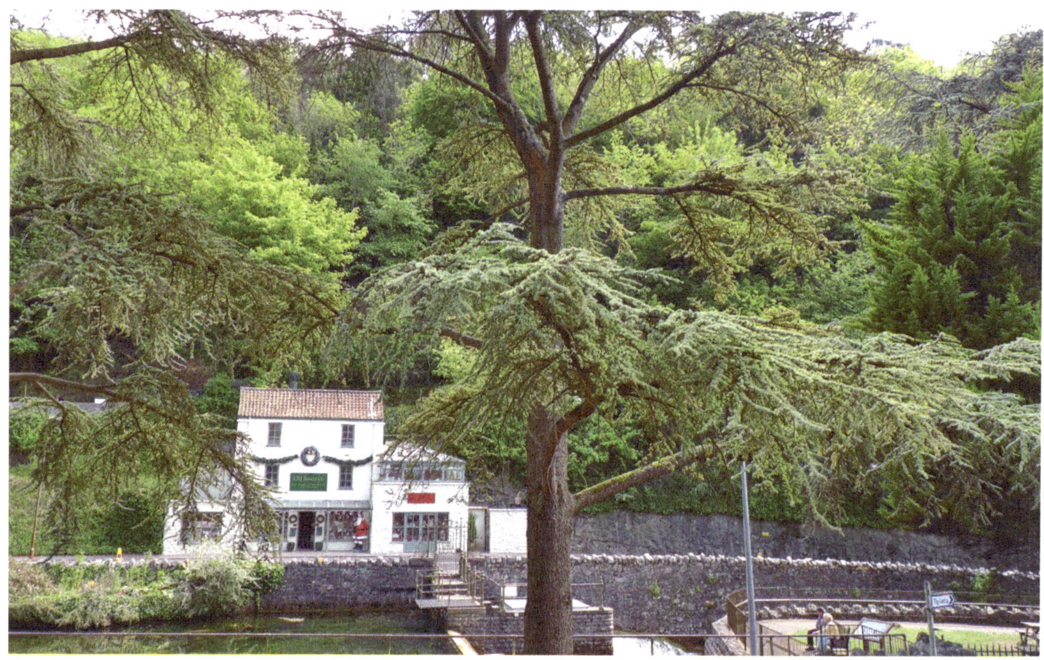

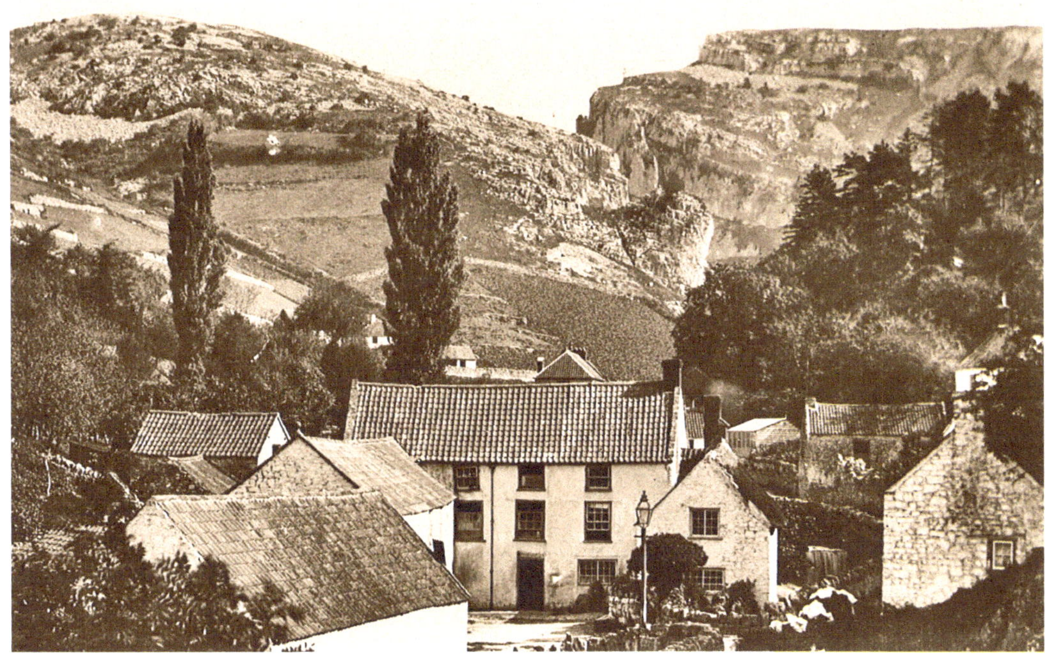

The Rotary Garden

Middle Mill was a corn mill over the road from Pavey's Temperance Hotel. Long since demolished, the site is now 'The Rotary Garden' funded by the local Rotary Club, and first planted in 1975. In the early photograph, Pavey's Mill is on the right from a view looking towards the Gorge; in the recent photograph, taken from Jacob's Ladder, the corner of Pavey's Hotel, now Old Rowland's Gift Shop, is to the left and the Rotary Garden is beyond the white car.

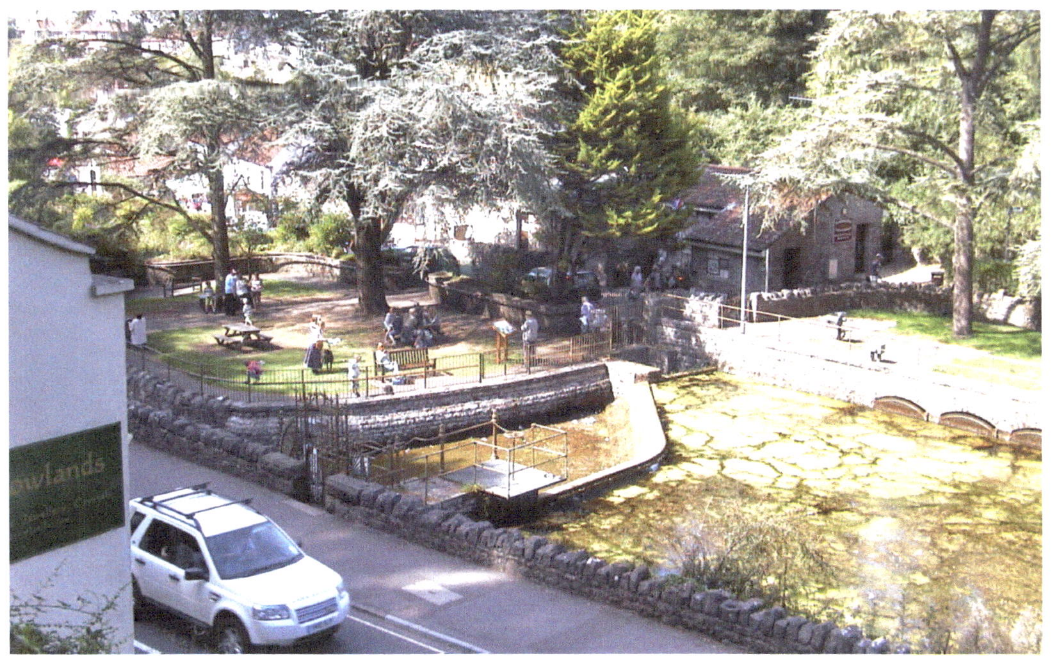

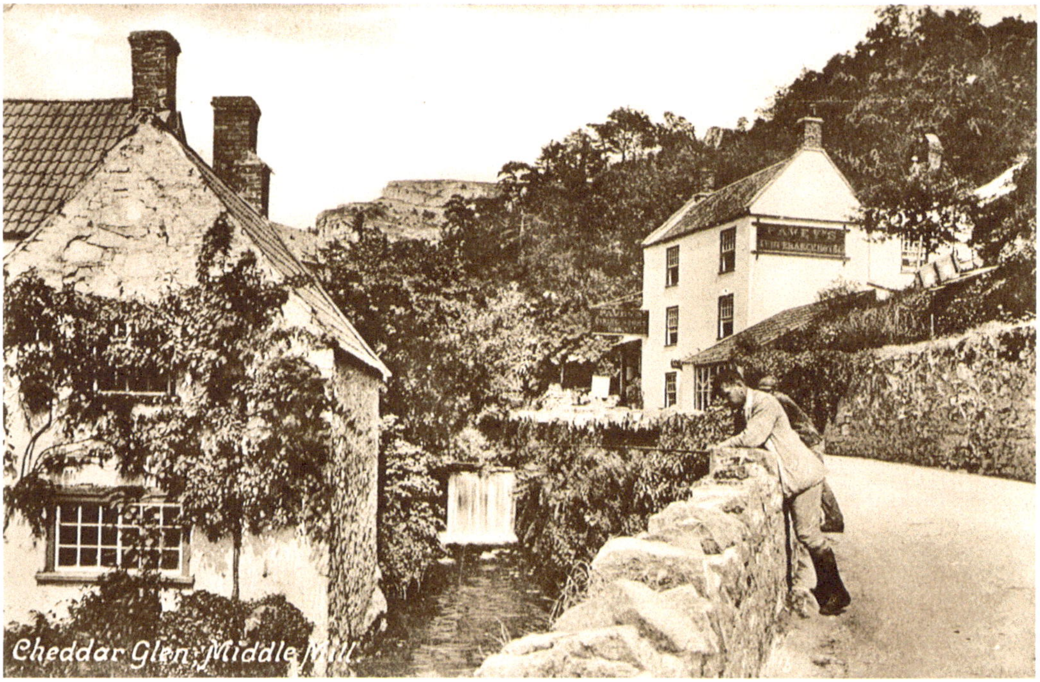

Middle Mill

The picture above appears to show men fishing in the mill leat between Pavey's Hotel and Middle Mill. Middle Mill may have gone, replaced by attractive overgrown rock gardens, but the fast flowing stream remains to delight Cheddar's numerous visitors.

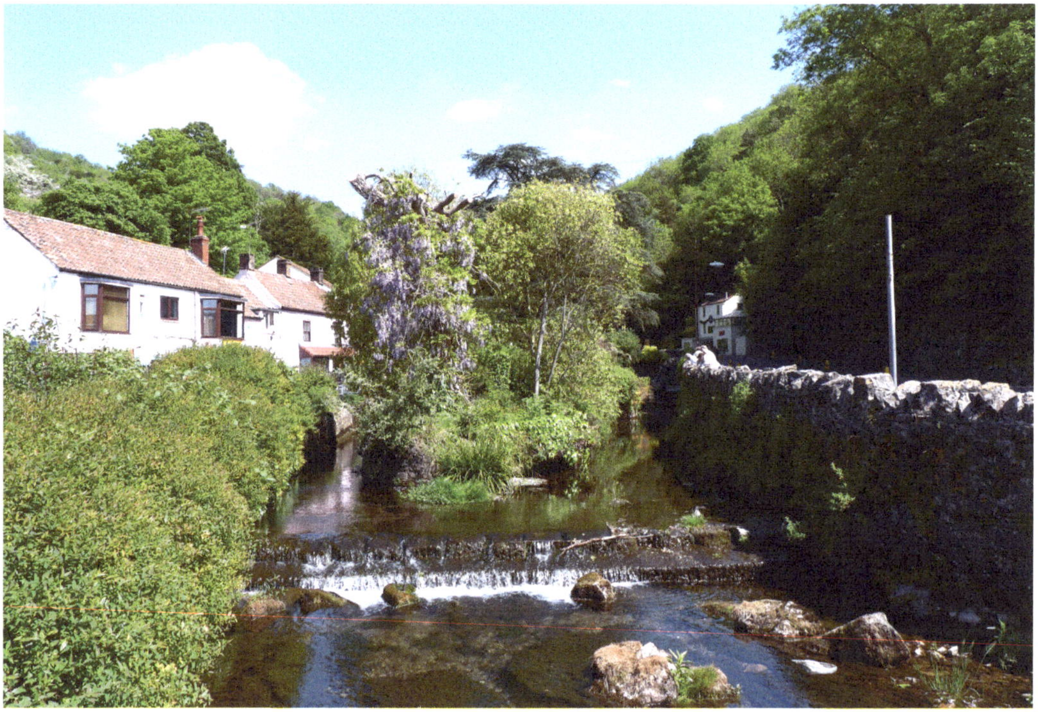

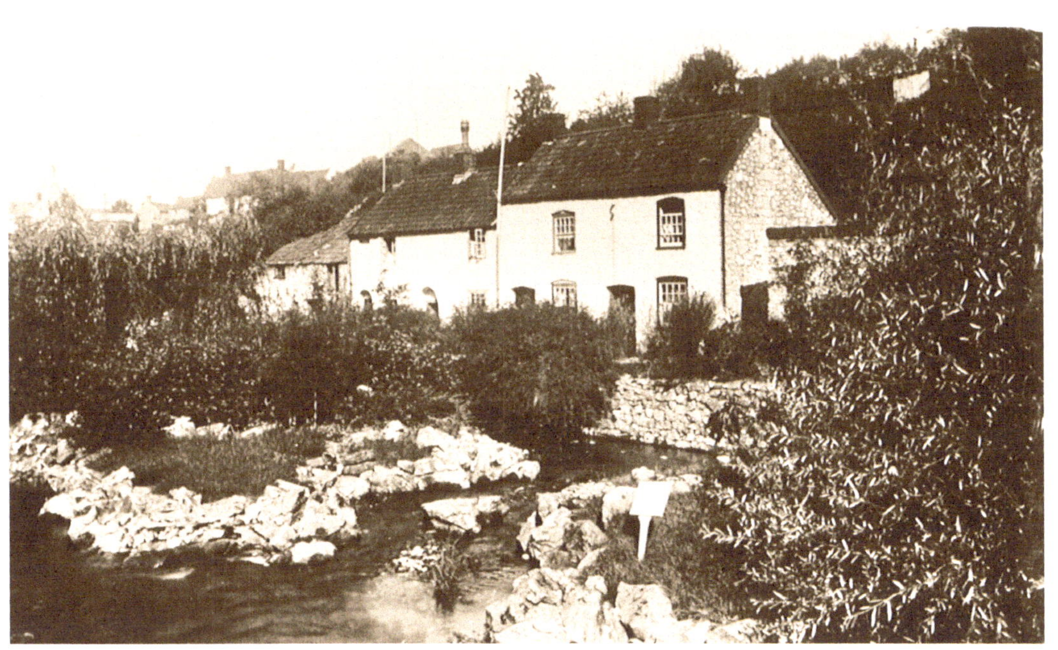

Daghole

Beyond the site of Middle Mill is Daghole, still an attractive and interesting row of cottages and shops. The archive image shows the Daghole cottages from across the lake.

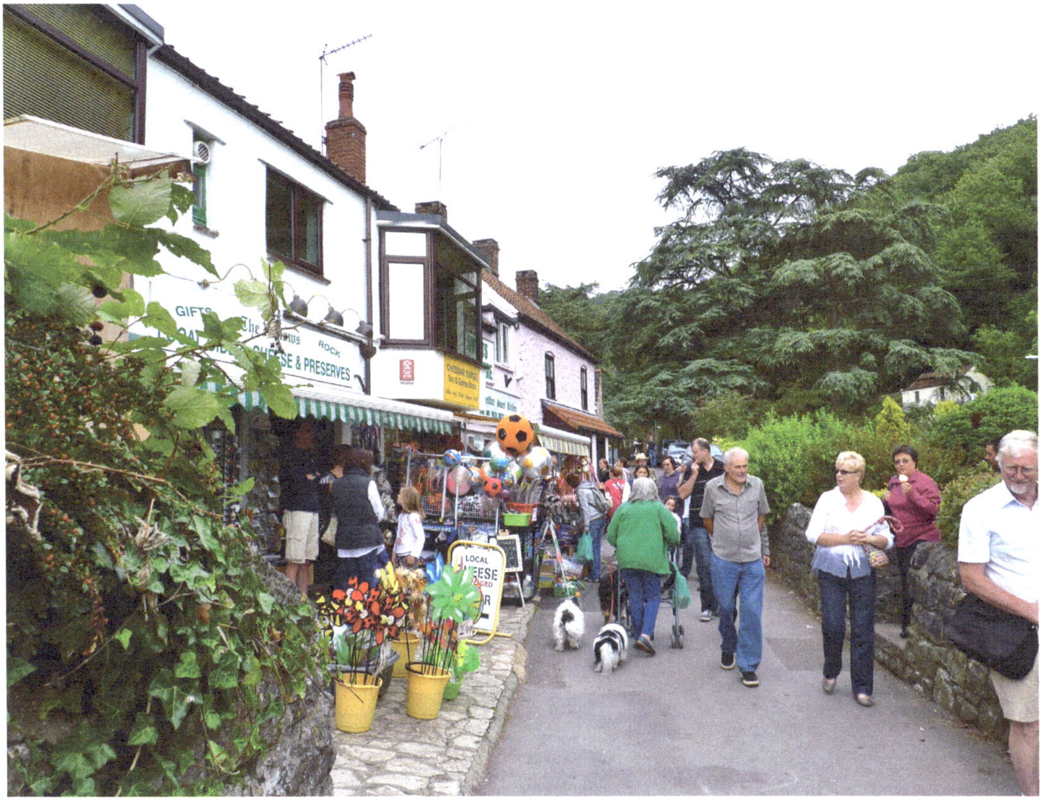

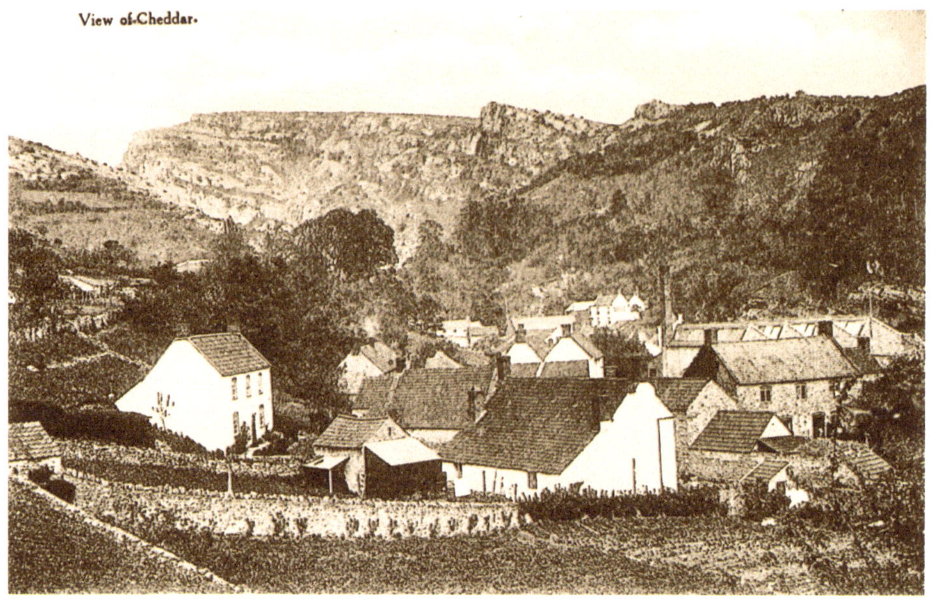

Shirt Manufacturing

The 1902 Ordnance Survey map for Cheddar identifies no less than three shirt factories in the village. For the reissue of this map, Mike Bone has written: 'Two of the old mills had been converted into shirt manufactories by 1902 and a third [...] on Tweentown. The making of shirts, blouses and detached collars of the time was quite significant in the late-Victorian economy of Somerset and North Devon [...]. The Cheddar factories were, apparently, quite short-lived. Production soon moved to Taunton, causing widespread unemployment and much emigration to America. Two of these factories survive, identified by their distinctive jagged north-light roof structures.' Those of the factory at the foot of the gorge, now housing shops and cafés, can be seen in both of the photographs on this page. Beyond its chimney (now gone) in the archive photograph can be seen the two-bay structure of Pavey's Temperance Hotel.

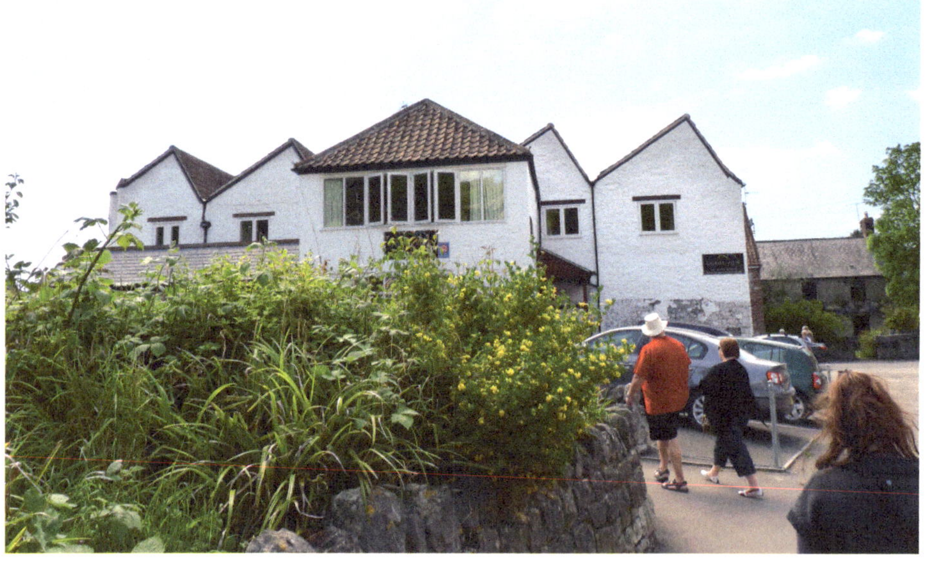

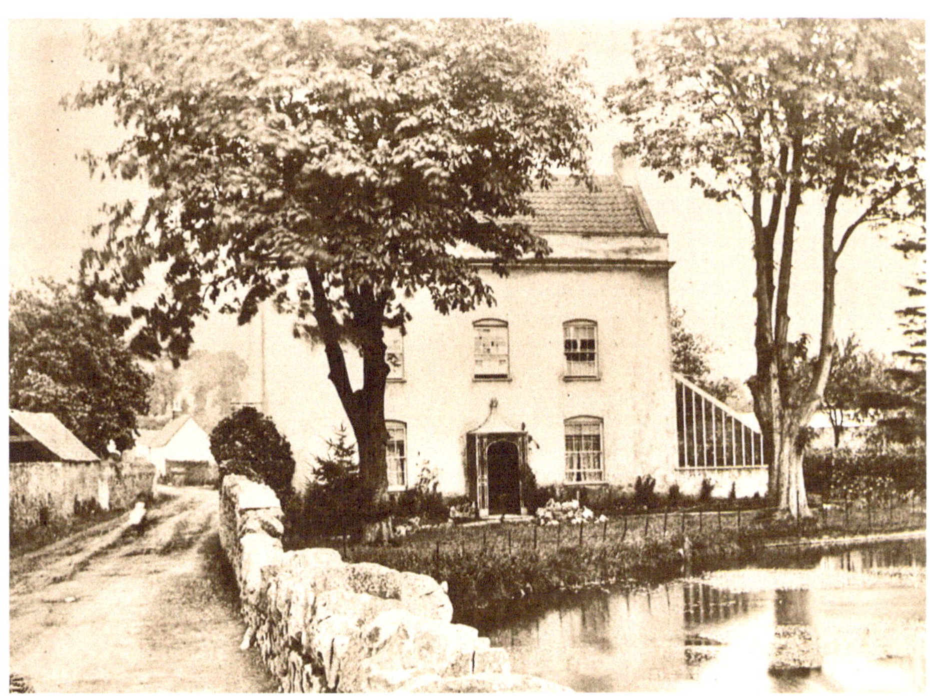

The Factory from the White Hart Inn

The modern photograph on this page shows the shirt factory from the parking bays beside the White Hart Inn. The manager lived nearby in the substantial house shown in the archive picture.

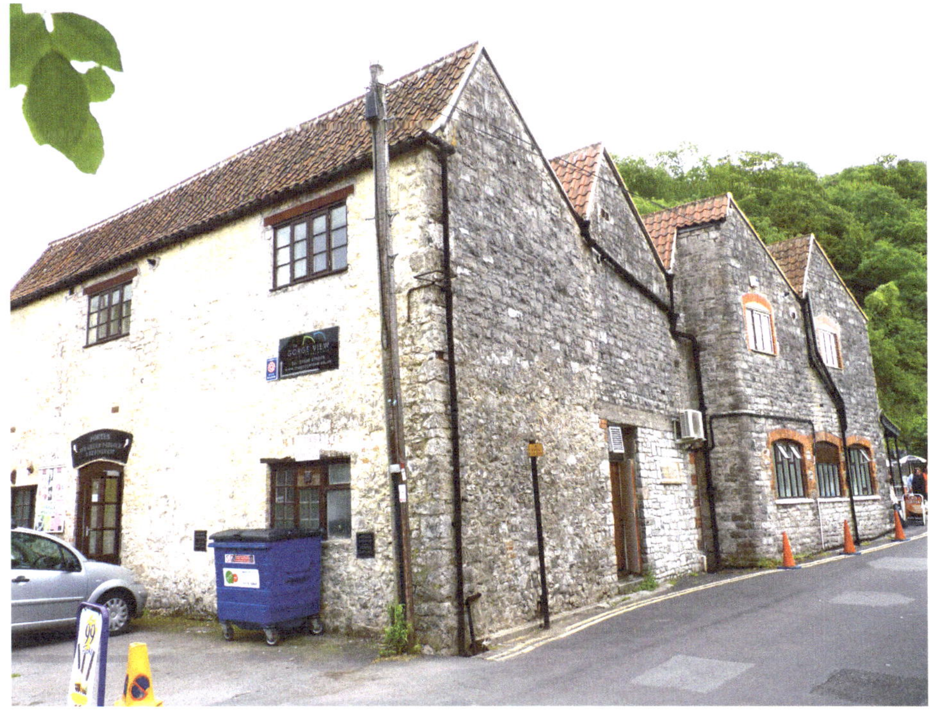

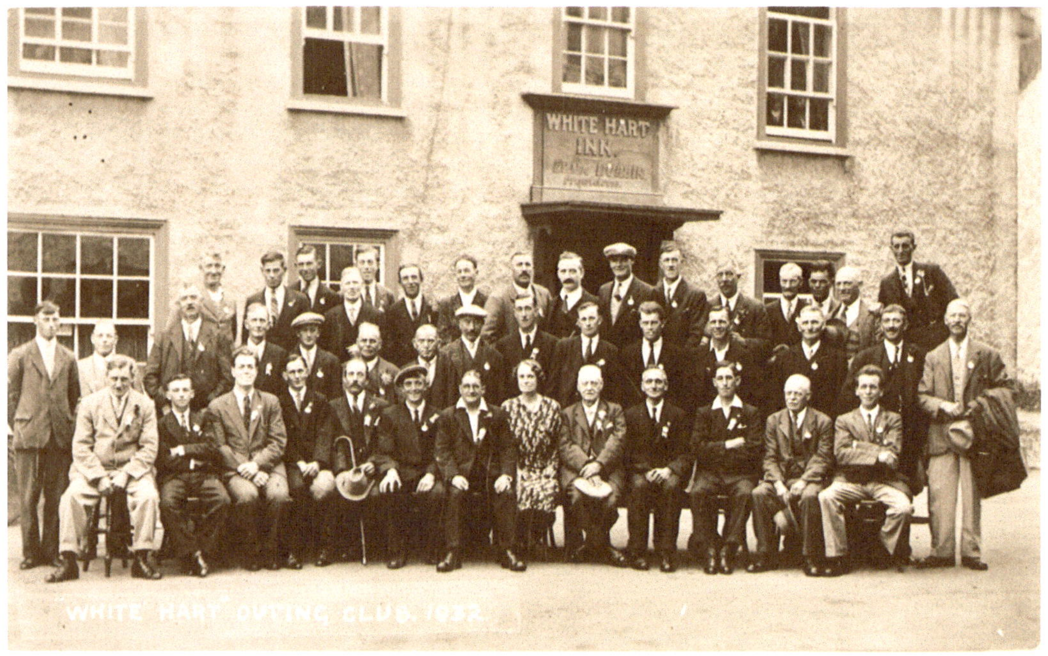

The White Hart

To the side of the old shirt factory is the White Hart in The Bays, a lane that runs parallel to the main street beside the cliffs. Taken in 1932, the photograph above shows members of the White Hart Outing Club. The Proprietor, Emma Durbin, presumably, is the lone woman sitting in the centre of what was clearly a gentleman's club. The White Hart remains a popular destination for thirsty and hungry tourists.

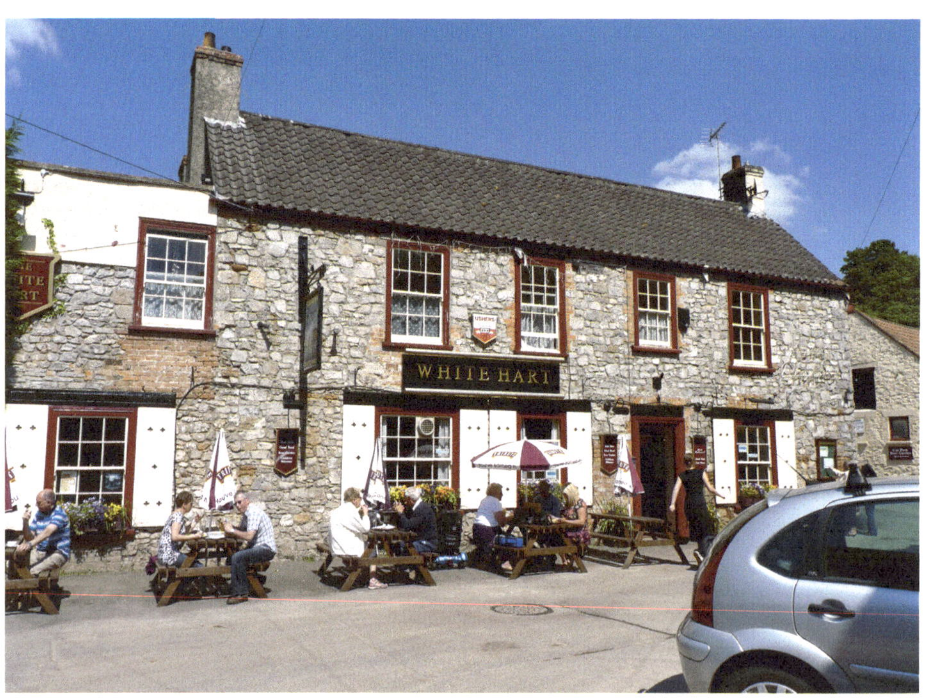

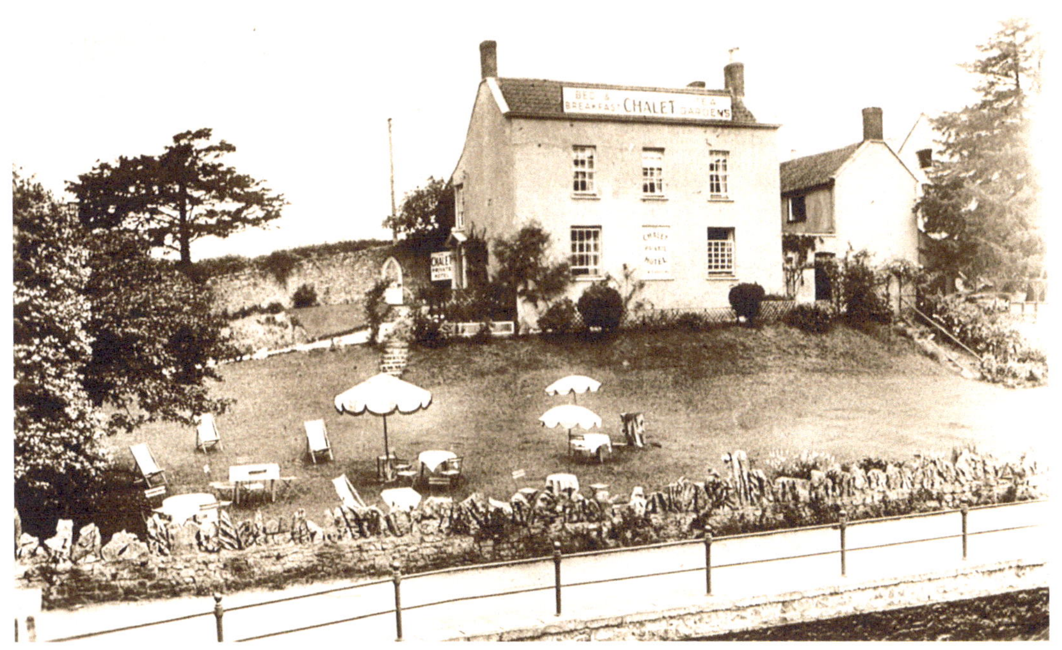

The Chalet Hotel

Below the White Hart is the Bays Pond, formed in 1827 in a bend of the river to serve the neighbouring mill. The Chalet Hotel, now a private house, occupied a prime position on The Bays on the far side of the pond. It provided another popular 'tea garden' with tables and umbrellas providing shade for summertime visitors.

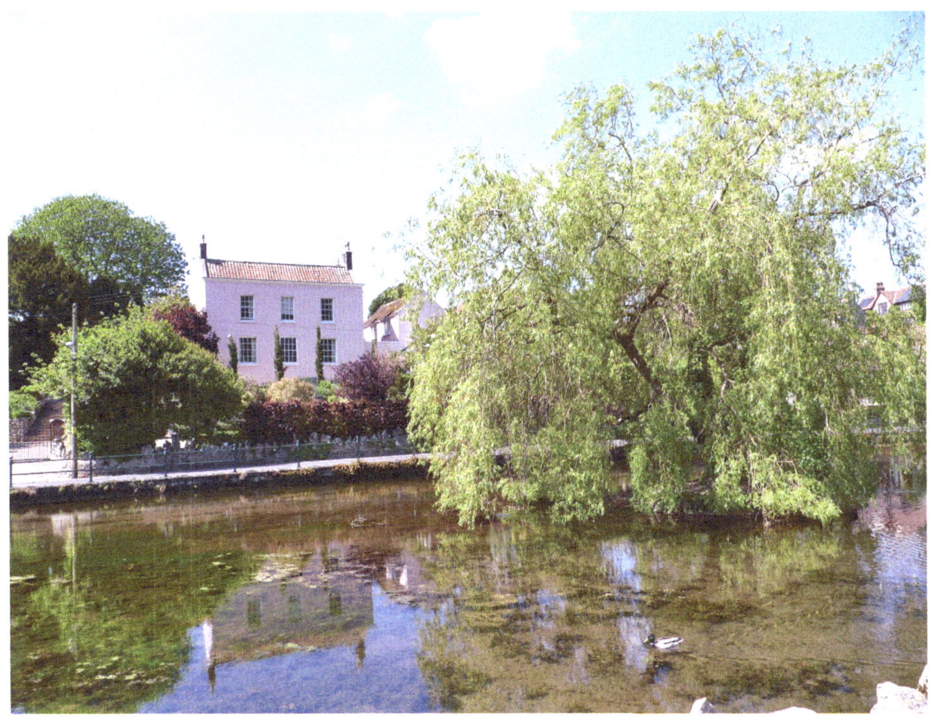

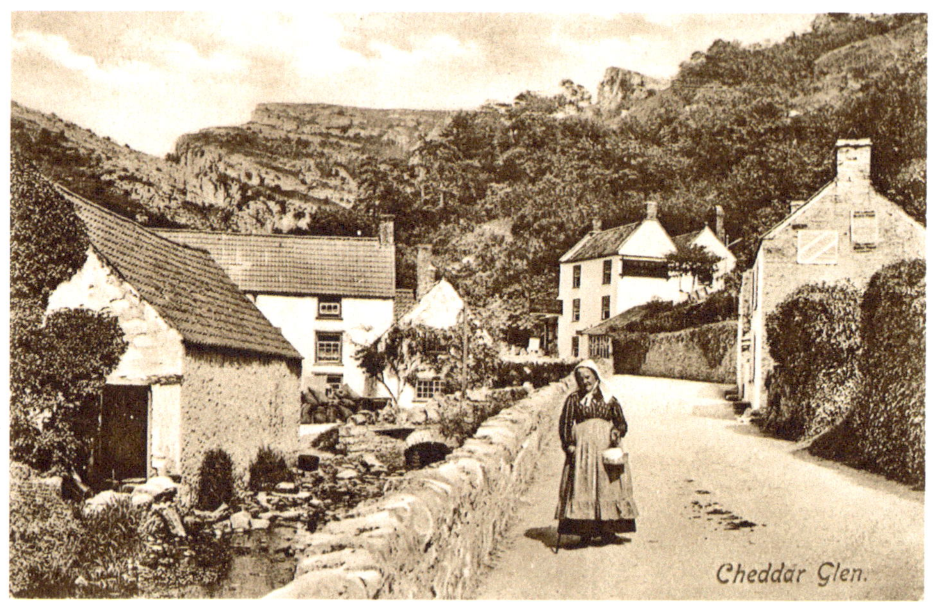

Betsy Card

The old photograph here shows a well-known local woman, Betsy Card (*see p. 57*), who used to sell pieces of spar rock from the caves to tourists. Behind her are clearly seen Middle Mill and Pavey's Hotel. Day-trippers, five-year-old Joshua and his three-year-old sister, Tegan, are pictured at the same location with their mum and dad. Traffic congestion has rather spoiled the view. The road at this point is now wider, and Middle Mill in the centre of the early picture has long since been demolished. The front bay of Pavey's and another commercial establishment, 'Cheese Cottage' as it was called in the 1920s, between Betsy and the hotel, were also taken down when the road was widened in the 1960s.

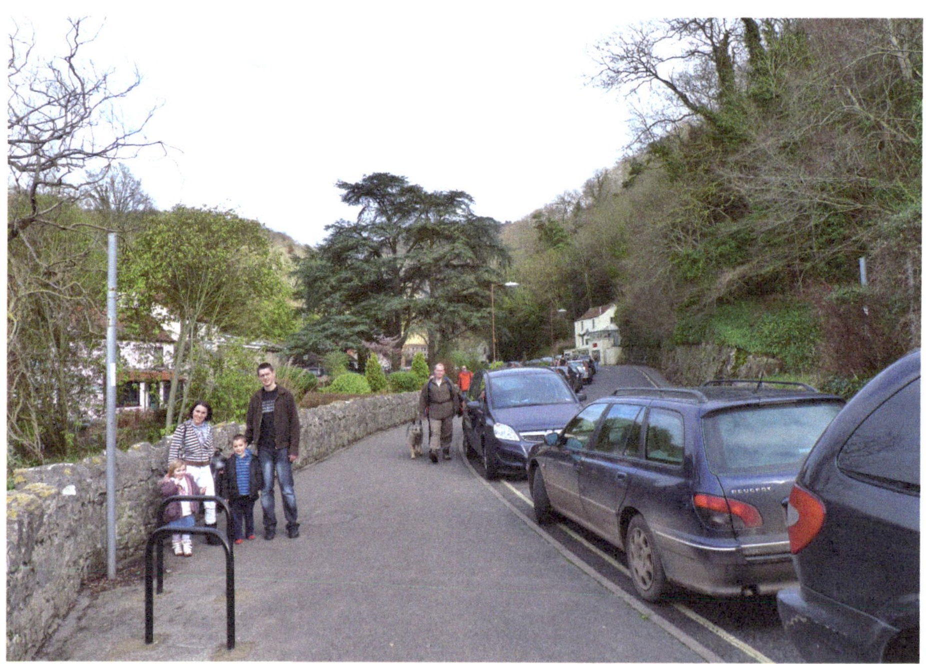

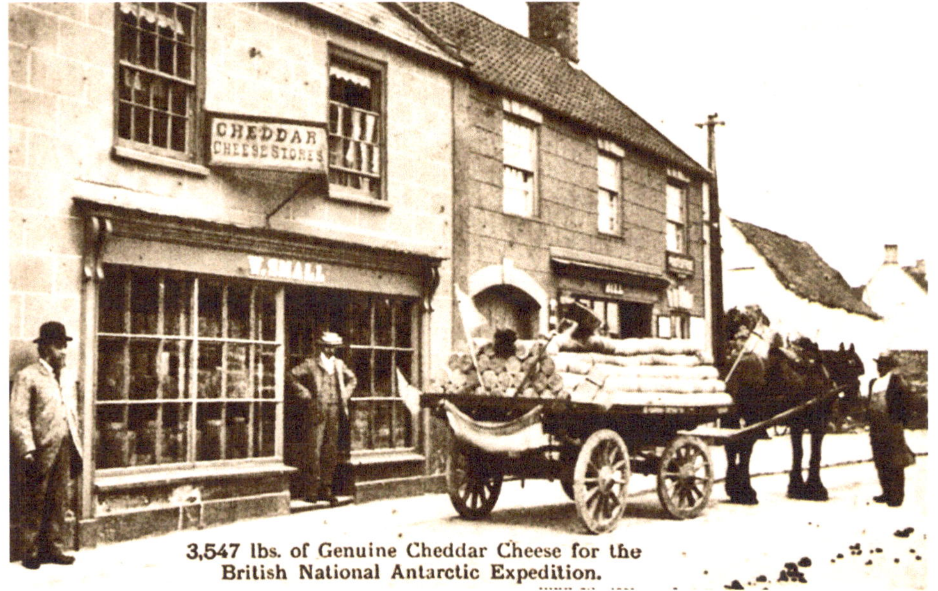

The Cheddar Gorge Cheese Company

A little further along The Cliffs, on the right, at the end of the gorge, is the award-winning Cheddar Gorge Cheese Company shop and exhibition offering customers the opportunity to taste a very wide range of cheddars; it sells its own rustic pottery platters, embossed with the phrase 'History in the Making', on which to serve them. It will deliver its cheeses to any address in the European Union. This is very much in the tradition of the village, which supplied cheeses to the court of Charles II in seventeenth-century London and, according to the caption of the photograph above, supplied 3,547 lbs of his Cheddar Cheese for Scott's 1901 Antarctic expedition from Mr Small's shop in Bath Street.

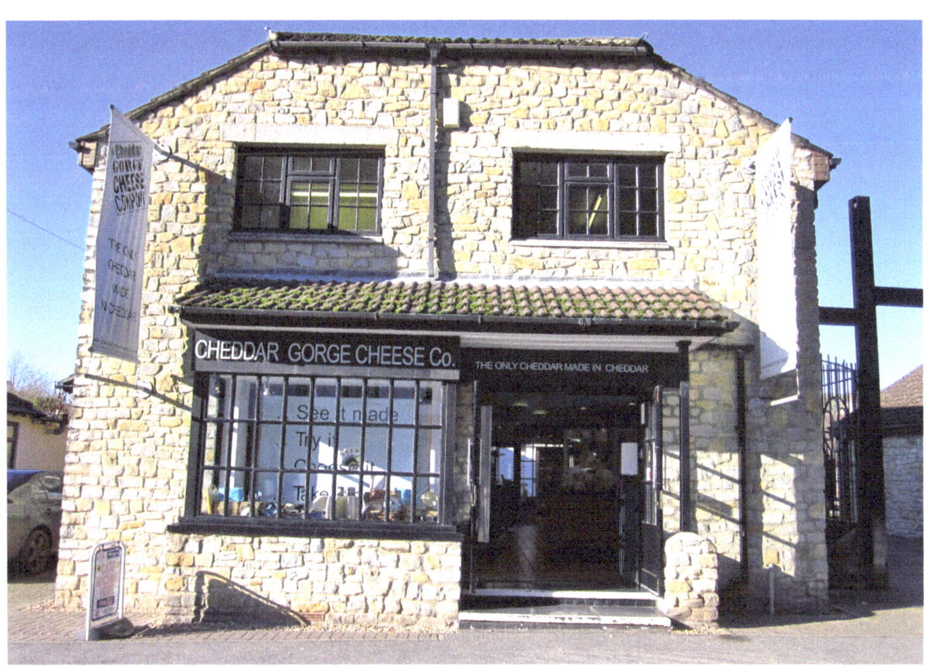

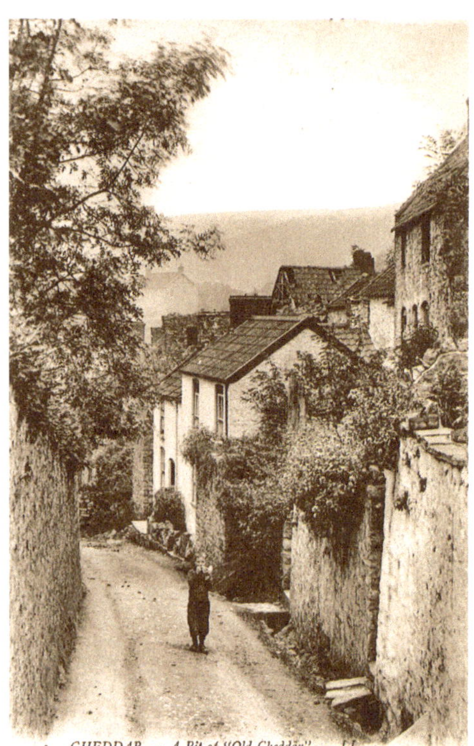

The Lippiatt

Over the road from the car park and terminus for the Cheddar Gorge tour buses is The Lippiatt, 'a bit of old Cheddar'; a steep narrow road, lined on one side with old cottages built on the steep slope that runs to the east of the village and connects Lippiatt Lane with The Cliffs. The curious name, Lippiatt, appears in various different forms on postcards dating from the first part of the twentieth century, including 'Lippet' and 'Lappats'. The word is thought to derive from an old English word for a cattle gate, which would have prevented cattle and deer from coming into the village. This is one of three old lanes with a similar affix that denotes their original function; the others are Wideatts and Venns Gate. A playful resident has renamed the first cottage on the left of the modern photograph 'Lilliput'.

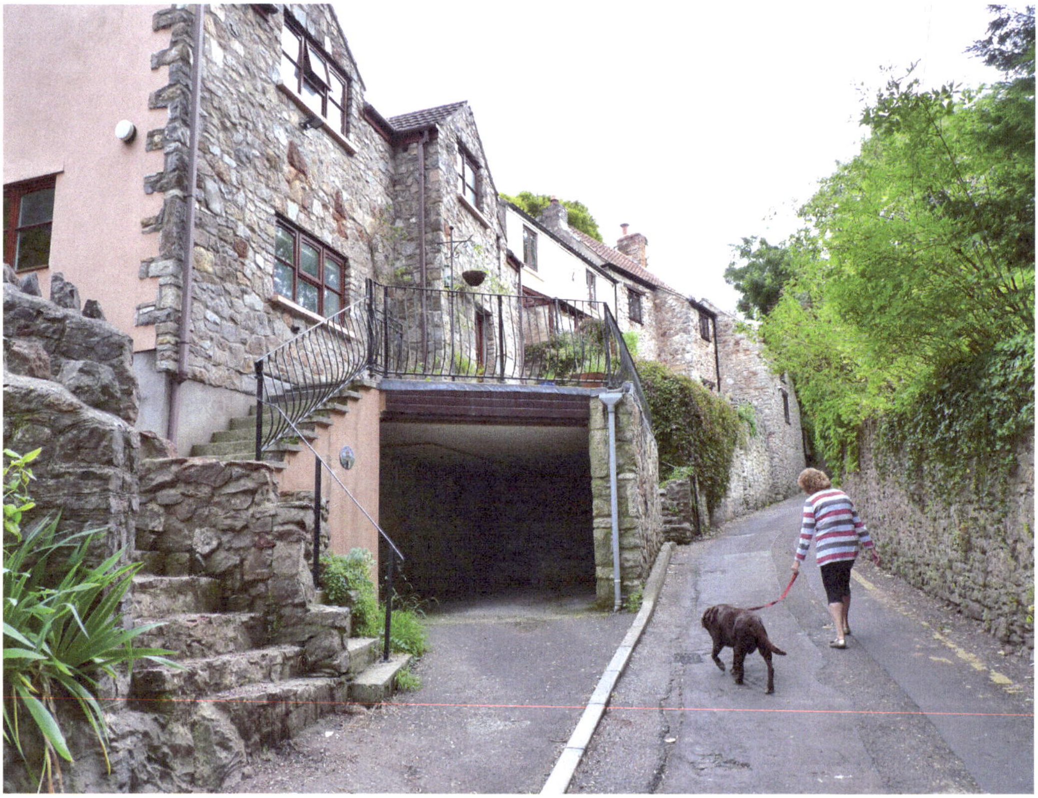

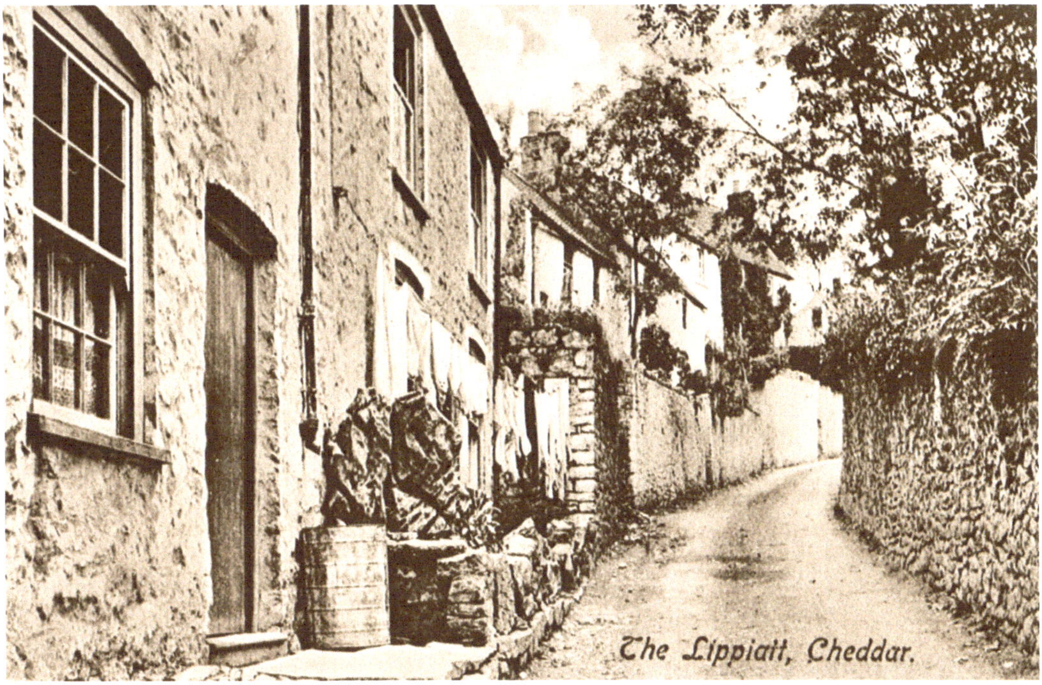

The Lippiatt, Cheddar.

The Woman in Black

At seven o'clock in the evening on 13 December 2004, Tina Nicholls (shown in photograph) was walking her dog, Oscar, along the lane when, at the point she is standing in the photograph but looking away from the camera, she saw in the gloom, coming towards her, the figure of an elderly woman in black with a white apron and cap who also had a dog with her, and there was a strong smell of tobacco smoke. Tina watched as the woman stepped to the right and disappeared into the bushes. Certain she had seen a ghost, she mentioned her frightening experience to a friend who promptly identified the apparition as the pipe smoking Betsy Card.shown on page 54.

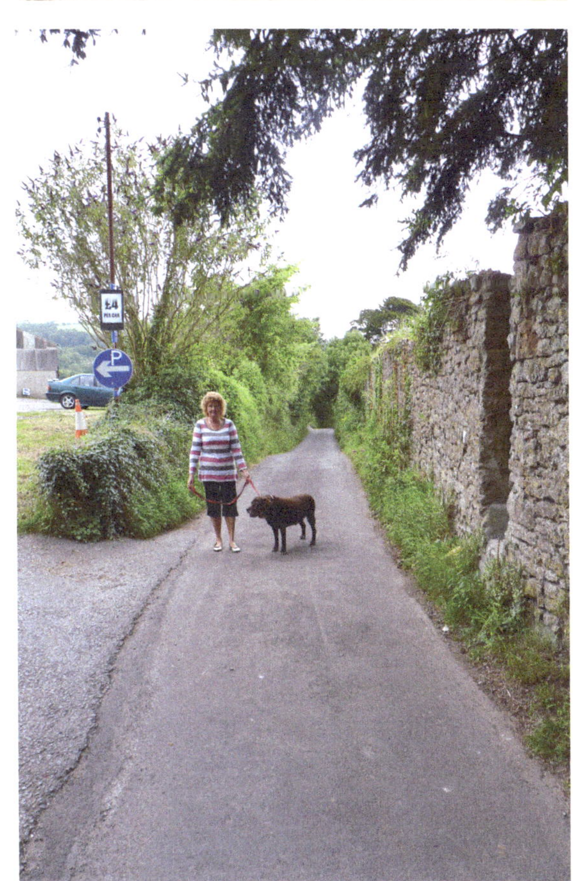

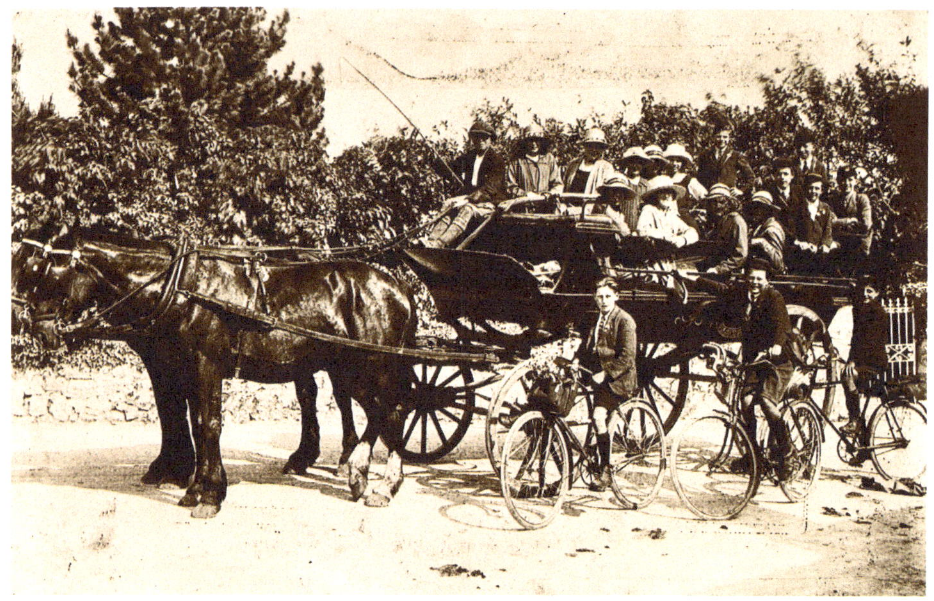

Bicycles Then and Now

You are highly unlikely to see a cart loaded with visitors in Cheddar these days, but the bicycle has been a regular feature of the Cheddar village landscape for over a century. Despite the great increase in motorised traffic, which makes cycling on the Mendips a precarious activity, every year thousands of visitors arrive at Cheddar on the seat of a bike. The bicycles in the recent picture have been parked just beyond the Cheddar Gorge coach terminus. The old photograph shows a group of boys and girls with, probably, their teachers. The boys are in school uniform of caps, blazers and short trousers. Notice how young the boy driving the cart appears to be.

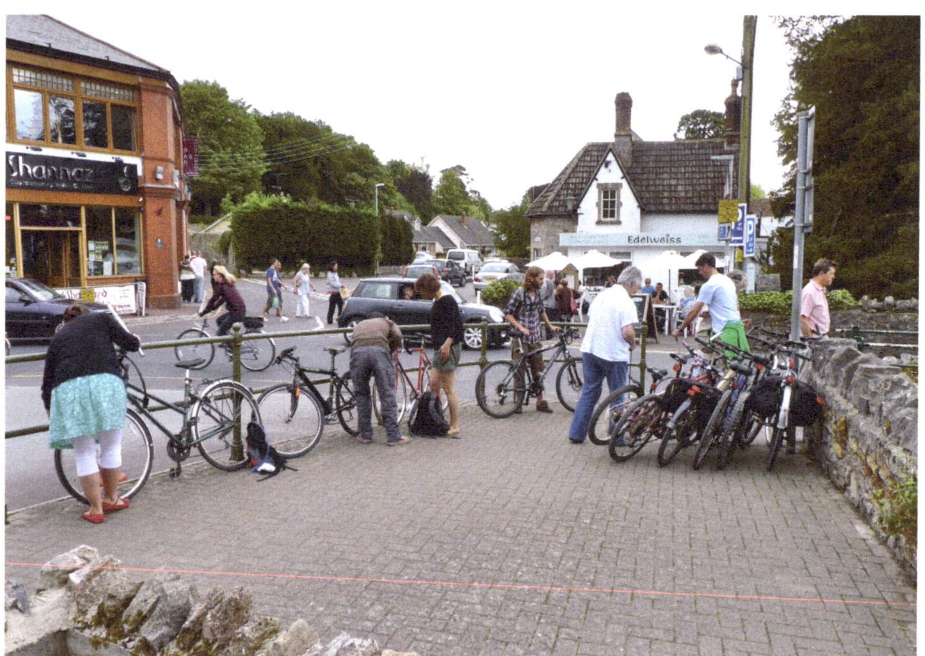

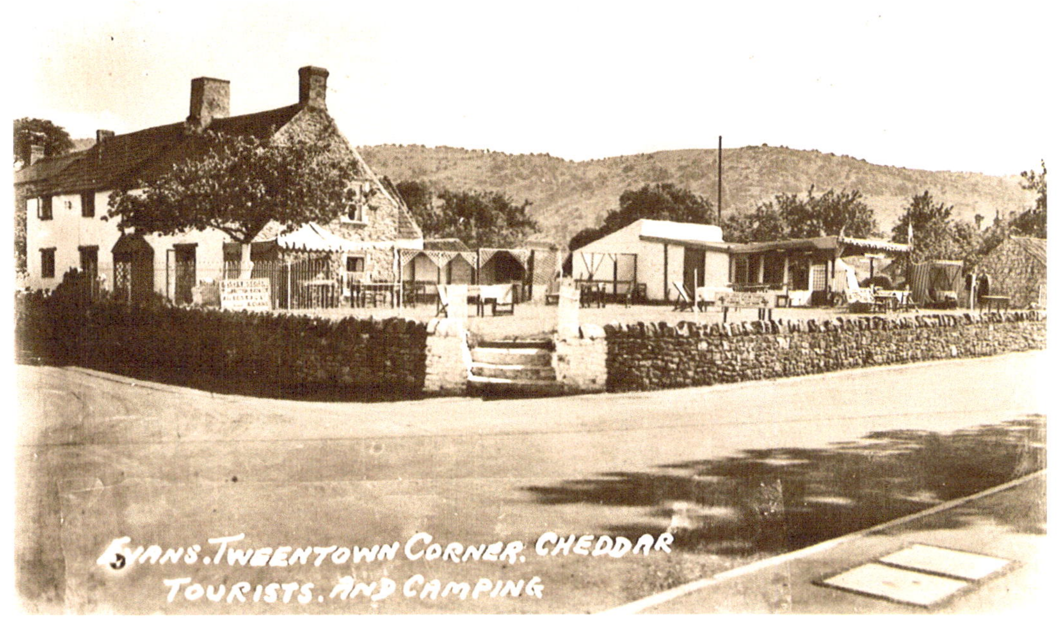

Tweentown Corner

Just beyond the junction of The Bays and Cliff Street, the road known as 'Tweentown' does, in a sense, as the name implies, divide Cheddar in two; with 'tourist' Cheddar to the north, along the Gorge, and residential Cheddar and the heart of the village to the south, east and west. The picture identifies Evans' campsite as being on Tweentown Corner. Evans' campsite was located on the junction of Tweentown and Upper North Street, a couple of hundred yards along the B3135. The campsite has gone but the retaining wall, with the entrance filled in, remains.

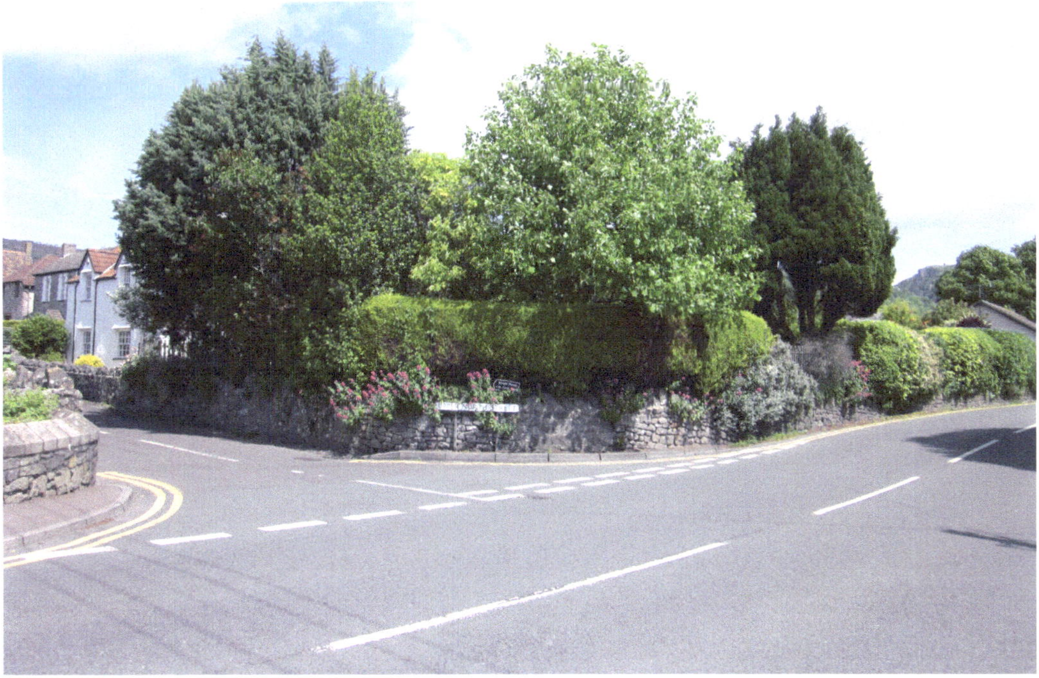

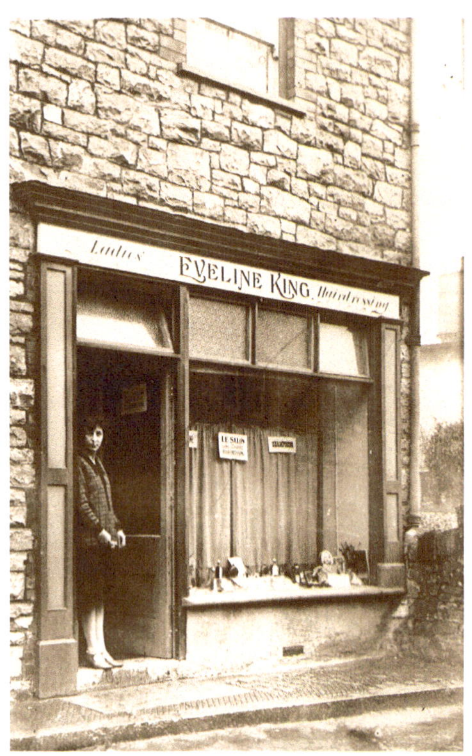

Evelyn King's Hairdressing Shop

A little further along Cliff Street on the right-hand side Eveline King's hairdressing shop could once be found. It is now a private residence named 'Roseneath', and its shop front has gone. However, several hairdressing premises can be found in Cheddar today including a barber's next to the Market Cross simply called 'Chop'. A 'Chop' shop, catering, like Eveline King back in the 1930s, for the ladies, is in Bath Street and another hairdresser's can be found in Union Street, aptly named 'Head Office'.

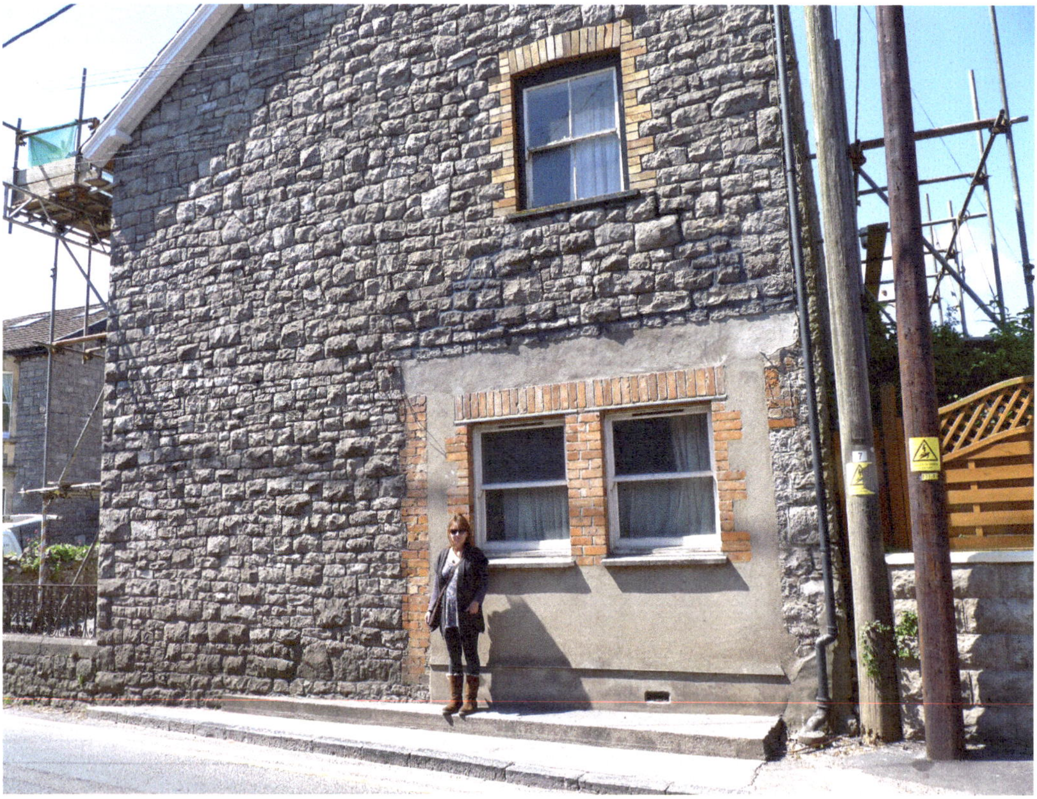

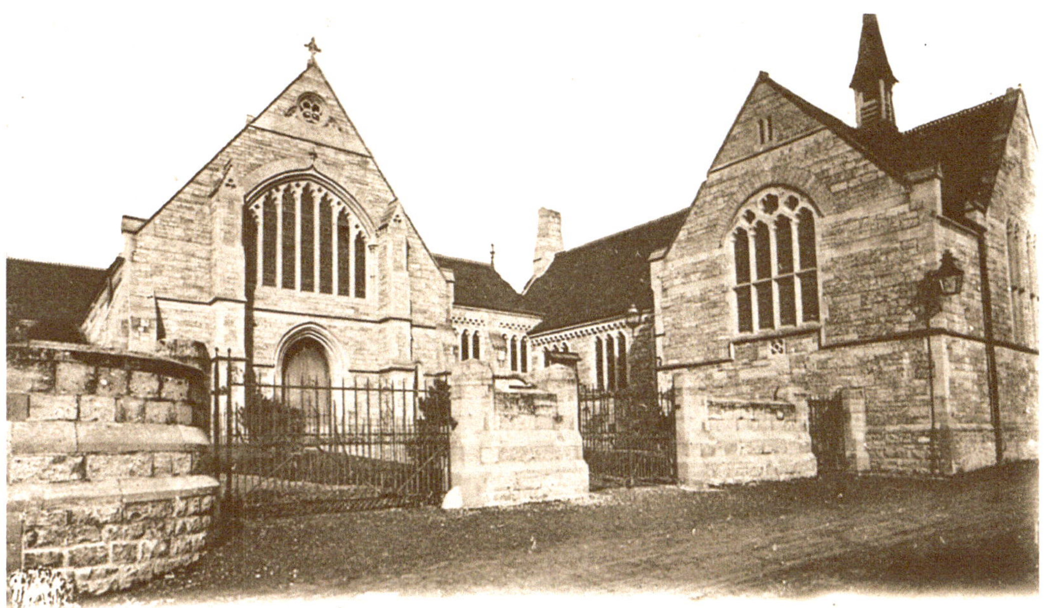

Wesleyan Schools, Cheddar & Church. H.B.& S.

The Methodist Memorial Church

The Methodist Memorial church further along Cliff Street was erected in 1820, with additions and alterations from then until 1897. Apparently no less than five churches constructed to the same design were built in the Cheddar Valley. In an era of diminishing congregations, the church proudly proclaims on its website that recently, for the first service of the Somerset Mendip Circuit, 'Cheddar soon filled up to overflowing'.

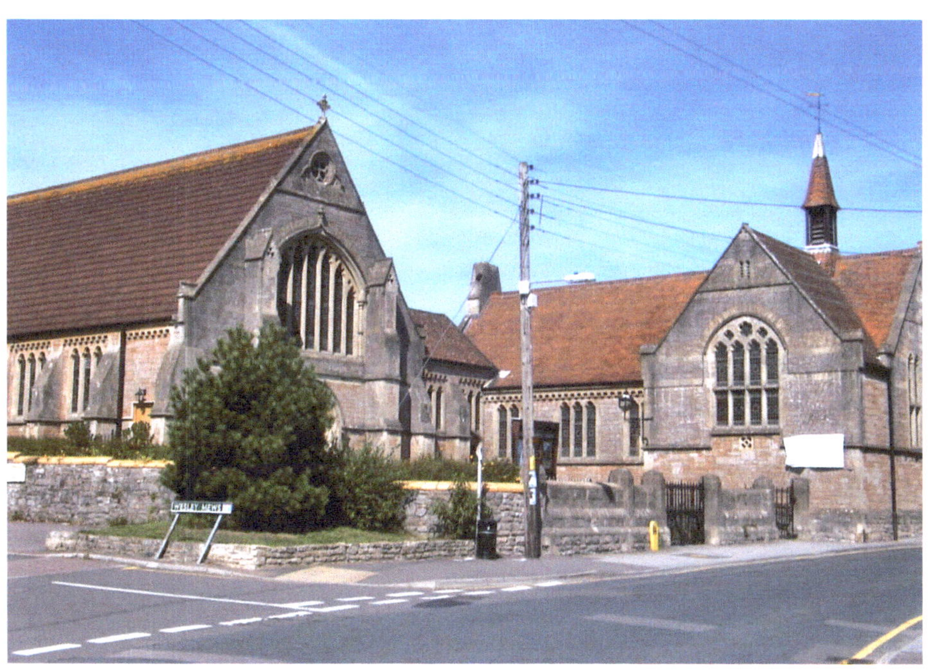

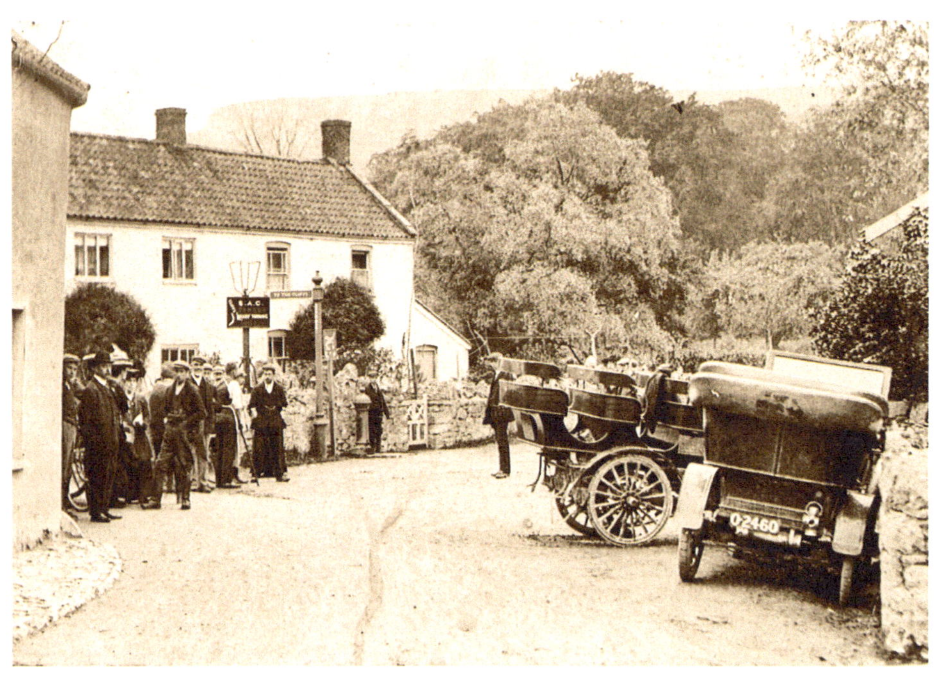

Car Collision

At the end of Cliff Street a car collided with a Burnell Brothers' 14-person charabanc in around 1910. The long building in the background on Coles Corner, where Cliff Street, Union Street and Redcliffe Street meet, is named Redcliffe Court and it houses a beauty salon.

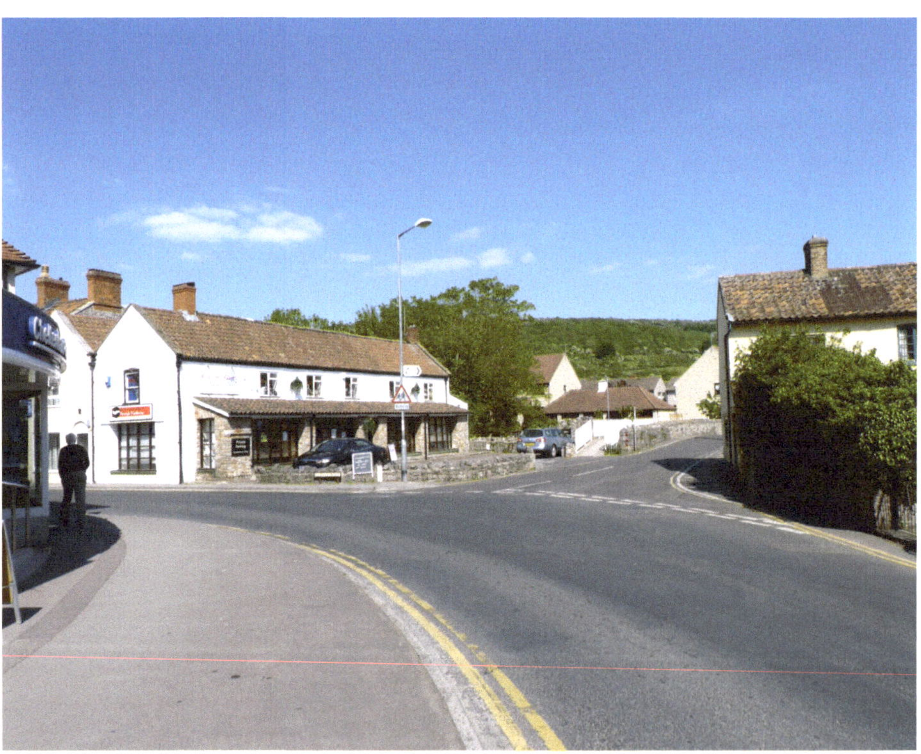

Reading, Writing, Arithmetic, Grammar, Geography and History

Just beyond the crash site, on the left, are two adjoining properties that once housed the Cheddar British School, which subsequently evolved into Cheddar First School, located in The Hayes. On its opening in 1845, it declared that 'The system of education to be adopted will be that of the British and Foreign School Society, which comprises the teaching of Reading, Writing, Arithmetic, Grammar, Geography and History. The only Religious Instruction given in the School, will be that derived from Scripture Lessons, and no Sectarian Catechism or Creed will be taught. The rate of payment will be one penny per week.' By the time the older photograph here was taken it had already relocated to its new premises in The Hayes. On the back is inscribed 'Aunt Susan outside her house', which is identified as 'Swiss Cottage', the name by which it is still known.

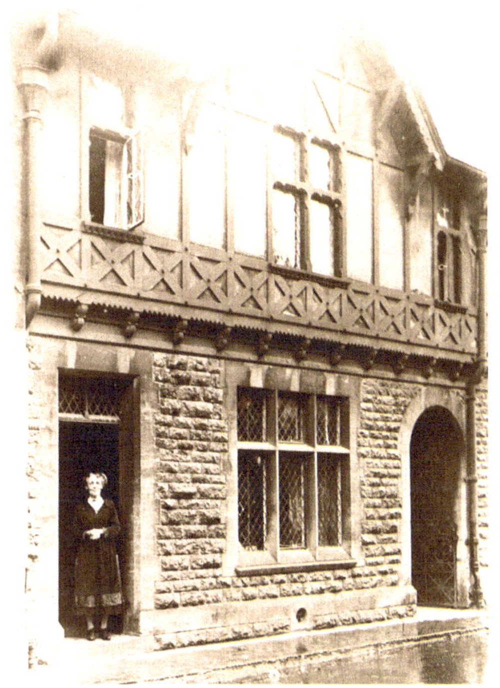

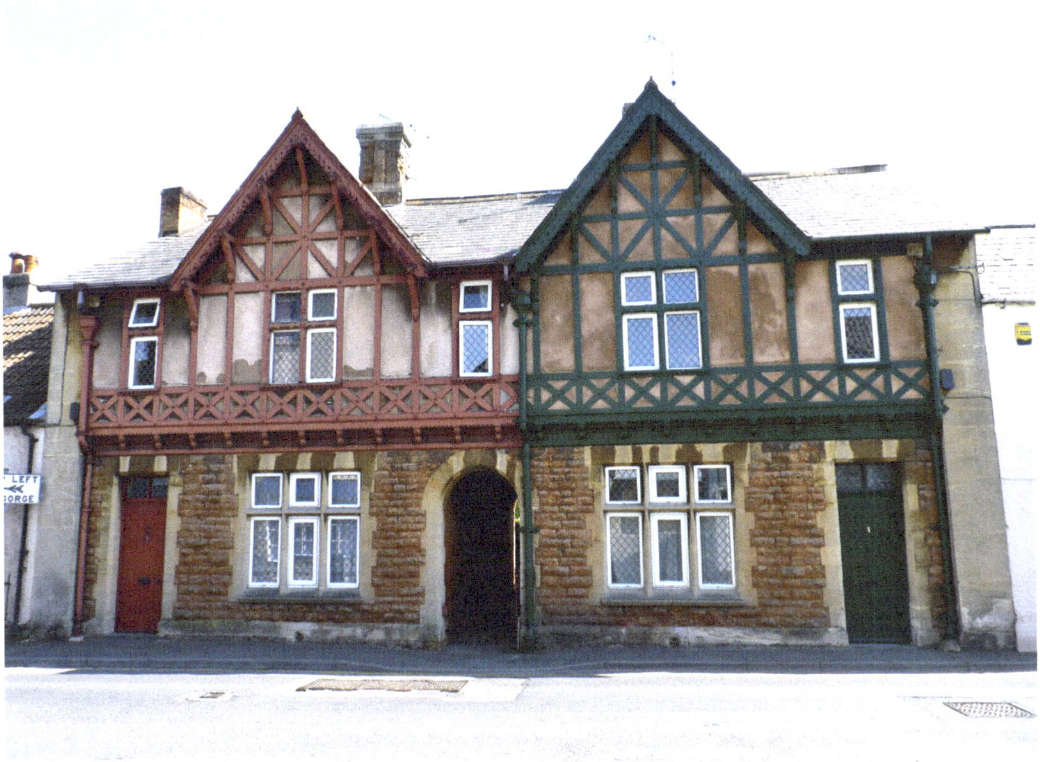

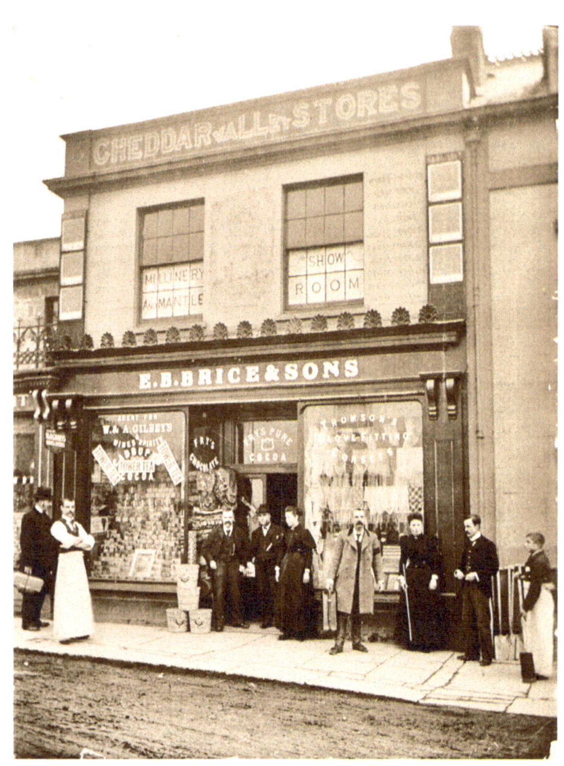

Cheddar Valley Stores

The premises shown in this splendid photograph of the 'Cheddar Valley Stores', since 1976, now house Cheddar's Library in Union Street. The Brice family continued trading next door until 1997. In addition to the tea, cocoa, wine, spirits, and 'Thomson's Close-fitting Corsets', the faded painted lettering above reveals E. B. Brice & Sons offered a range of other goods and services including boots, shoes, and tailoring.

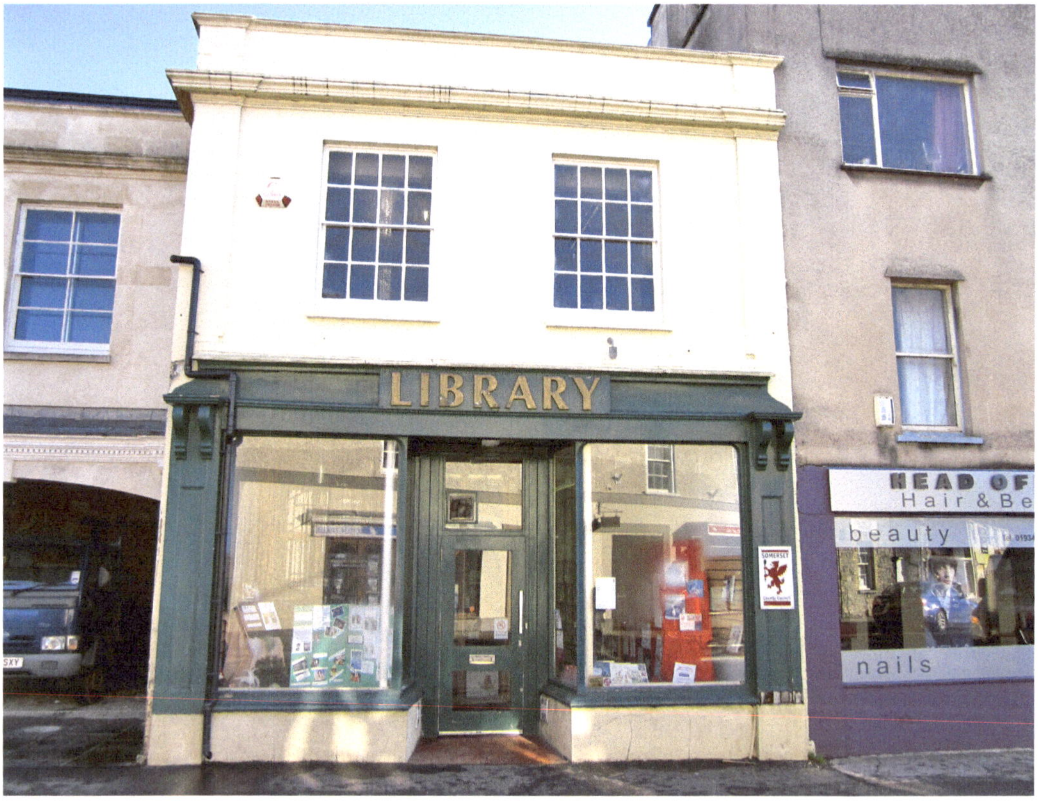

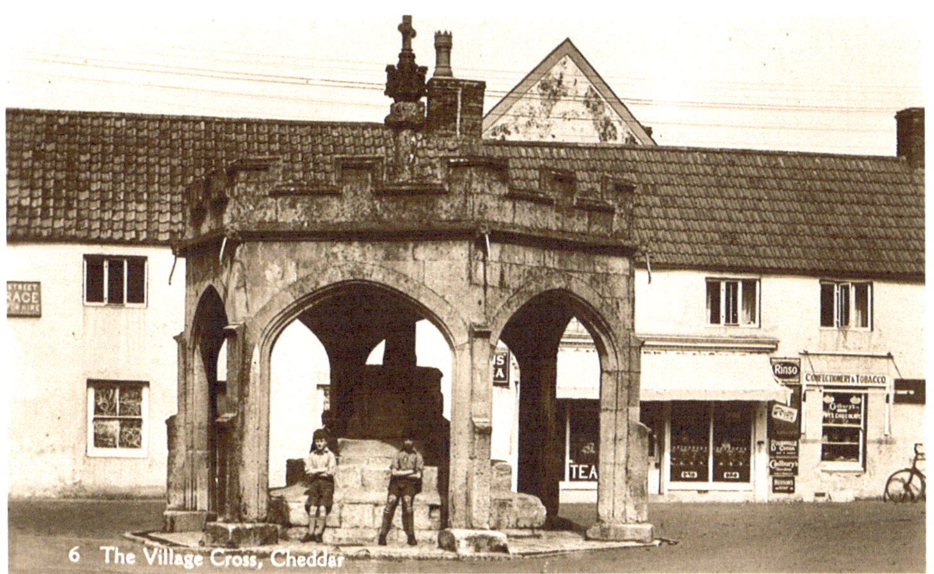

The Market Cross

If Cheddar village has a centre it is its fifteenth-century market cross, or 'butter cross', upon which its three main streets – Bath Street, Union Street and Church Street – converge. Bath Street and Union Street formerly shared a single name: High Cross Street. On the evidence of these two photographs, it would appear that the Market Cross has not suffered any kind of damage in the decades since the older picture was taken. In fact, the half of the structure facing the camera was badly damaged in a traffic accident in January 2000, and its restoration was not completed until 2002. In the fifty years or so since the earlier picture here was taken the appearance of the buildings on the far (gorge) side of the Market Cross, on the corner of Union Street, has scarcely changed. The premises once occupied by the grocer's on the right-hand side are now available to let and the sign for Bath Street Garage, advertising hire cars, has gone. The rather unsightly telegraph wires in the earlier picture have also gone and it is likely the soon-to-be-obsolete television aerials in the recent photograph too will be removed in the near future.

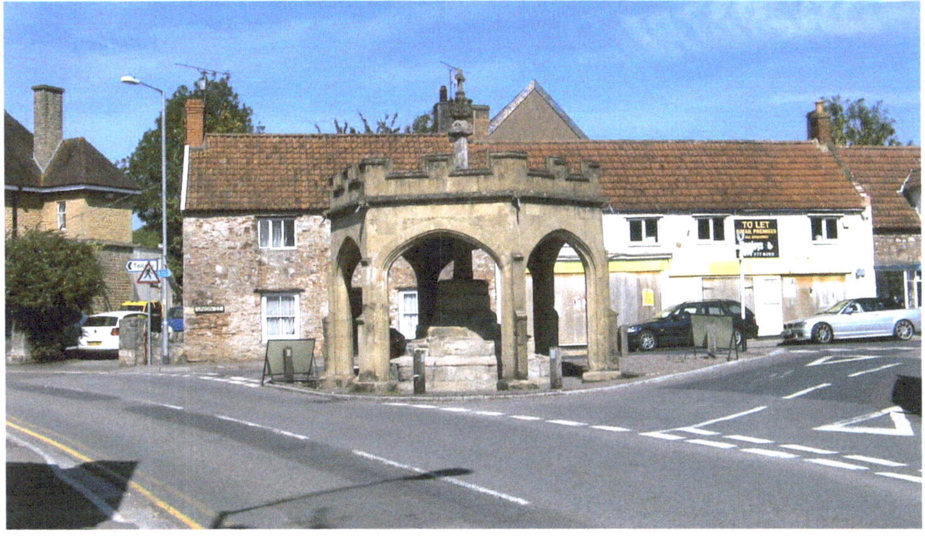

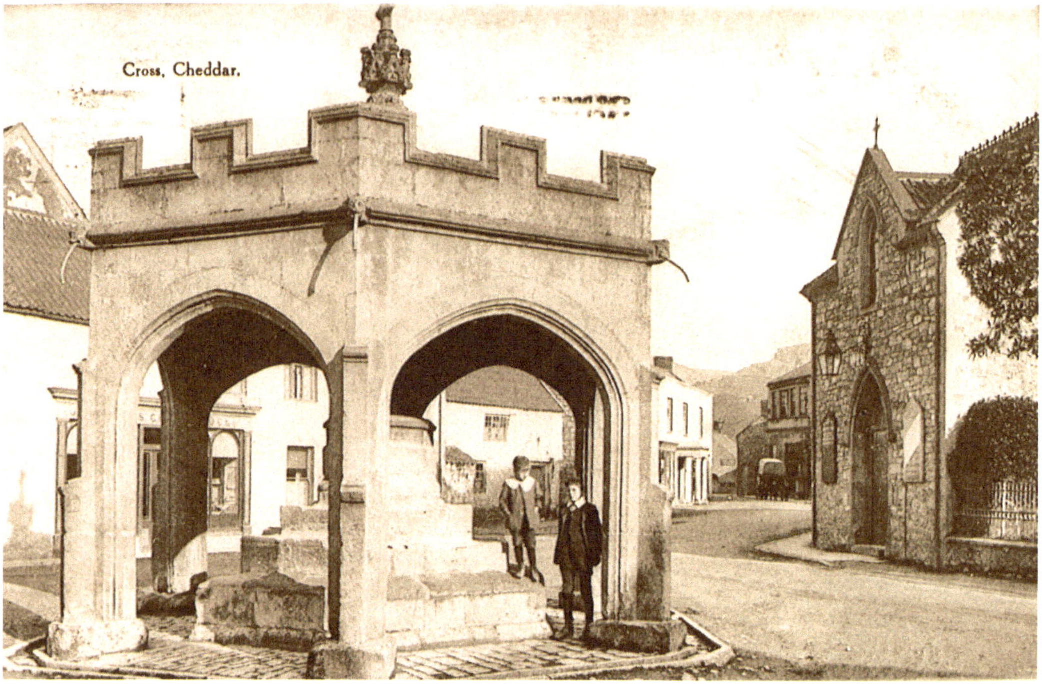

Cross, Cheddar.

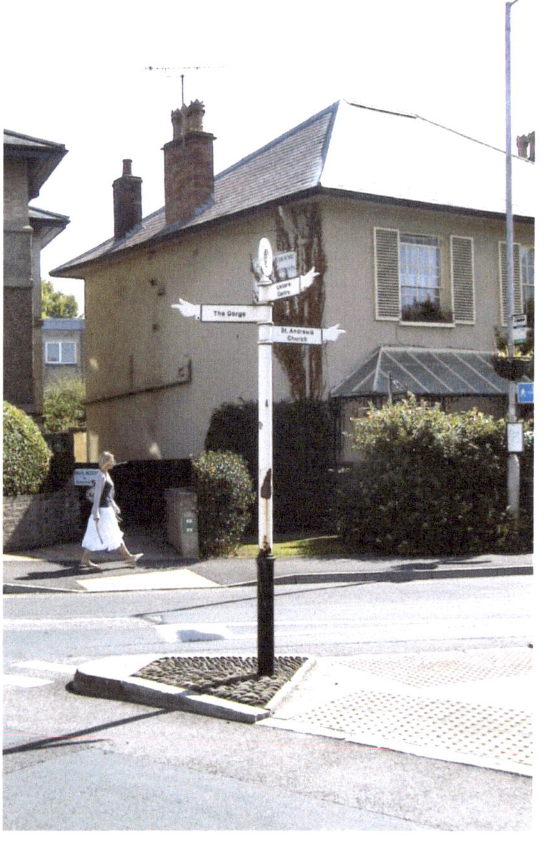

Christ Church

Beyond the two boys sporting Edwardian 'Eton' collars, on the corner of Union Street, is a substantial chapel, Christ Church, a place of worship for the Reformed Episcopal Church. Before its demolition in 1939, Christ Church served as a store for Brice's – the department store that occupied the premises now housing Cheddar Library. The attractive, old-fashioned way sign adjacent to the Cross is a relatively recent addition.

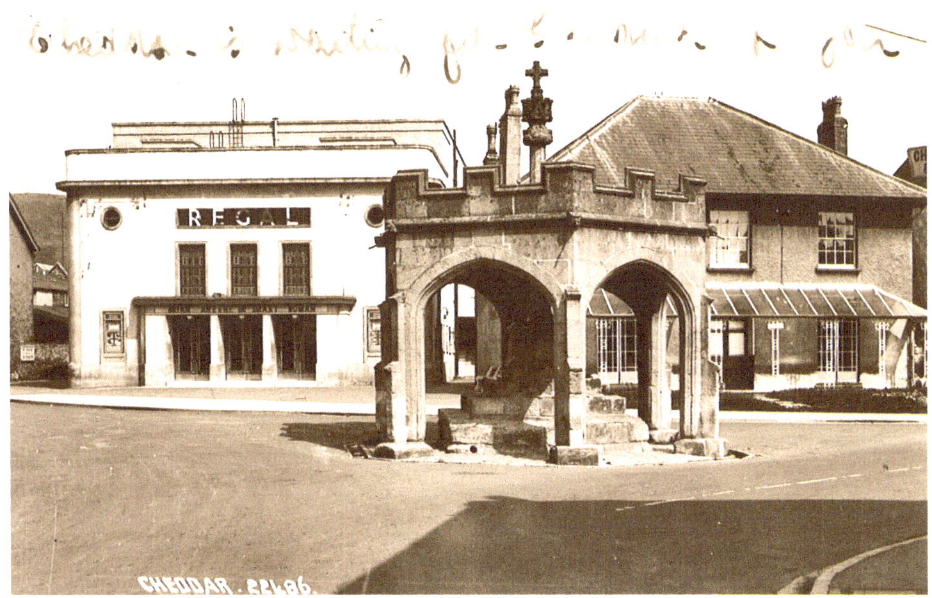

The Regal Cinema

In 1939, the Regal Cinema was built on the site of Christ Church and opened just a couple of weeks after the outbreak of the Second World War in the September of that year. At the time this photograph was taken it was showing a film called *Smart Woman*, which was made in 1948. The Regal could seat 400, but its days were numbered with the advent of television, and it eventually closed in 1958. The Regal eventually became a car showroom before it too was demolished and replaced by the 'Homestead' retirement apartments shown in the recent photograph. The older photograph is annotated: 'Cheddar is waiting for Grandma and You'.

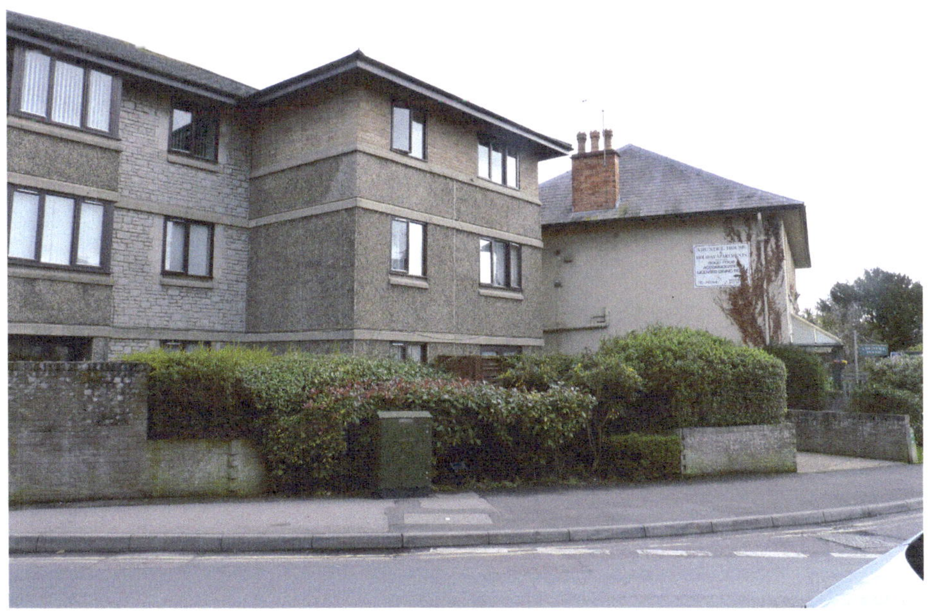

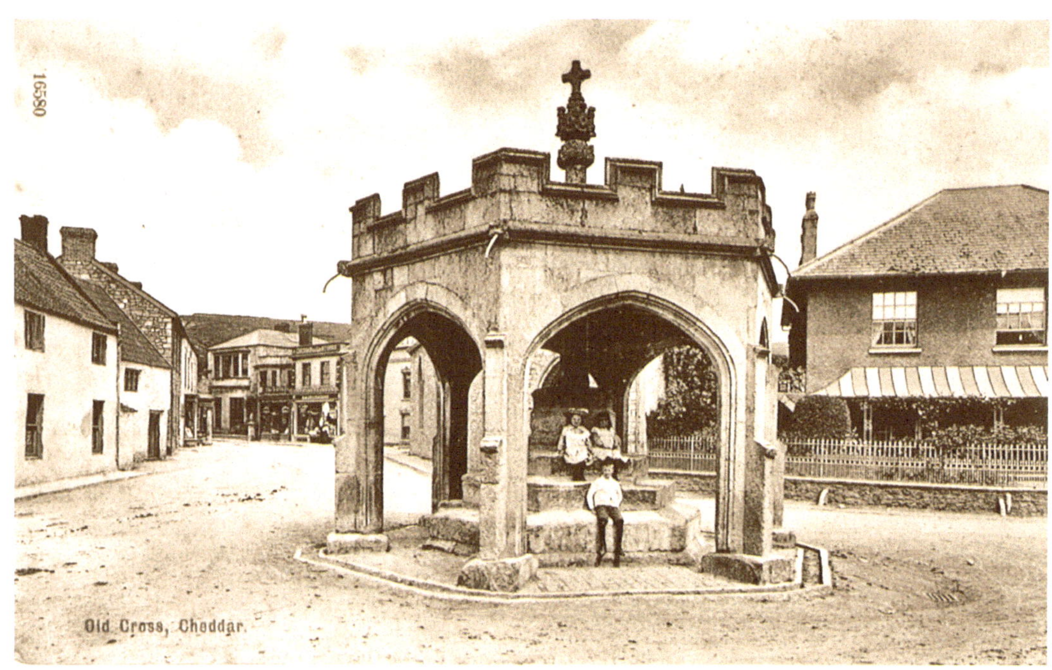

Market Cross Hotel

Next door to the Christ Church / Regal Cinema / Homestead site stood the Market Cross Hotel, now Arundel House, sporting what appears to be a fabric canopy in the earlier photograph before it was replaced with one made of glass. Next door stands Christ Church and in the background, in Union Street, is Brice's department store. To this day, Arundel House retains its distinctive and attractive canopy; the shutters are more recent additions.

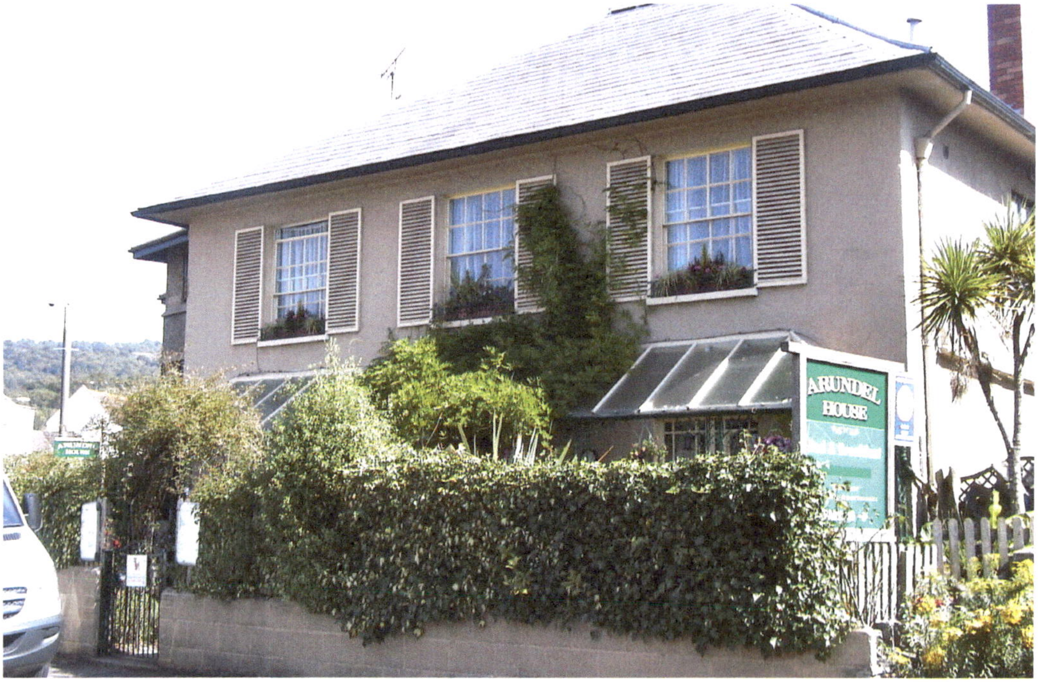

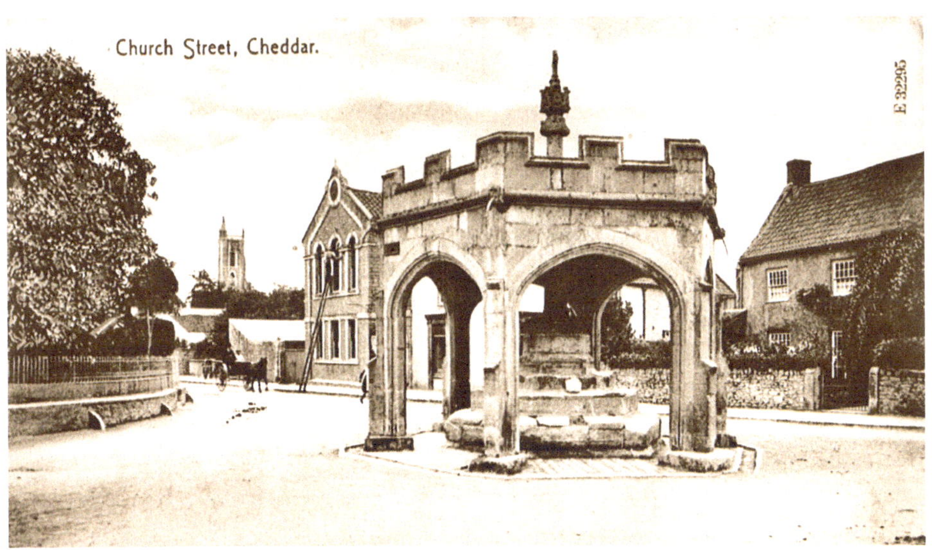

The Parish Hall, Among Others

This rather grand building next door to Court House in Church Street now houses the Parish Hall, the Sedgemoor District Council Sub-office, the Council Information Point, and the Cheddar Village Snooker Club. Formerly it served as the village's Literary Institute, established some time before 1870. Over the years it was a canteen for servicemen in the Second World War, a place for card players to meet (strictly by invitation only!), and a space for concerts, readings and other cultural activities. In the old photograph someone is up a ladder, possibly cleaning the building's windows, as a horse and gig rattles by. St Andrews church tower is in the distance. The building to the right was demolished not long after the photograph was taken. Court House, just beyond the Parish Hall, can be seen in the modern photograph.

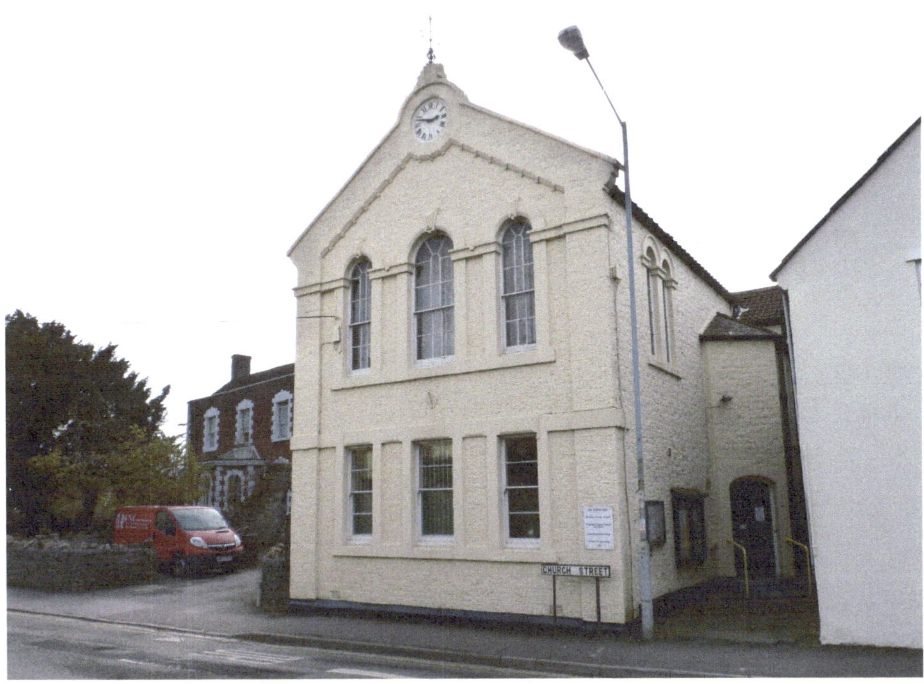

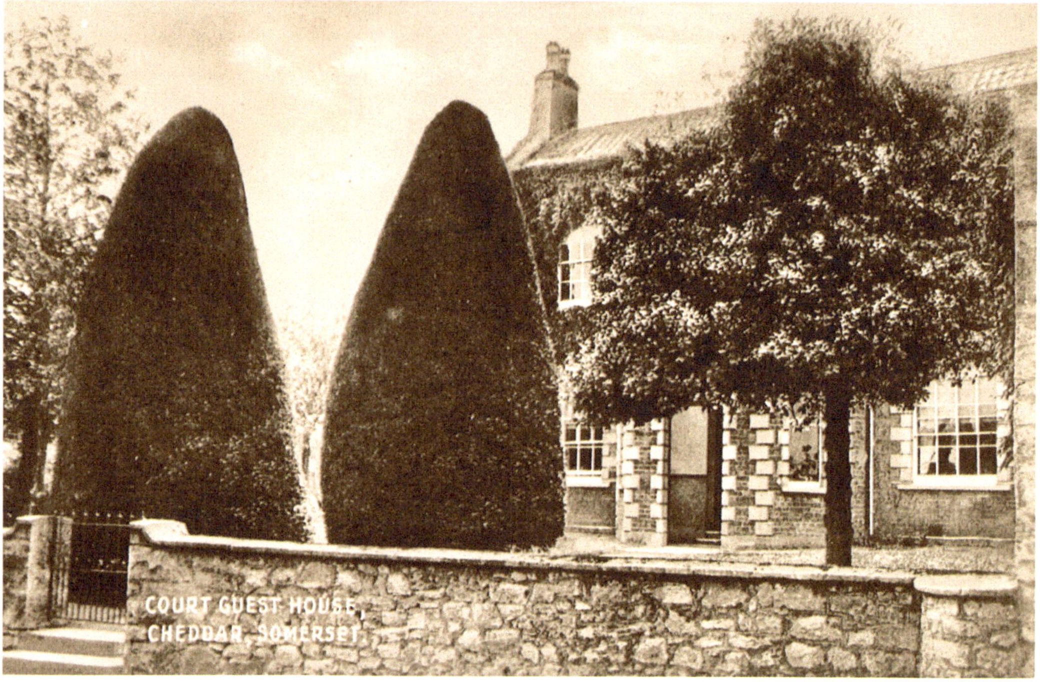

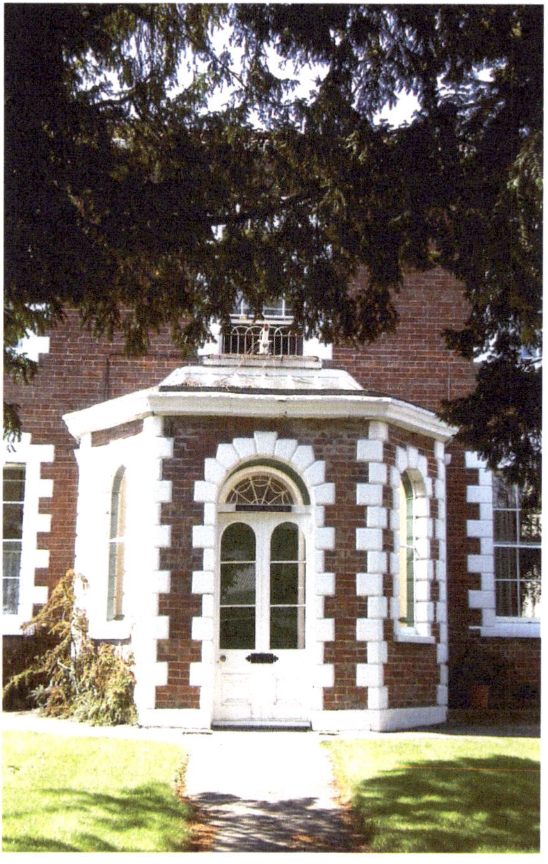

The Court House

The Court House was largely rebuilt in red brick on the site of much earlier structures in Victorian times. Manorial court sittings were held here since medieval times.

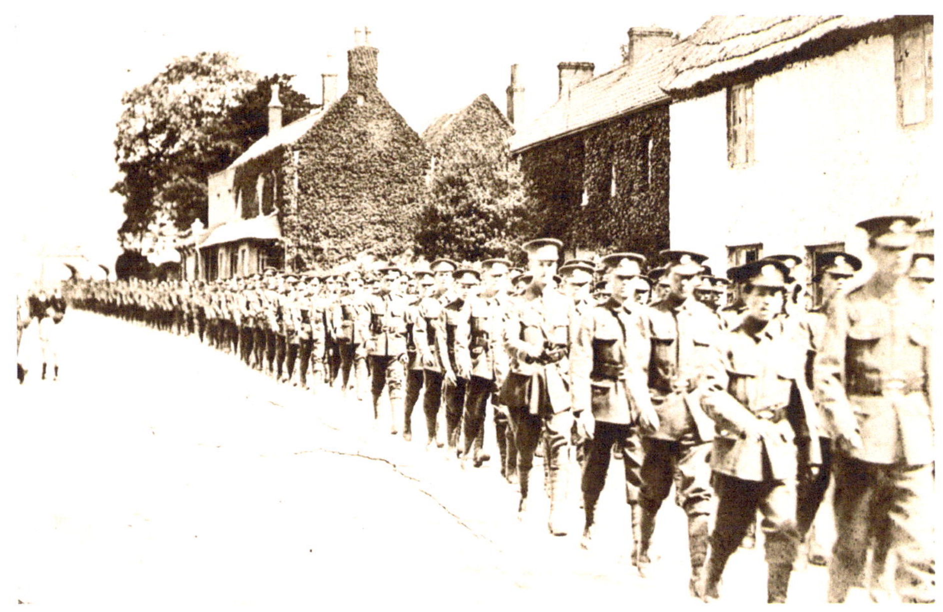

The Royal Gloucestershire Hussars Imperial Yeomanry

The archive photograph here shows off the Royal Gloucestershire Hussars Imperial Yeomanry who camped at Cheddar in May, 1904, on the site of what subsequently became the Axbridge Reservoir. They are shown marching along Church Street, on the other side of the road to Court House, and in the direction of St Andrews' church. Large numbers of children skipped school to watch them parade through the village. Note the canopy in front of the property to their left; this, and another one next door, much like that which adorns Arundel House, have survived to the present day. The Butter Cross can be seen in the background of both pictures.

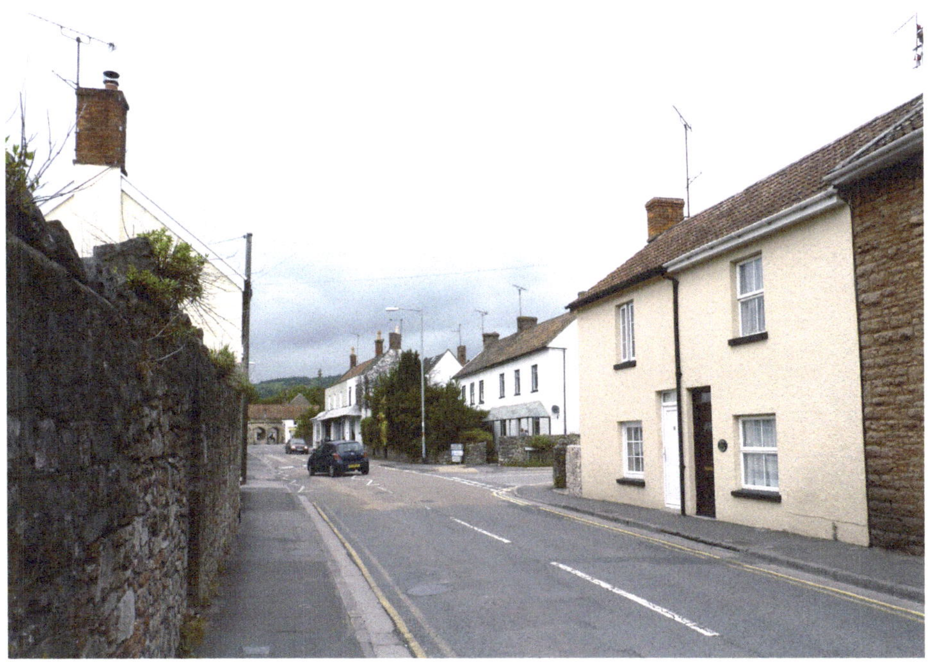

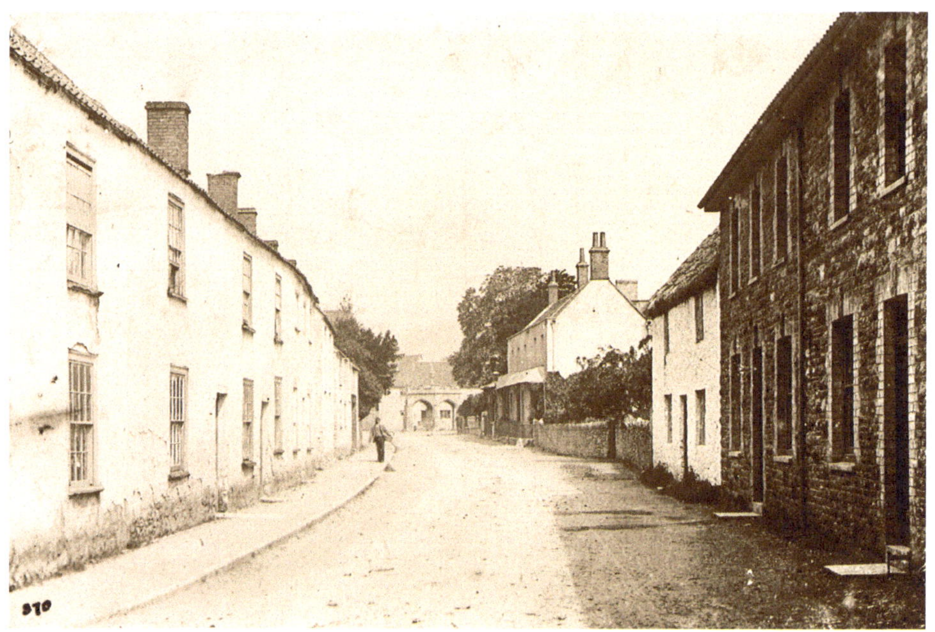

The End of Church Street

The houses at the end of Church Street, shown on the right of these photographs, have changed very little over the years. The earlier whitewashed cottage is no longer thatched, and the houses next door have gained a pavement but lost their boot scrapers. The modern photograph shows an archway at the end of the terrace and what was probably a store room into which heavy objects could be winched up from a cart stationed under the arch below. The terrace on the left was demolished to accommodate the large hall, Church House, constructed opposite the church sometime before it appeared on the 1902 Ordnance Survey map.

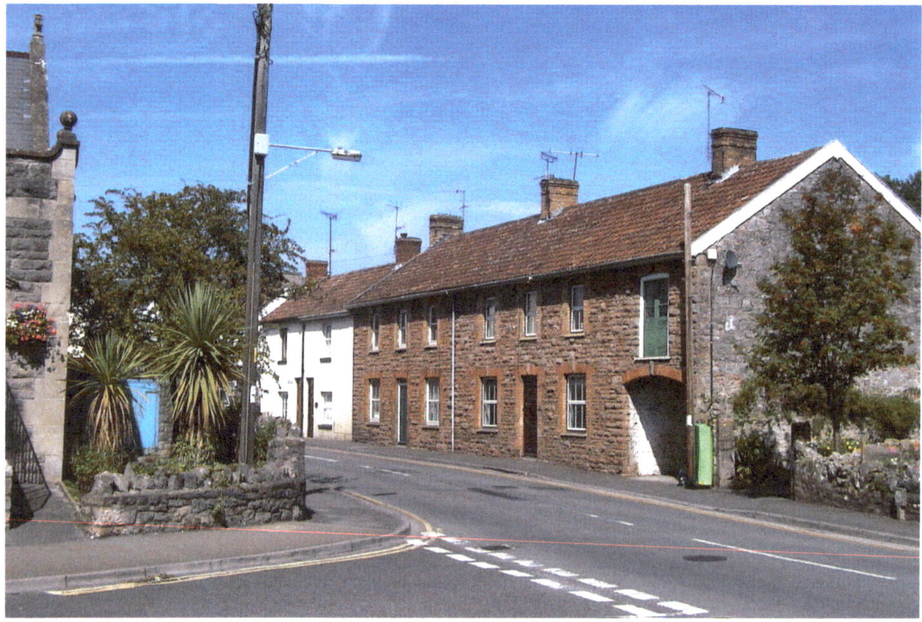

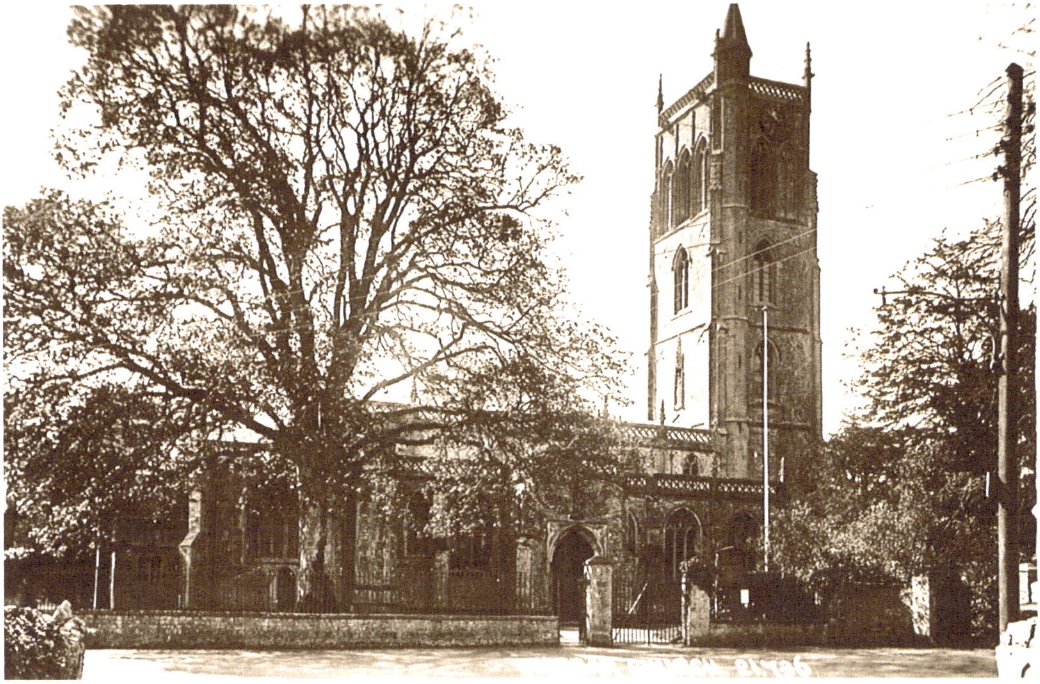

St Andrew's Church

Built between 1350 and 1450, St Andrew's church has changed little since it was restored in 1873 by William Butterfield. The 30m-tall tower, dating from around 1423 and considered the finest example of the Cheddar Valley type, houses a mid-eighteenth-century bell made by Thomas Bilbie. Originally based in nearby Chew Stoke, the men of the Bilbie family of bell-makers were reputed to have been long haired and savage looking. Legend has it that they would only ever cast their famous bells by the light of a full moon at midnight.

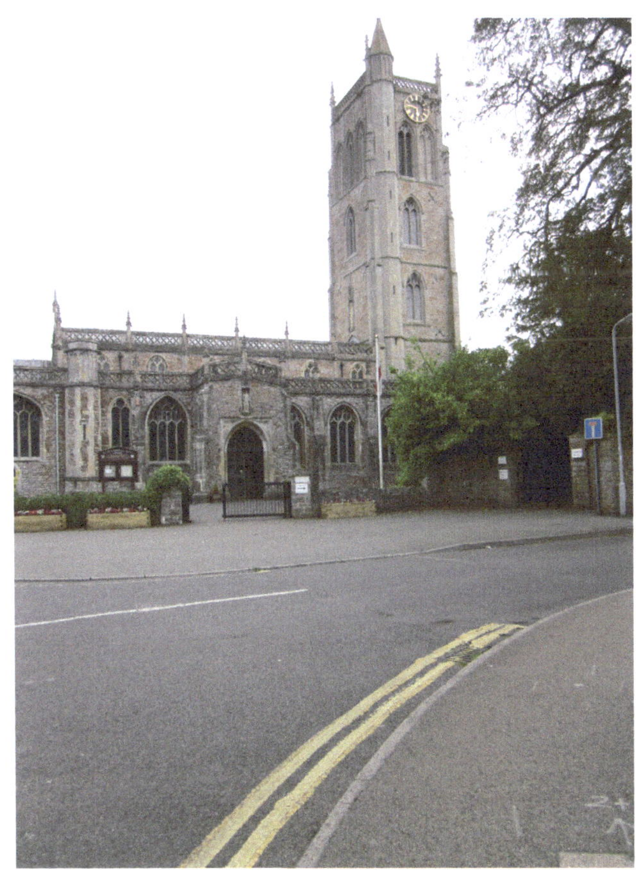

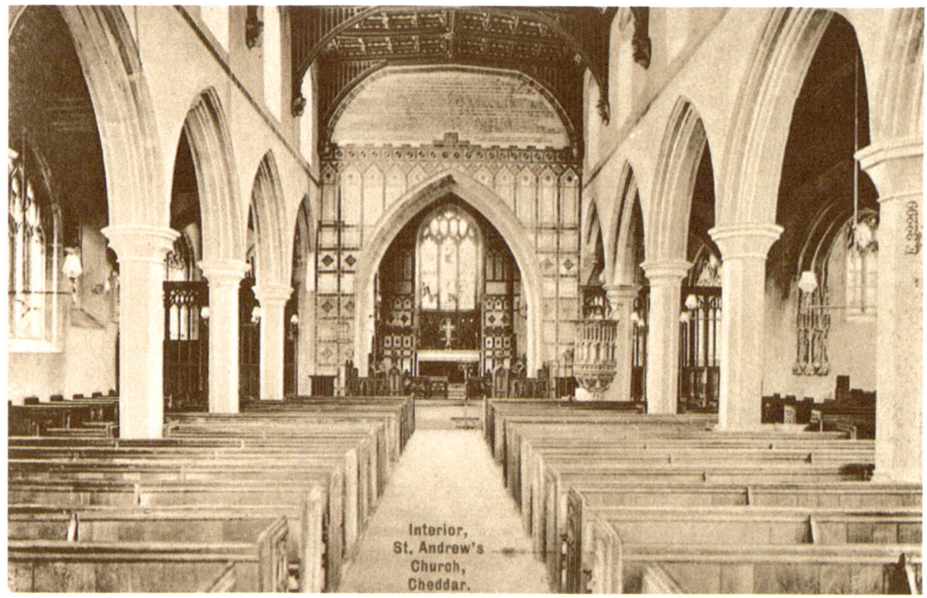

Interior Decoration

The obliteration of earlier wall decorations in medieval churches is usually associated with the Puritans of the seventeenth century but this pair of interior photographs clearly reveal how the practice of eradicating all trace of earlier intricate designs has continued into recent times. The covered-over decorations from the early-twentieth-century photograph are tiles, placed on the chancel arch and on the wall behind the communion table by Victorian 'gothic' revivalists.

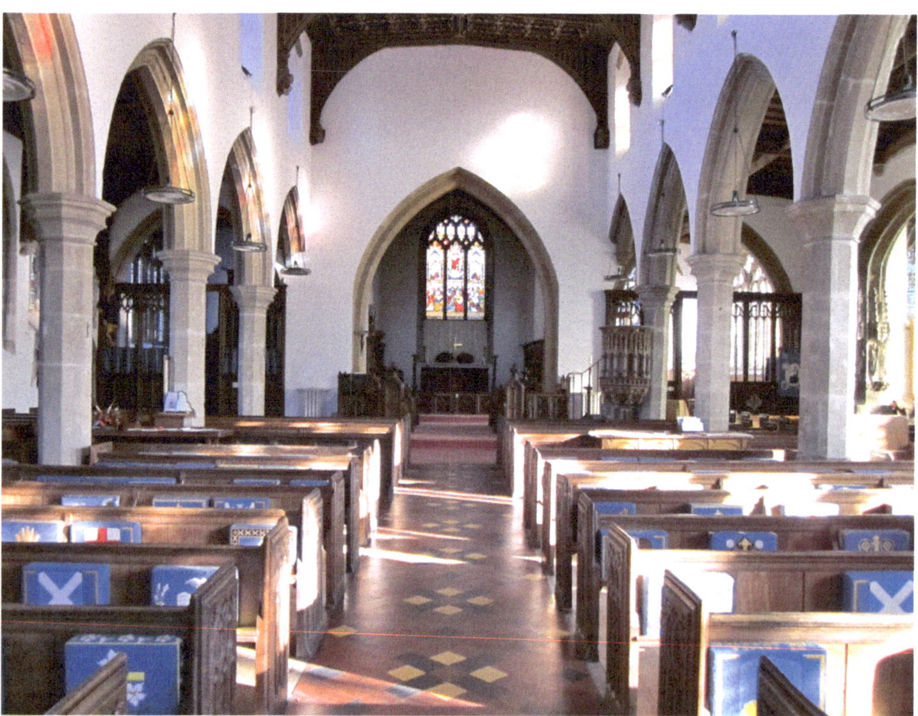

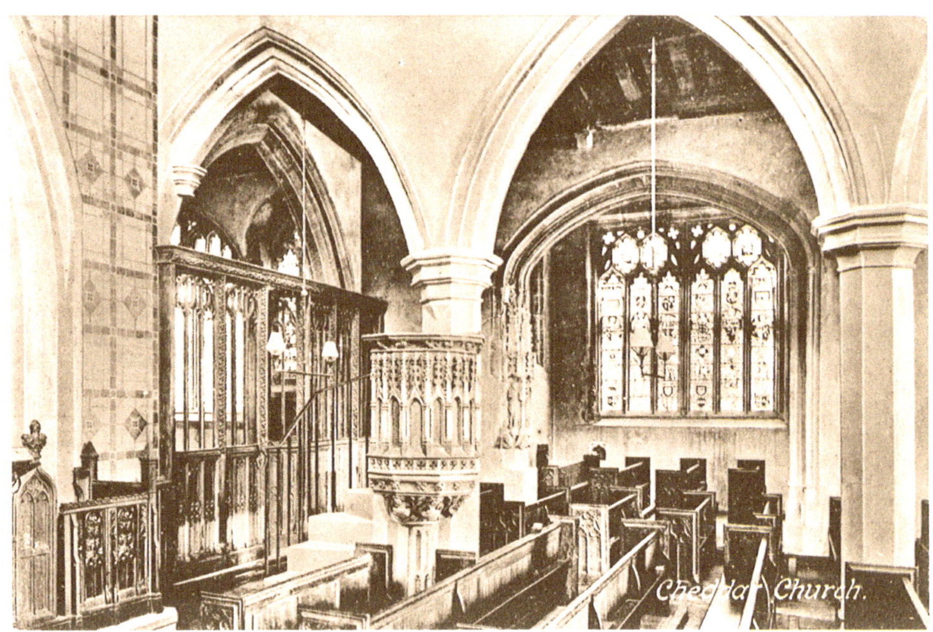

The Vicarage

St Andrew's boasts many fine examples of ecclesiastical architecture and decoration. The pulpit dates from the mid-fifteenth century and a good deal of beautiful and intricate carving has also survived, including several striking bench ends. Three in the north aisle represent the deadly sins of deceit, gossip and evil speaking – all three sins of the tongue. Although the vicarage still stands, largely unaltered, it no longer houses the Vicar of St Andrew's who instead occupies more modest premises in Station Road. The present incumbent is the Reverend Sue Rose. One of her predecessors introduced in 1883 a tradition from Oxford whereby children in his congregation would climb the steps to the top of the church tower on Ascension Day and sing the hymn 'Hail the day that sees Him rise'; the custom continues to the present day.

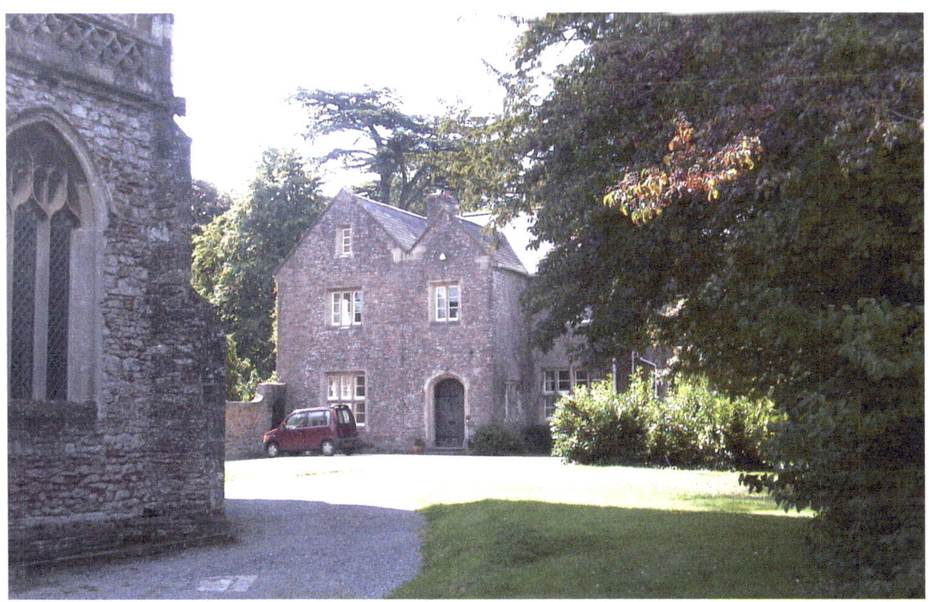

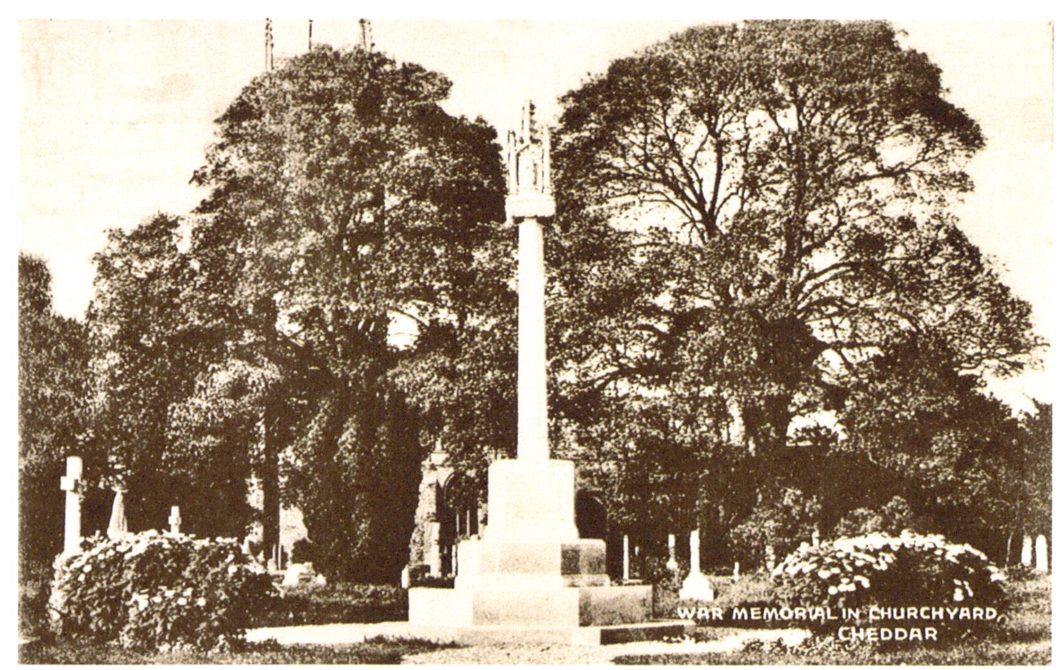

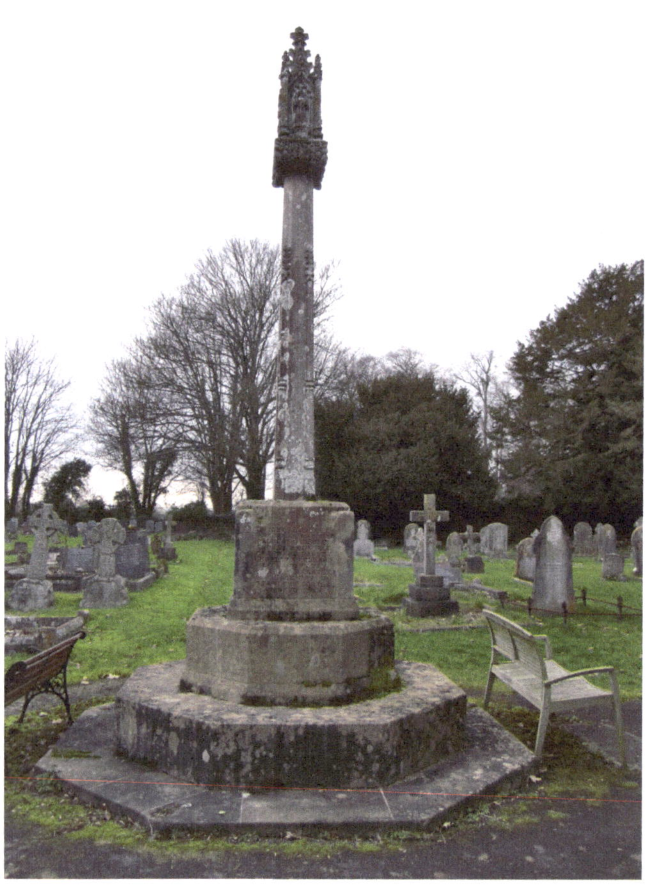

Memorial

A memorial to the 'Men of Cheddar' who fell in the First World War can be found in St Andrew's churchyard. This has a closed lantern cross mounted on a tapering stone column set on a square plinth, and it is decorated with carvings depicting St Michael, St George, the Virgin and Child, and Christ's Crucifixion.

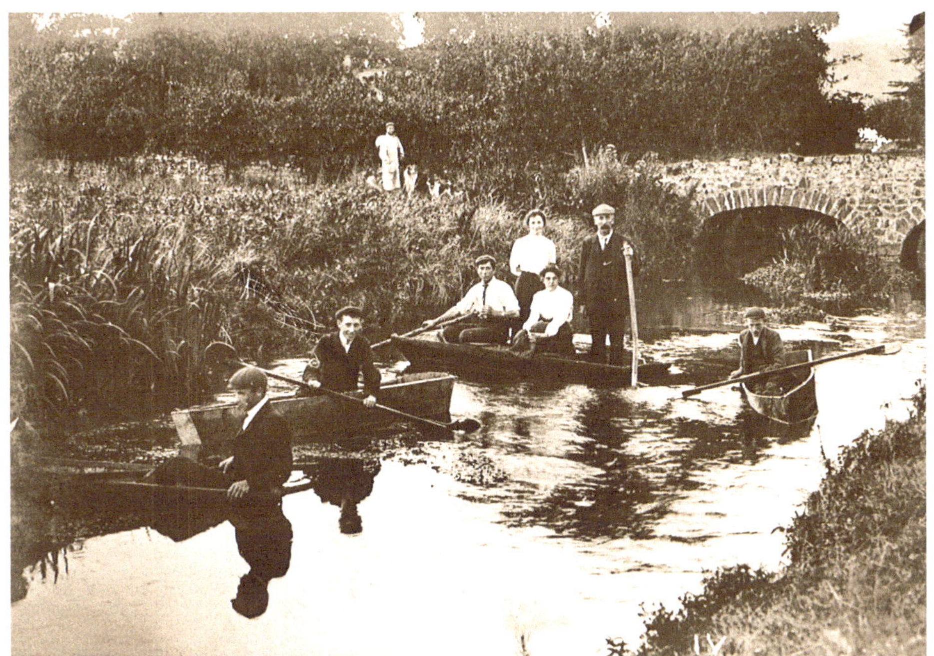

The Cheddar Yeo

Unlike its immediate surroundings, the Cheddar Yeo and its packhorse bridge directly behind St Andrew's church remain largely unchanged. The party of people in the earlier photograph, taken *c.* 1905, are afloat in wooden canoes and a punt. They include several members of the Hill family, residents of Cheddar. Since their photograph was taken, a 'gypsy caravan' has found a permanent home on the bank.

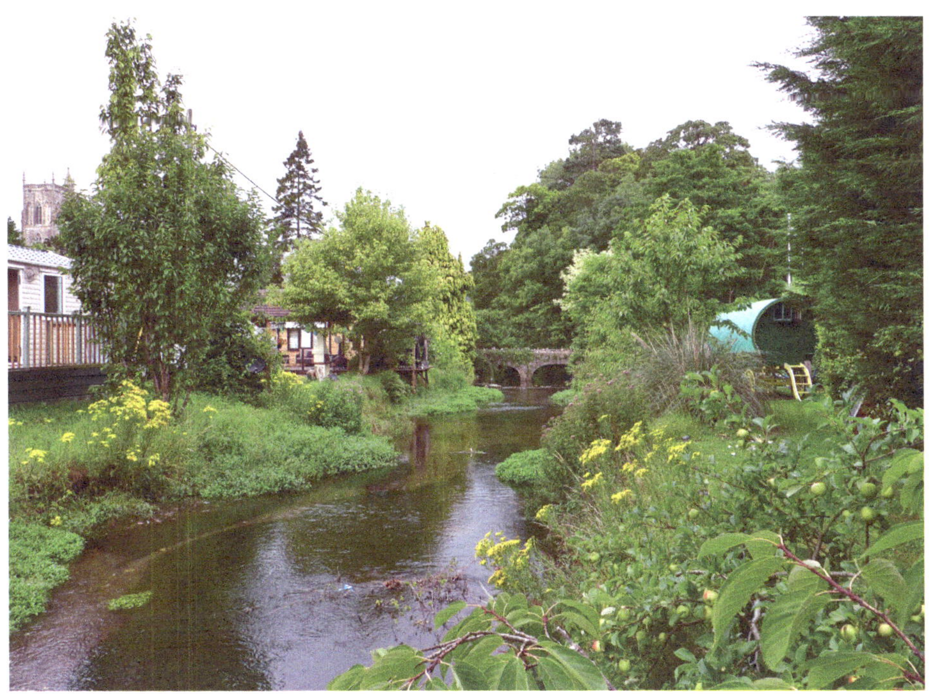

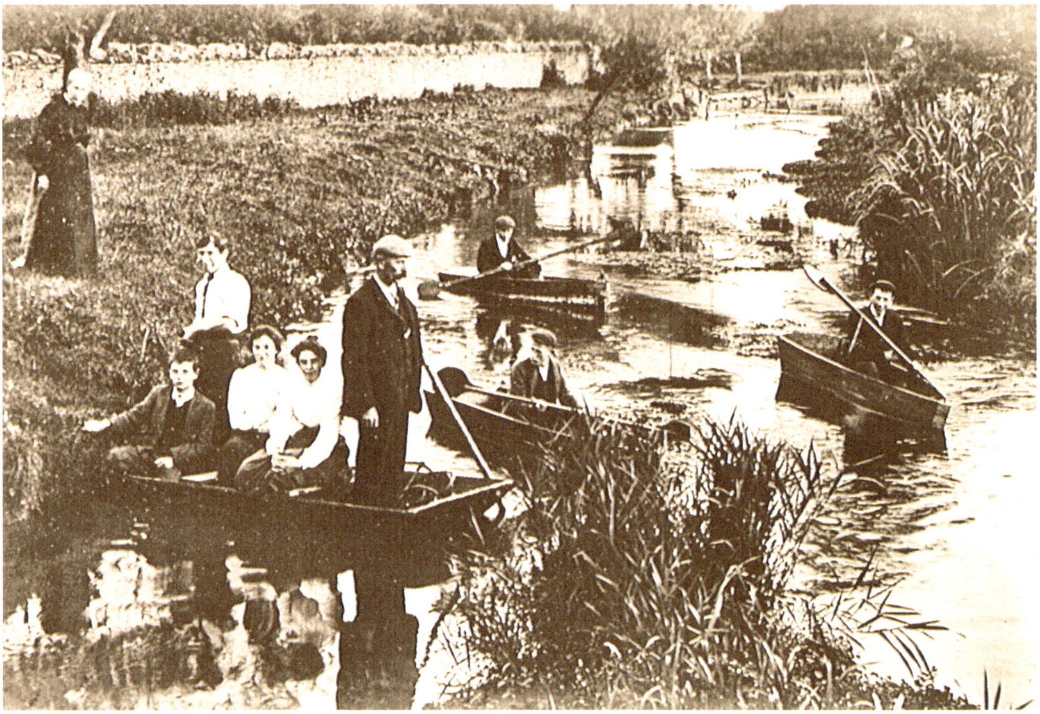

Boating on the Yeo

In this picture the same boating party is photographed in a setting looking along the Yeo away from Church Bridge. The land adjacent to the river on the right now houses the Cheddar Bridge Touring Park. Beyond it is St Andrew's church.

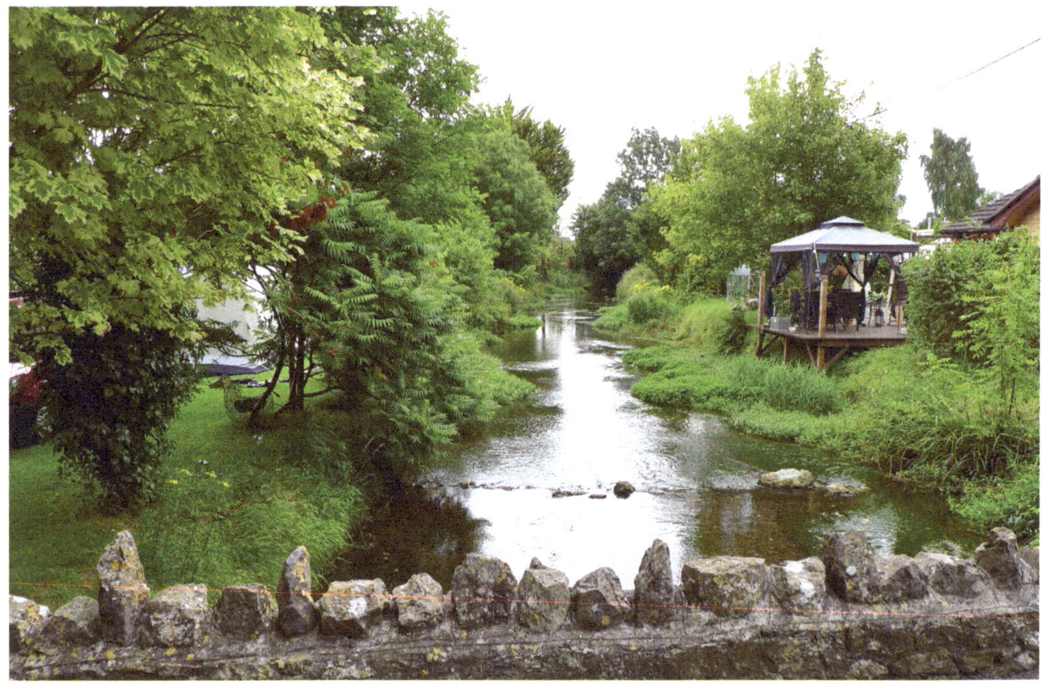

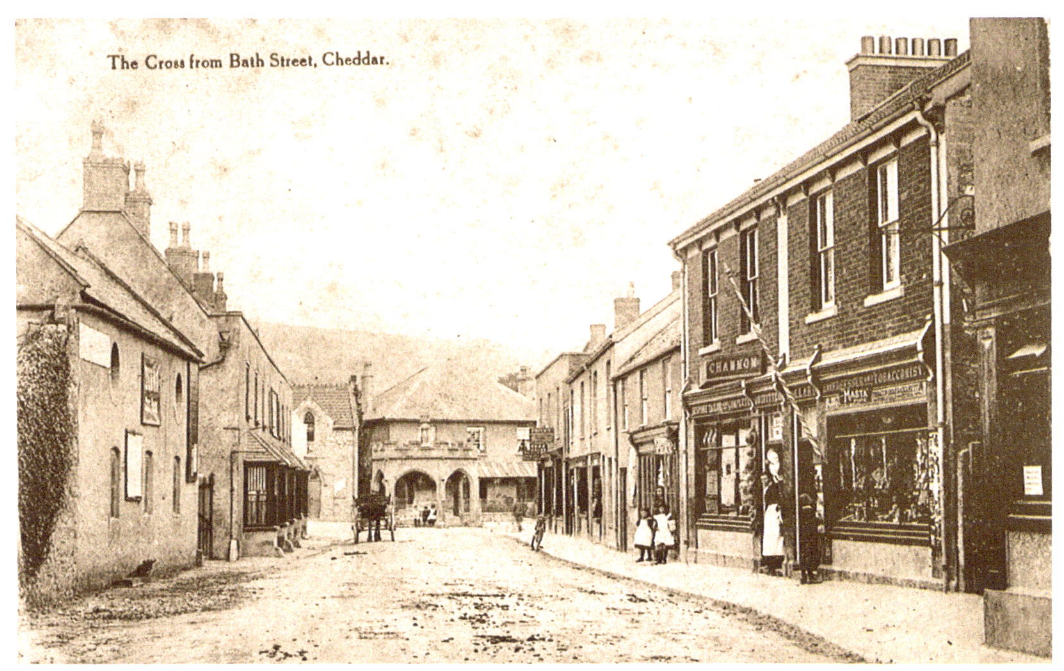

Bath Street

Returning to the Market Cross, Bath Street – which runs to the west – remains the commercial heart of the village of Cheddar. The buildings on the right are largely unchanged. The buildings at the end of Bath Street on the left were the former premises of the Bath Arms Hotel, demolished when the hotel was rebuilt in the 1930s. Adjacent to the hotel is a property that served as a store for an auctioneer.

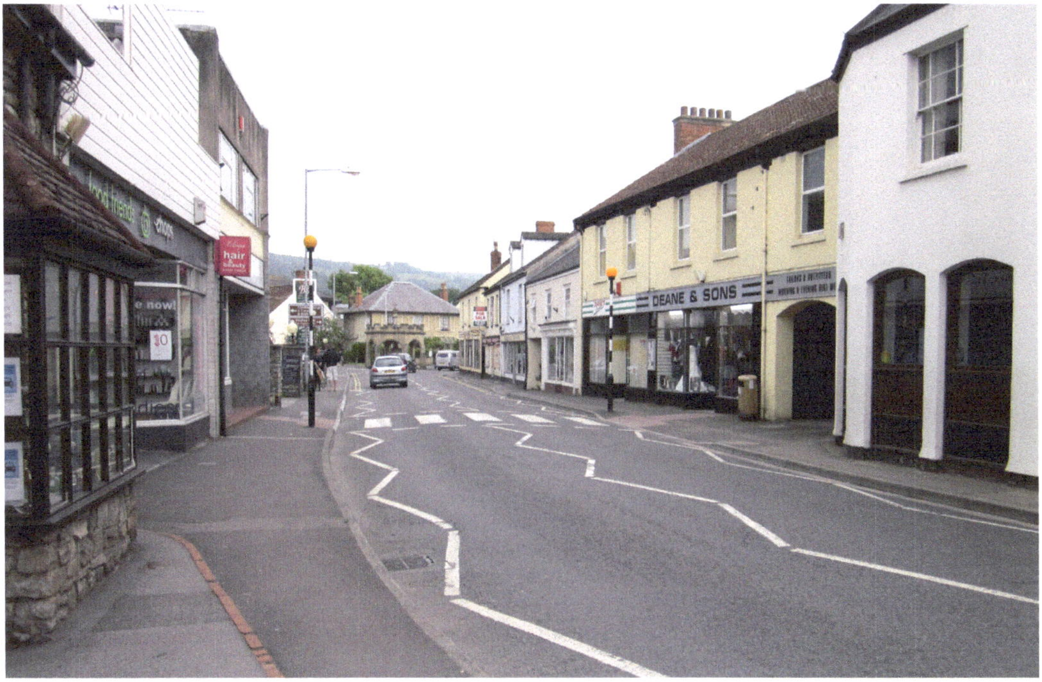

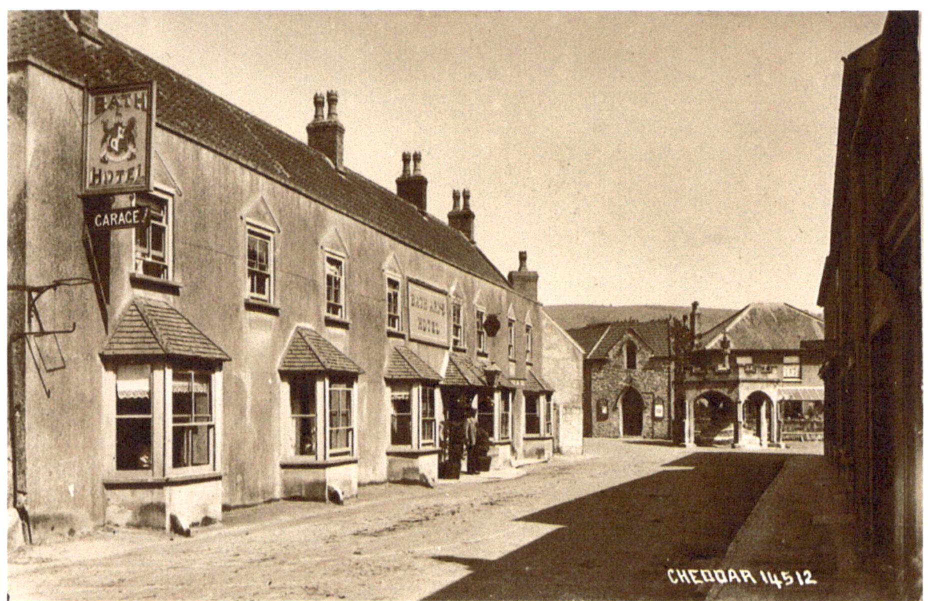

The Tragic Story of Charles Tyley

The present car park for the Bath Arms Hotel replaces the earlier buildings and, presumably the hotel grounds behind. Of these Nicola Sly has related the tragic story of Charles Tyley who died in 1878, aged twenty-nine: 'The son of a prosperous farmer in Cheddar, he had inherited some property on his father's death and, according to the contemporary newspapers, had somewhat largely indulged in stimulants for a few days [...]. For his own safety, Tyley was placed in the care of his brother-in-law, Joseph Pavey [...]. However, at three o'clock in the morning, Tyley managed to escape. His body was found late the following afternoon in the gardens of the Bath Arms Hotel [...]. Tyley apparently scaled the 8ft-high wall separating the hotel from the road but had fallen from the top, landing face down. When found, his nostrils were filled with earth; it was believed that he had stunned himself when he fell and was suffocated by the garden soil.' (Sly N (2010) *A Grim Almanac of Somerset*)

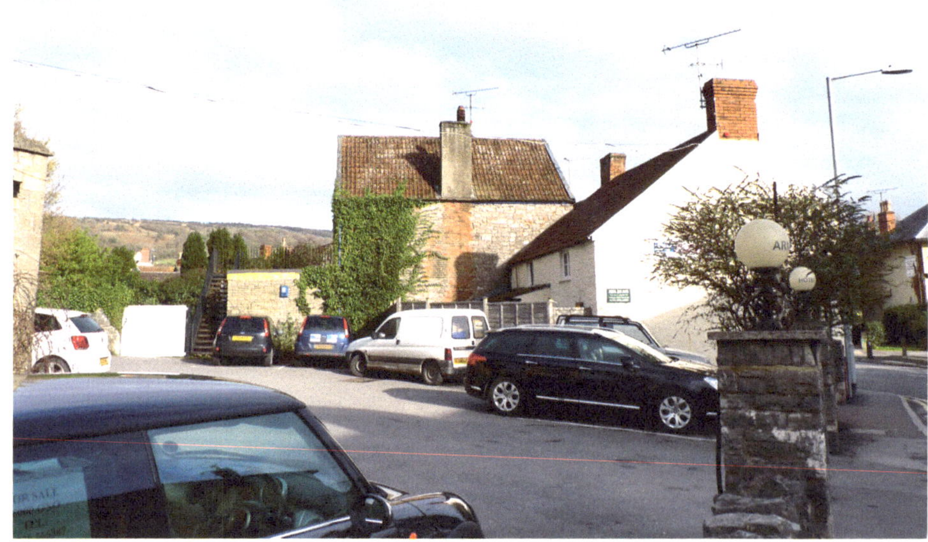

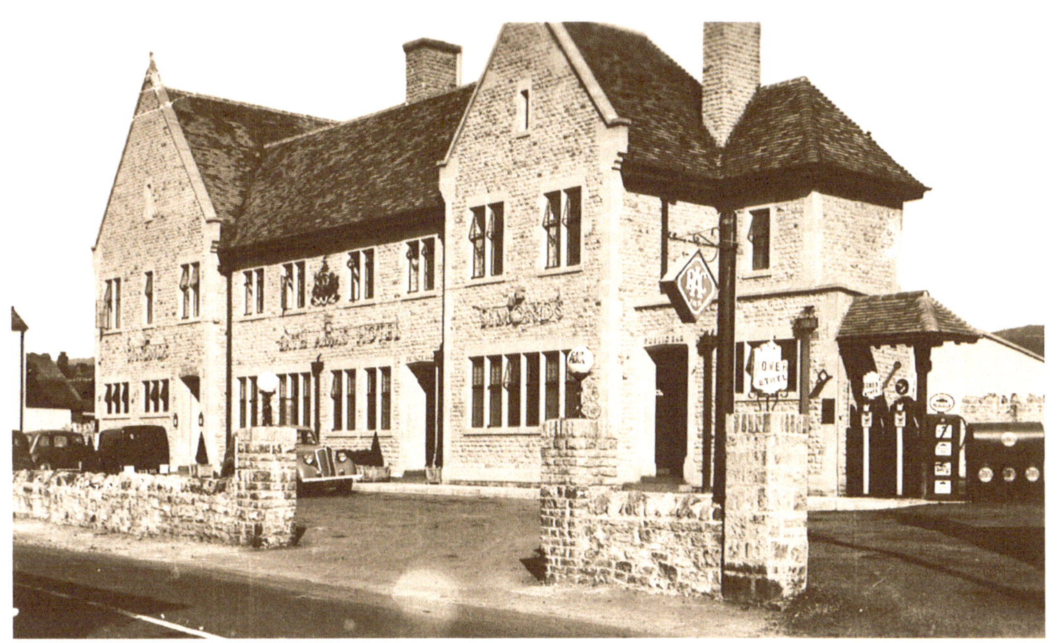

The Bath Arms

The scene of a political riot in 1892, when its windows were smashed by an angry crowd in pursuit of the Radical candidate it was sheltering, the Bath Arms was rebuilt in the late 1930s. Canopies have been added and the 1940s petrol pumps have long since been removed. Famous visitors in the past include Hannah More, the romantic poets – Coleridge and Southey – and King George VI. The 'Bath' in its name refers to Lord Bath after whom the pub was renamed in 1830 in recognition of his commissioning the restoration of the nearby Market Cross; prior to this it was known as 'The George' or 'The George and Dragon'.

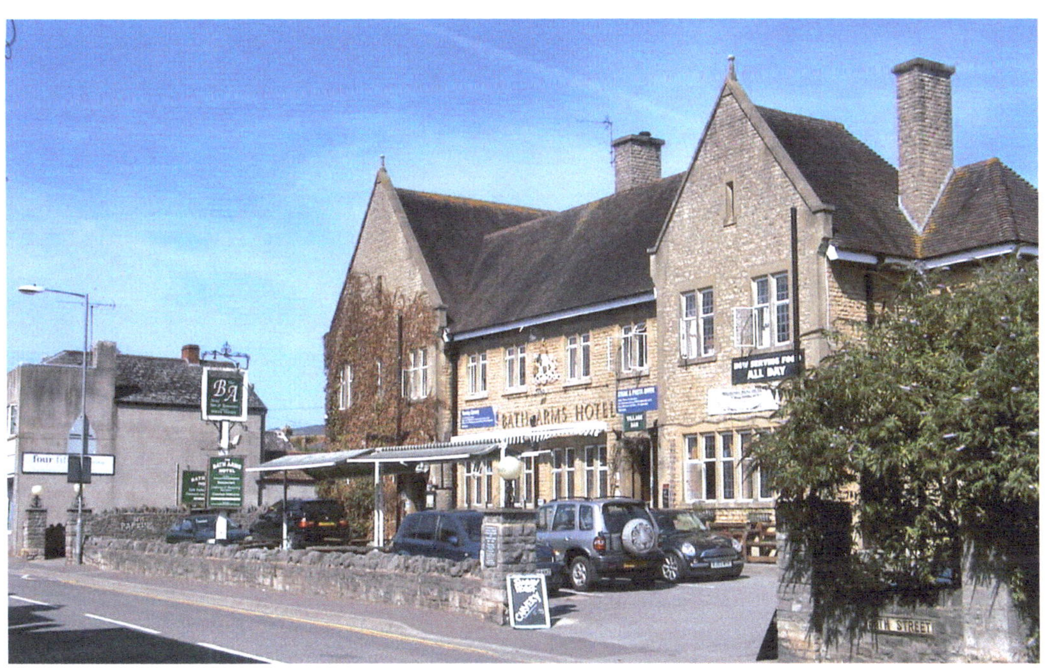

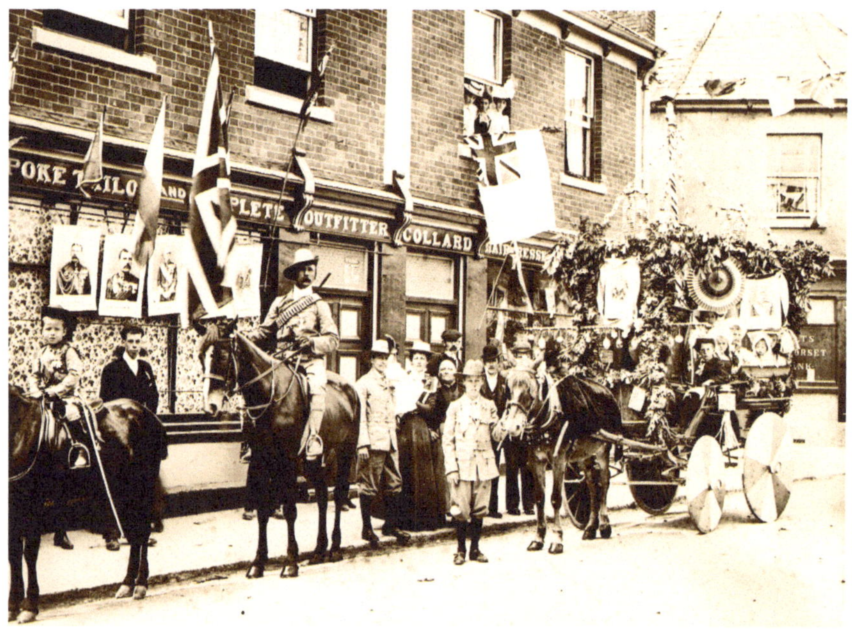

Relief of Mafeking

This early photograph here records a parade along Bath Street to celebrate the relief of Mafeking, besieged for several months during the Boer War, on 19 May 1900. The parade culminated in a thanksgiving service held at St Andrew's church. The uniformed rider is Robert Channon, grandfather of Rex Thomas who provided the image. The buildings behind the procession were largely unaltered in the following century. Channons, the tailors, was open until fairly recently. The Wiltshire & Dorset Bank has become the National Westminster Bank. The 1900 photograph was taken by Mr C. H. Collard who was a professional photographer as well as a hairdresser. His hairdressing premises can be seen in the picture; they are now occupied by Deane & Son.

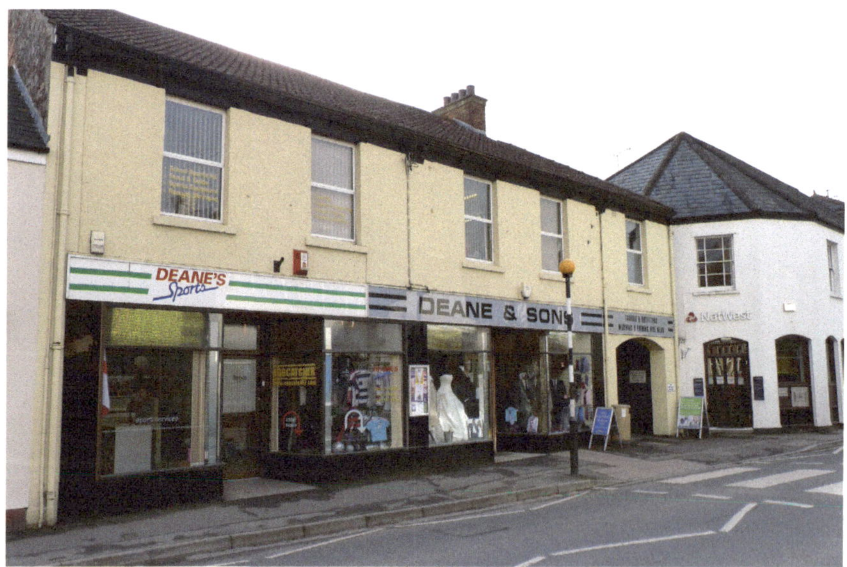

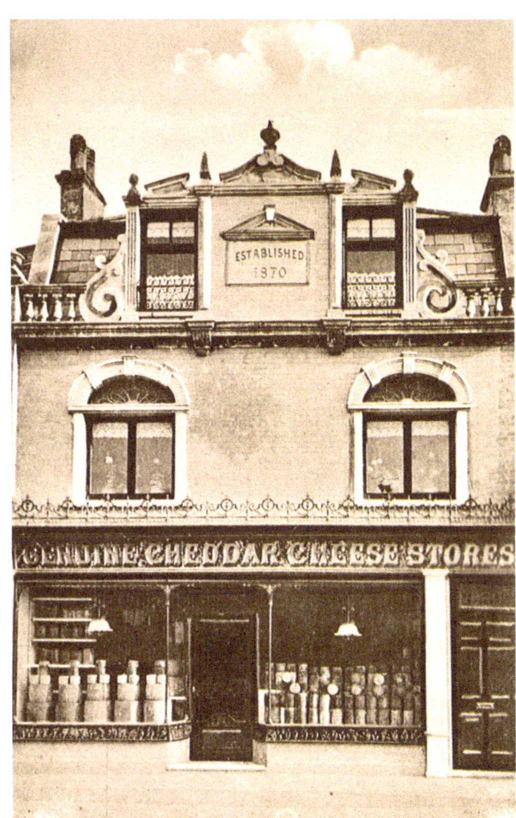

Mr Small

Mr Small, Cheddar's main purveyor of Cheddar cheese at the end of the nineteenth century, had a substantial and ornate shop in Bath Street. The premises are now occupied by a shop selling second-hand items for a local charity.

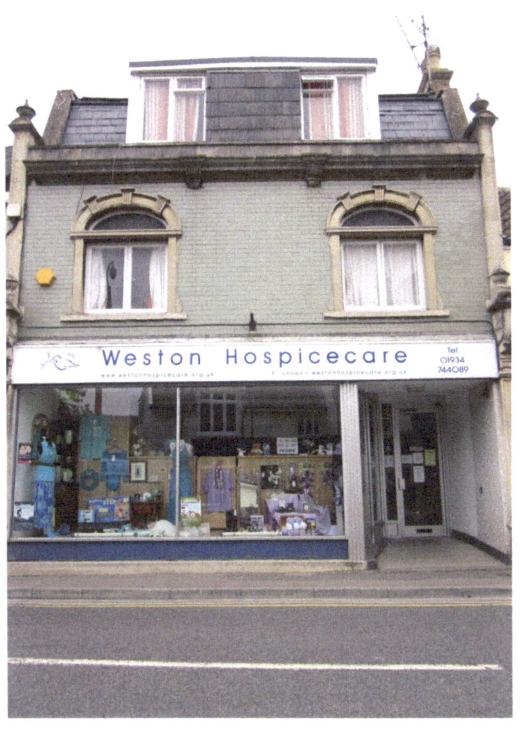

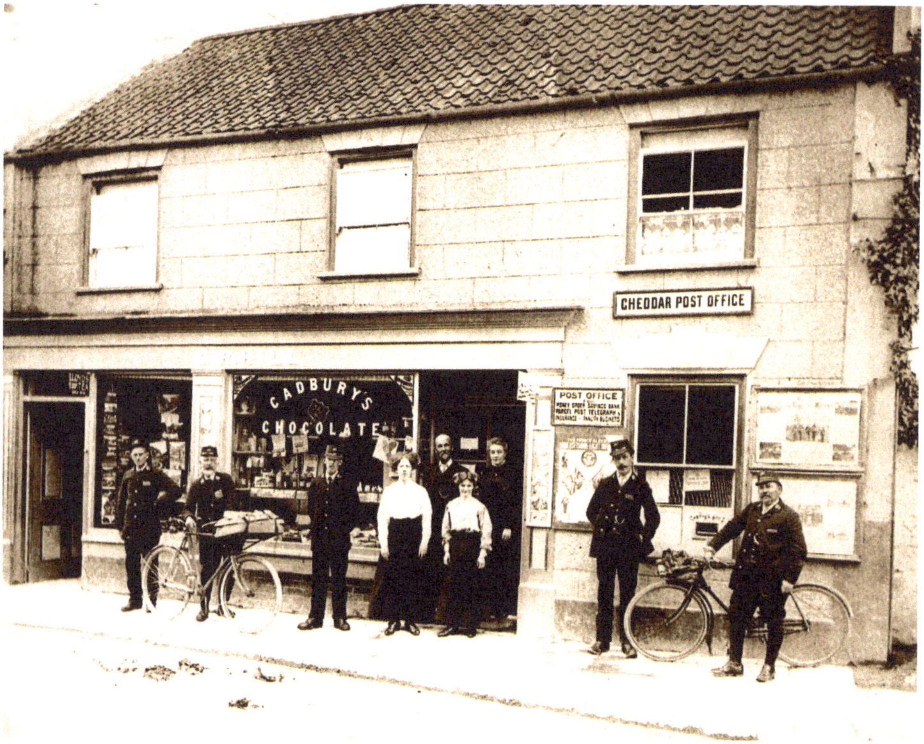

Cheddar's Post Office

Cheddar's post office has occupied the same premises in Bath Street since *c.* 1860.

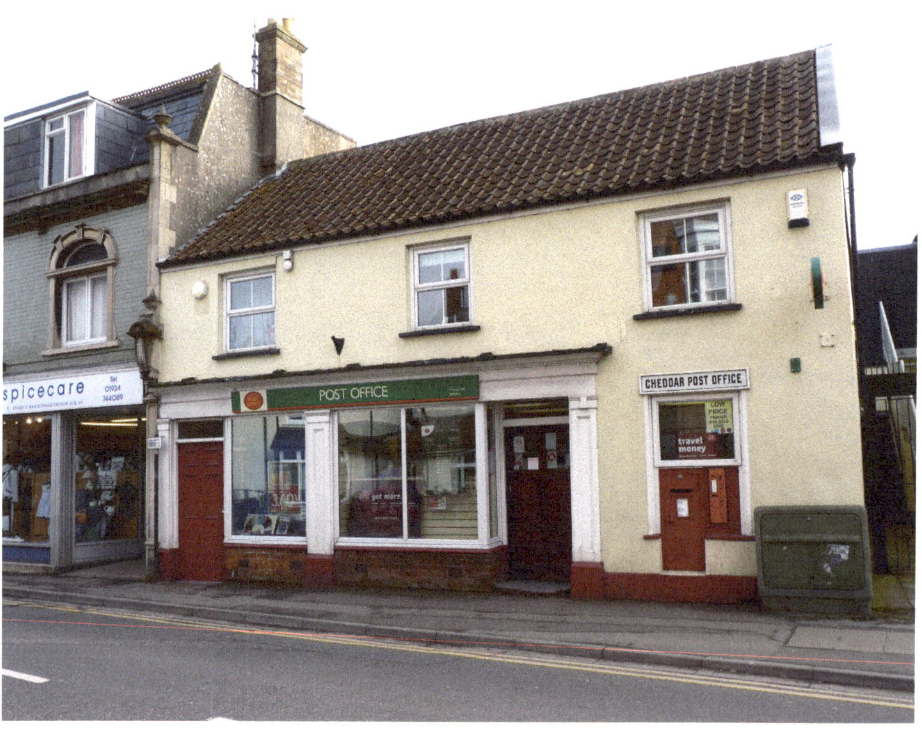

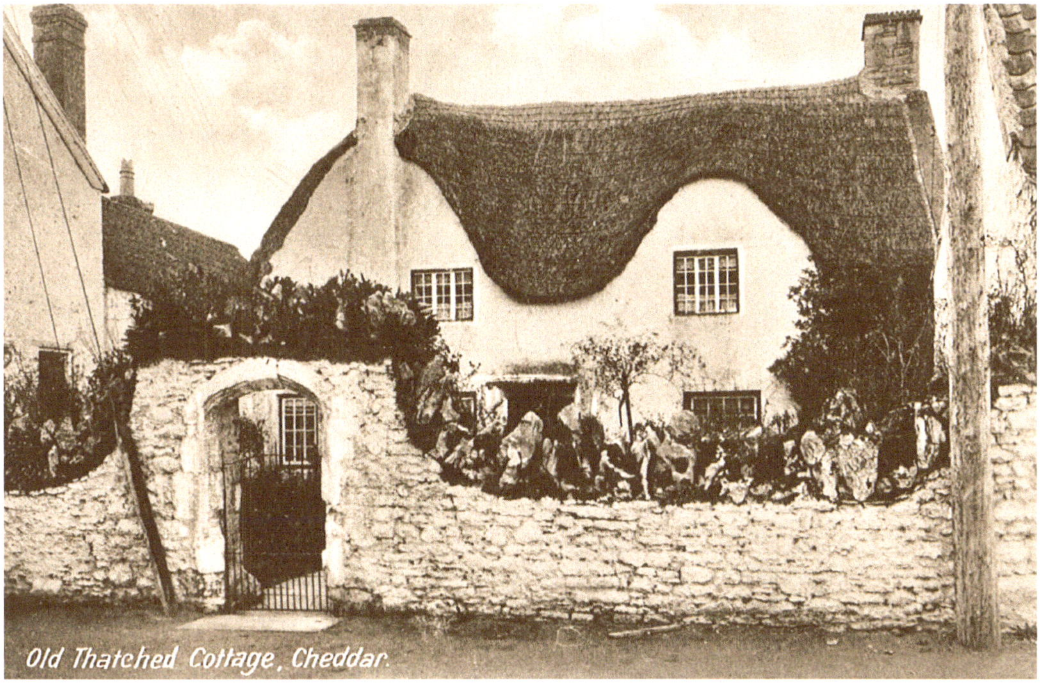

Old Thatched Cottage, Cheddar.

Dare House

The charming cottage, now replaced by an ugly, utilitarian shop, is Dare House and it stood next door to the post office. It was built by James Dare, owner of the *Western Mercury* newspaper. It was demolished around 1950.

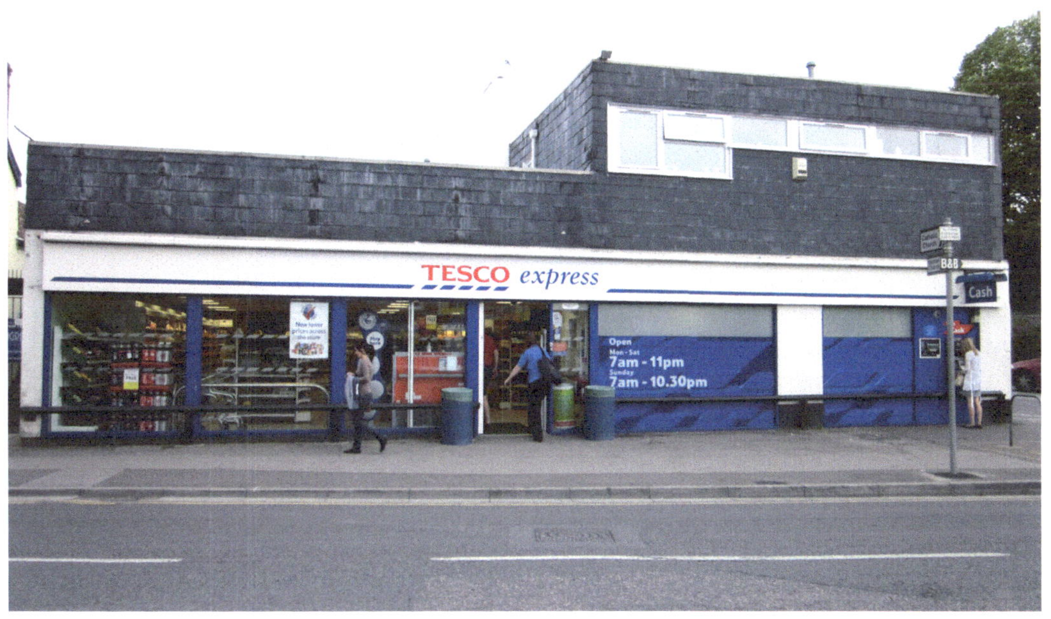

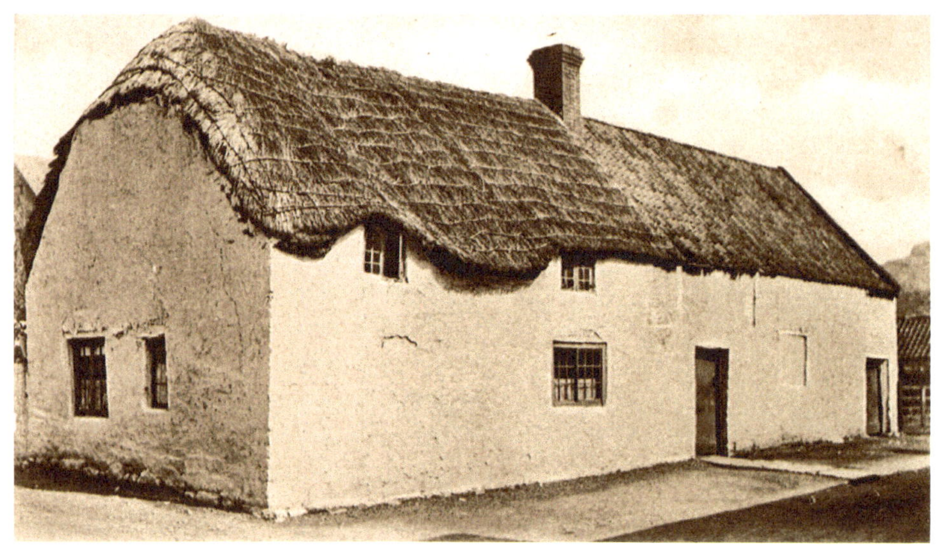

Hannah More's Cottage

In Lower North Street, which runs off to the right at the end of Bath Street, can be found one of Cheddar's most historically significant buildings – Hannah More's Cottage. The original cottage structure is the end adjacent to the road. The farther end was an extension of housing educational pioneer Hannah More's schoolroom on the site of an earlier shed for oxen. The school for the poorer children of the village was endowed by More's friend, the anti-slave-trade campaigning MP, Sir William Wilberforce. When the Sunday school first opened in 1789 – just nine years after Thomas Raikes had opened the first one in Gloucester – 140 children attended the opening day, which was celebrated with a service at St Andrew's church. The attractive thatched roof of the older part of the building, as elsewhere in the village, has been replaced with tiles in more recent times. Since 1953 it has been owned by the parish council and it is used for meetings by various local organisations. The earlier photograph appears on a postcard, which was stamped on 2 October 1909.

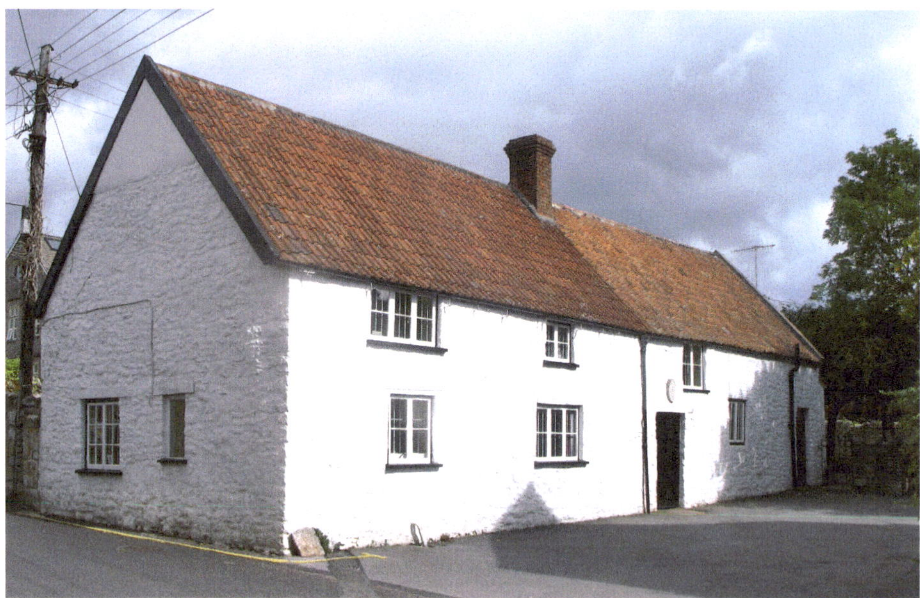

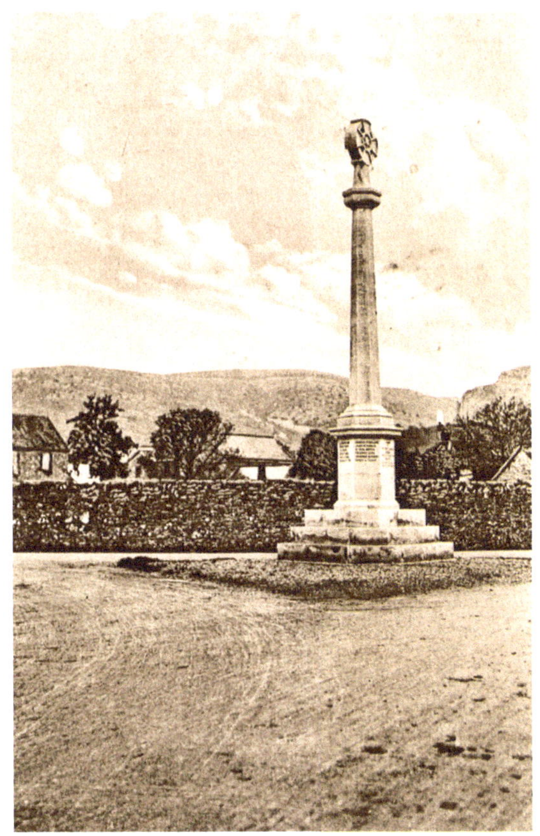

'Ye Who Live On...'

Bath Street runs into Station Road, formally called Play Street or Plas Street, possibly because of its close proximity to the site of Cheddar's famous Saxon 'palace' in the grounds of the Kings of Wessex community school. The war memorial stands at the junction of Station Road and the A371 in Cheddar. In the earlier photograph, the names of those who fell in the First World War are carved into a hexagonal column. The postcard is inscribed 'Ye who live on 'mid English pastures green, Remember us, and think what might have been.' The recent picture shows the subsequent addition of brass plates carrying the names of the dead of both World Wars. The area has gradually become more built up where the war memorial stands.

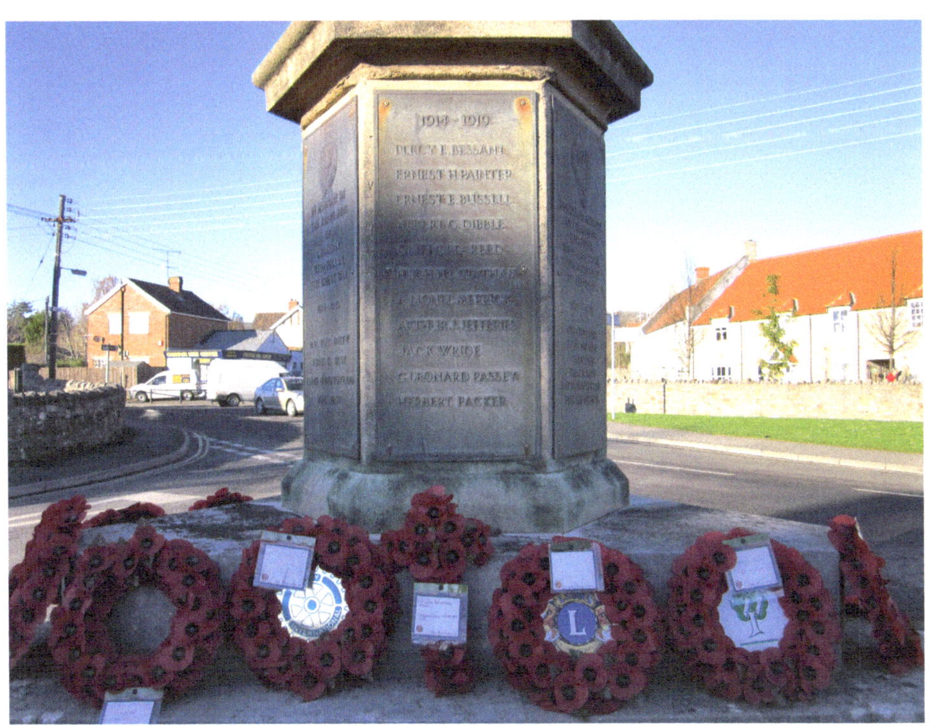

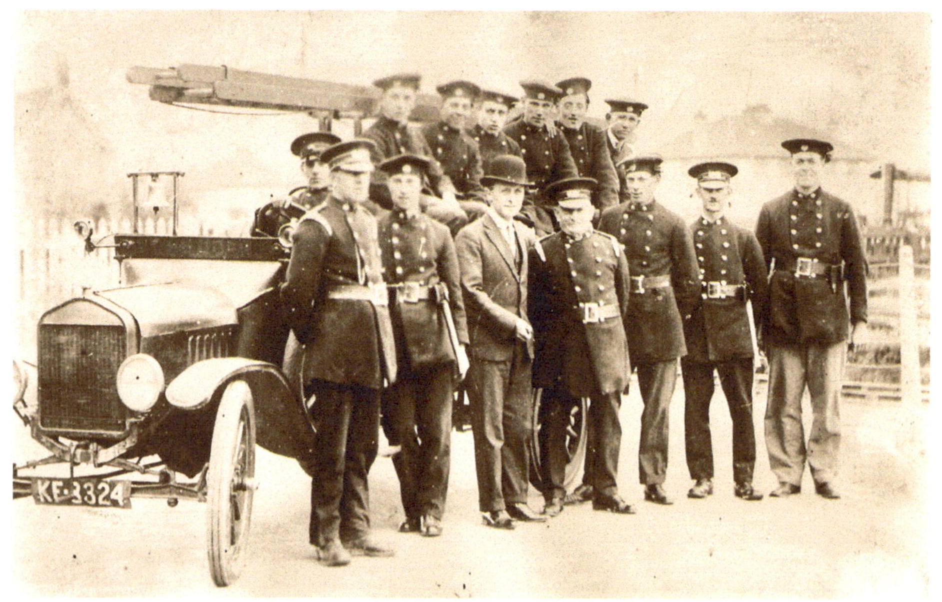

The Fire Station

Where Station Road meets Wideatts Road (identified as 'Widgett's Lane' on the 1902 Ordnance Survey map) can be found The Hayes, along which are sited three important community buildings. Cheddar's fire station, a couple of hundred yards up the Hayes, on the right, was built in 1936. Its roof was specially designed to amplify the sound of its siren, giving warning of air raids in the Second World War. The firemen in the photograph above (*c.* 1930) are standing in front of their Leyland fire engine. To the right is part of the main station building where the engine was housed until the building of the fire station a few years later. Cheddar has had its own fire brigade since 1906. In 1906 it comprised a captain, a lieutenant and ten officers.

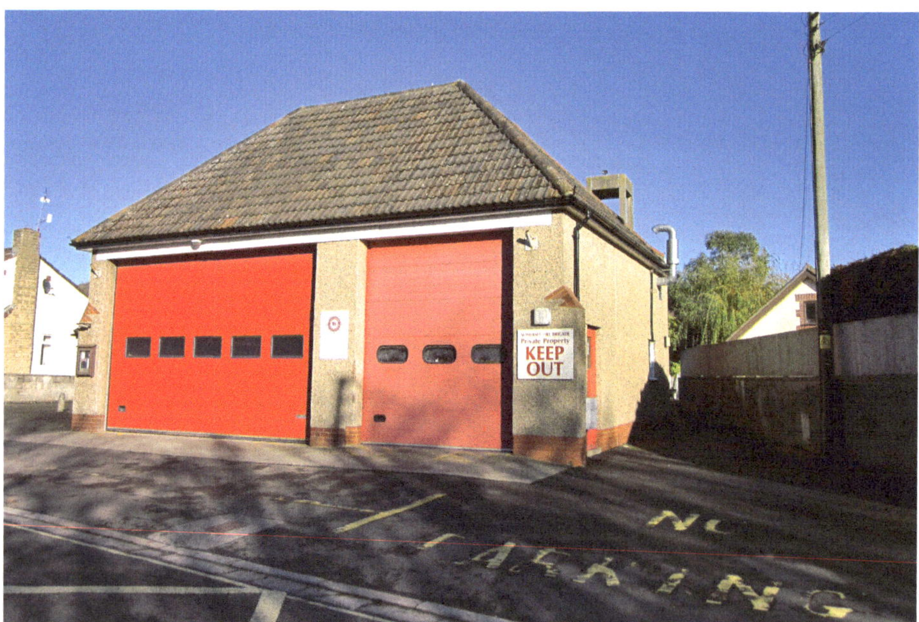

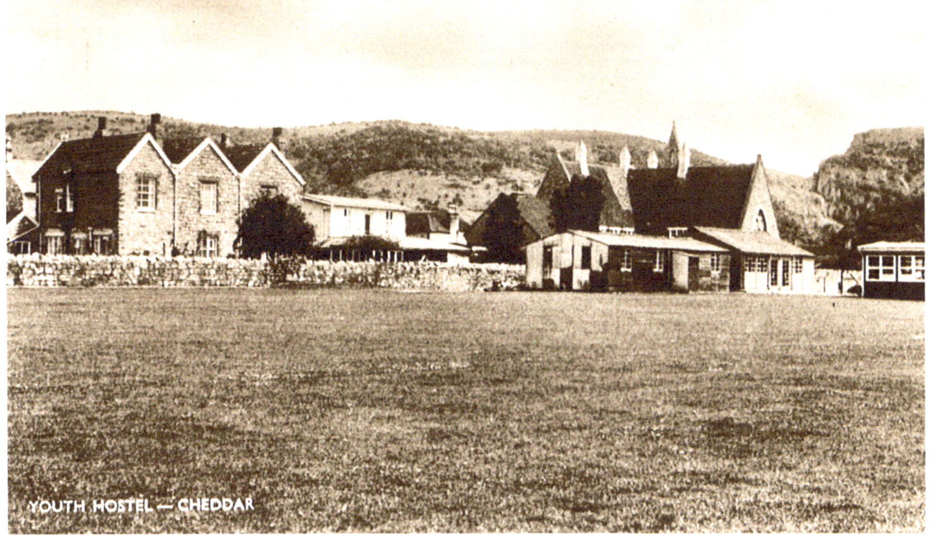

The British School

Cheddar's British School, just over the road from the Fire Station, was established in 1872; shortly after the 1870 Education Act introduced secular rate-supported elementary schools. On opening it had seventy-two pupils. The village's infant school, Cheddar First School, occupies the surviving buildings of the original structure. The older picture shown here dates from around 1905.

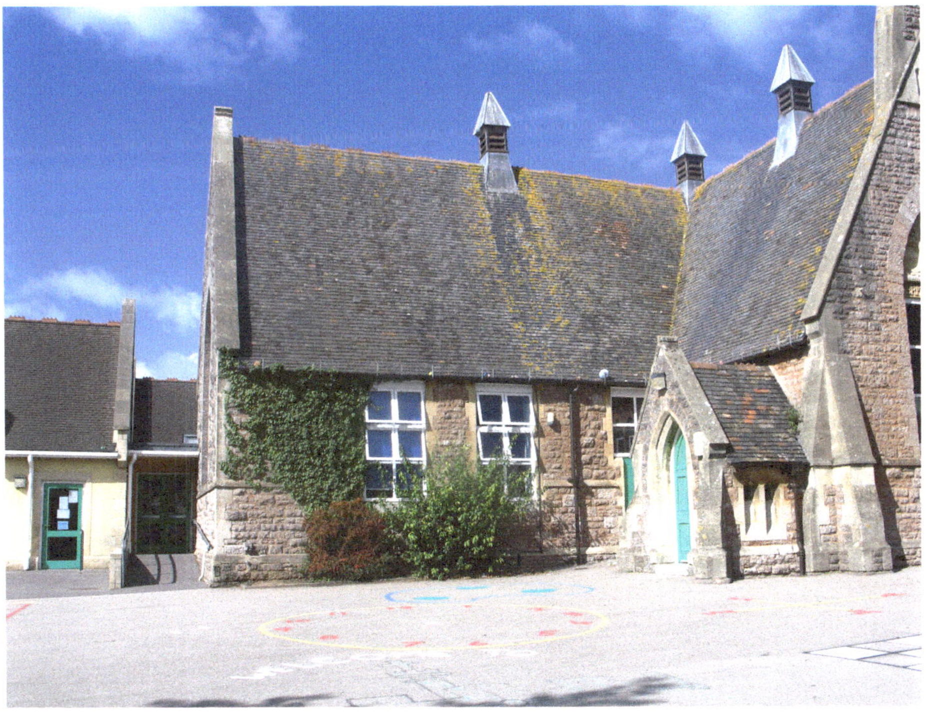

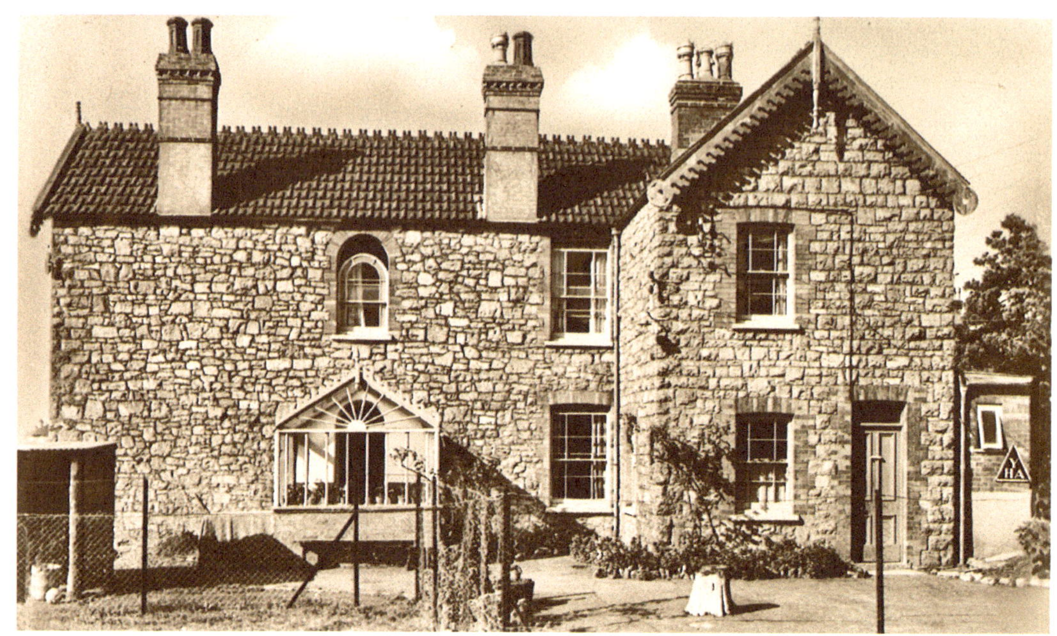

Hillfield

'Hillfield', Cheddar's Youth Hostel, which is located directly behind Cheddar First School, continues to occupy the same Victorian premises shown in the earlier photograph. Although the interior has been modernised and several ancillary structures have appeared in its grounds, essentially the building is unaltered.

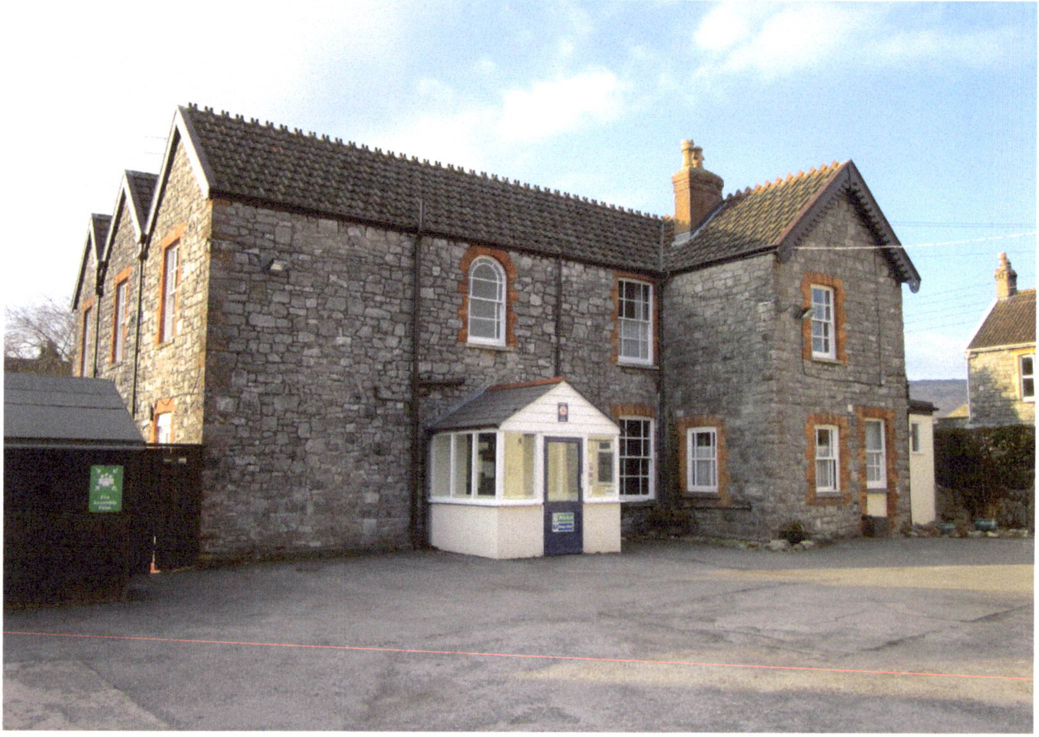

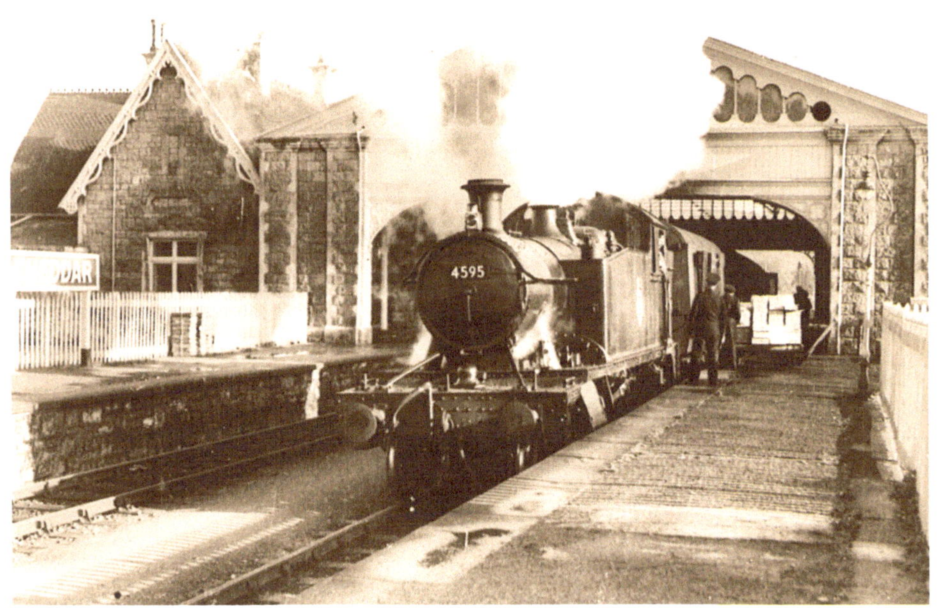

The Railway Station

Returning to the A371, between Wideatts Road and Station Road are the largely intact remains of the old railway station. Cheddar's station was opened in 1869 by the Bristol & Exeter Railway Company, which became part of the Great Western Railway in 1876. The new station boasted a roof built to a design by Isambard Kingdom Brunel. The engine in the archive picture is a Prairie type, one of 175, built sometime before 1930.

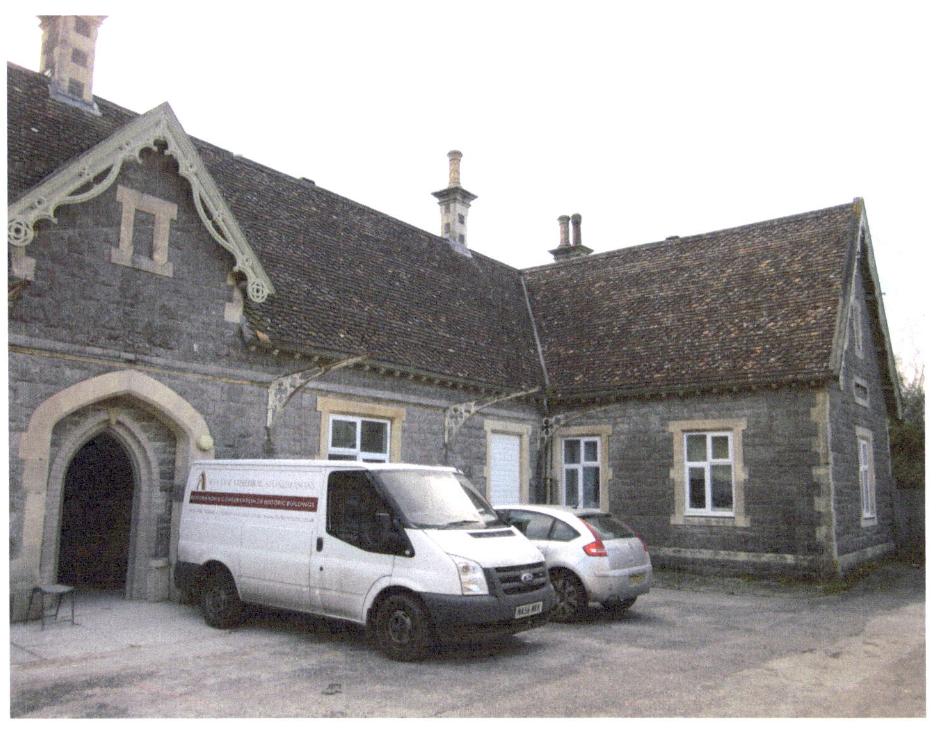

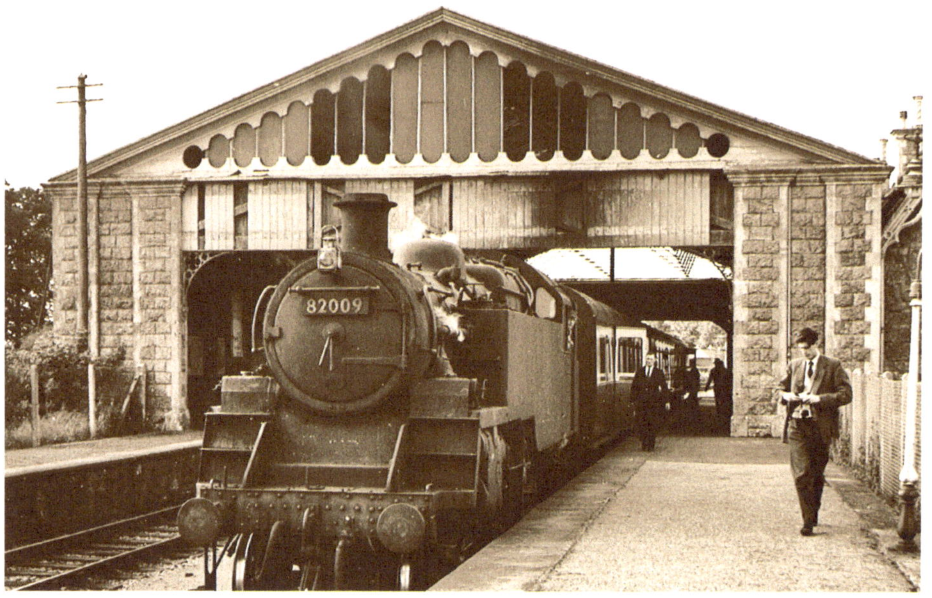

Cheddar's Railway

Although Cheddar's railway carried passengers, mostly pupils of Wells Cathedral School and Wells Blue School, and light goods, including, of course, strawberries, most of its carriage was that of heavy goods – stone from the Batts Combe and Crow Catchpole quarries and lime produced by the Carrow Rock Lime Company. By 1886, it was laying on five passenger trains a day to carry tourists to the view the famous sites at both Cheddar and Wells. The stationmaster's house is now a private residential property with the name 'Station House'. The engine shown in this archive photograph is BR Standard Class 4 Tank, one of 155 built between 1951 and 1957.

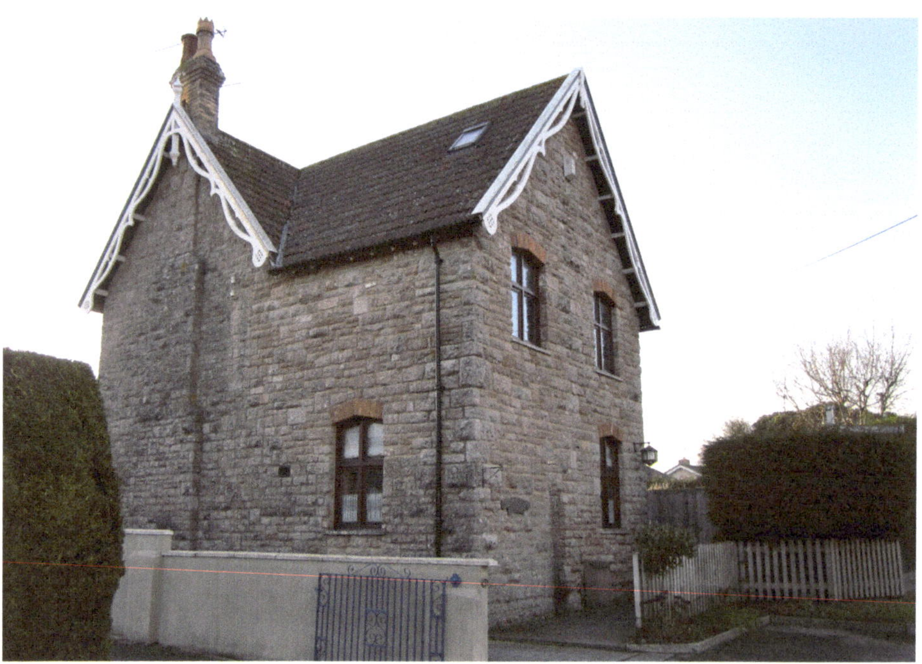

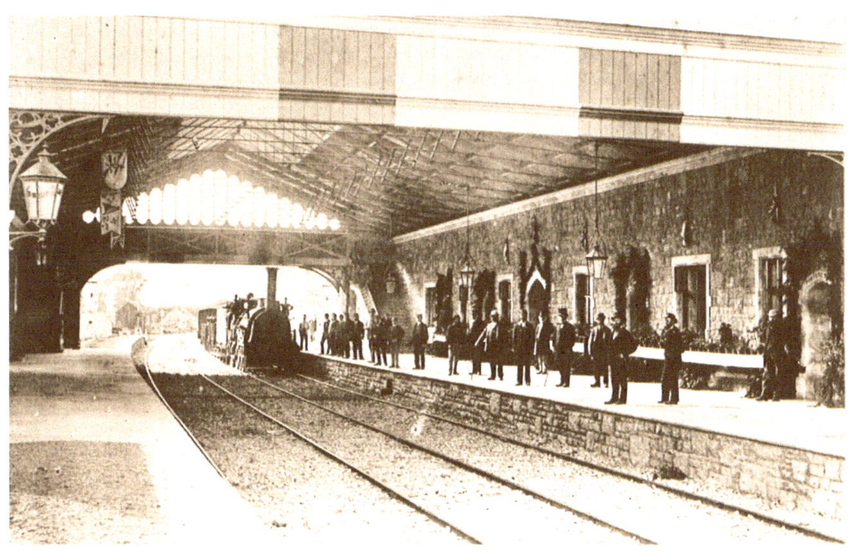

Wells Cathedral Stonemasons

At the time of the official opening of the line a Bristol newspaper commented: 'At Cheddar the directors were invited into the station where an elegant refection of cake and champagne was prepared for their refreshment. The vicar said he was deputed to welcome them to Cheddar. In his opinion the main cause of the prosperity of the railway was that the directors were a God-fearing body (*hear, hear*). They had not run on the Lord's Day those monster excursion trains by which the people were demoralised. He wished them all success for their line (*loud applause*). Several bottles of champagne were then opened and the usual toasts were drunk without stint.' (Coysh A. W., Mason E. J., Waite V. (1954) *The Mendips*, Robert Hale, p. 125) Since 1984 the station has been home to Wells Cathedral Stonemasons, specialists in the restoration and conservation of historic buildings for over thirty years.

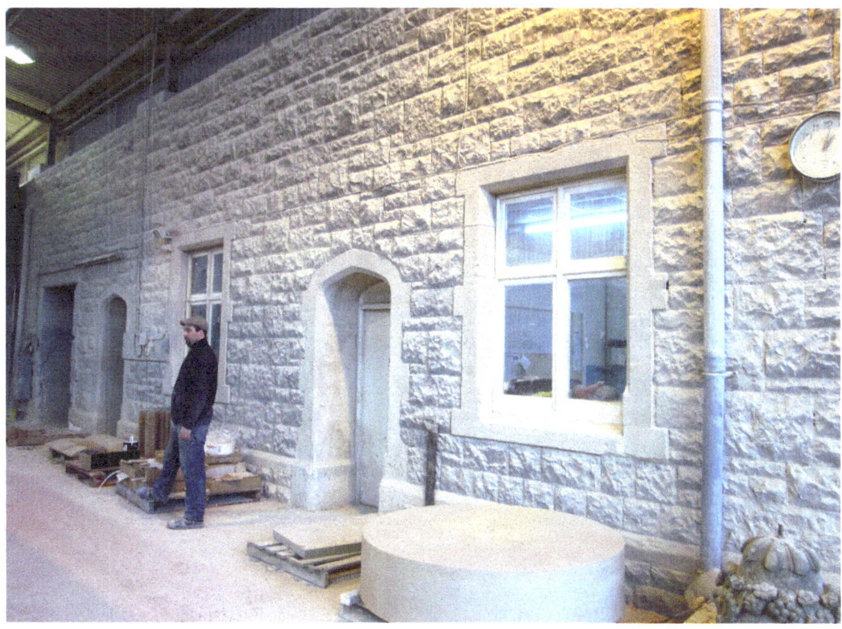

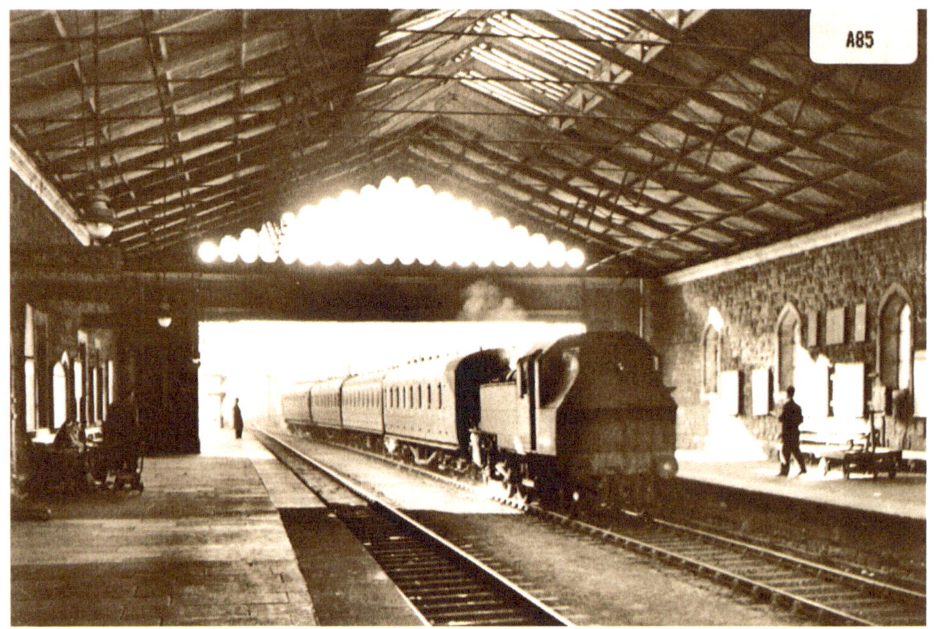

Cheddar's Railway History

Although the rails have long since been lifted, plenty of evidence remains to remind the visitor of Cheddar's railway history including this bridge. Shortly after its opening a Bristol newspaper reported: 'Leaving the main line at Yatton the branch proceeds through nearly ten miles of the most beautiful and picturesque scenery of mid-Somerset. The making of the track for a considerable part of the route has been comparatively easy; the natural level of the valley has been followed as much as possible, and the line passes over and under some half a dozen bridges in its course.' (Coysh A. W., Mason E. J., Waite V. (1954) *The Mendips*, Robert Hale, p. 125)

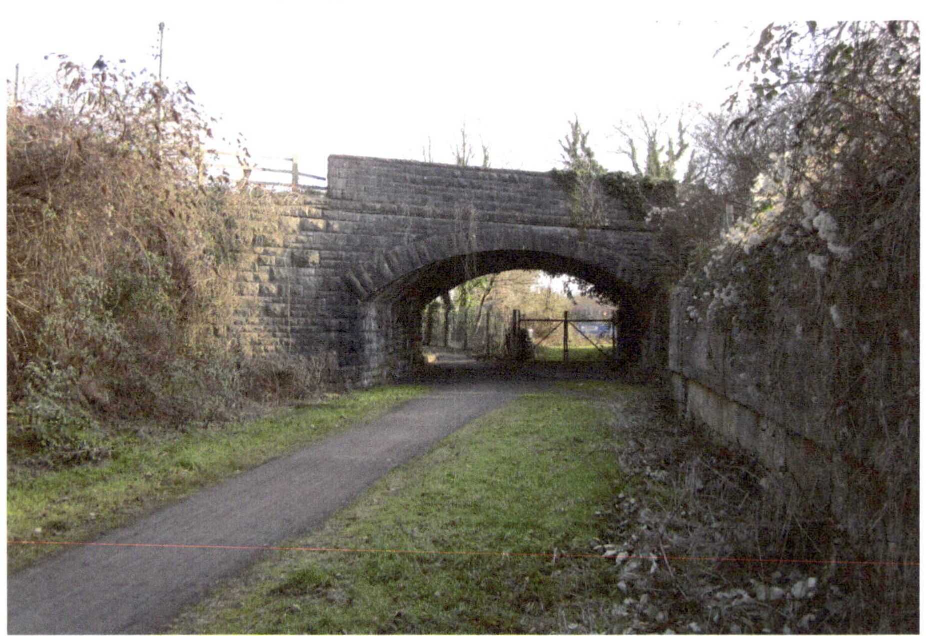

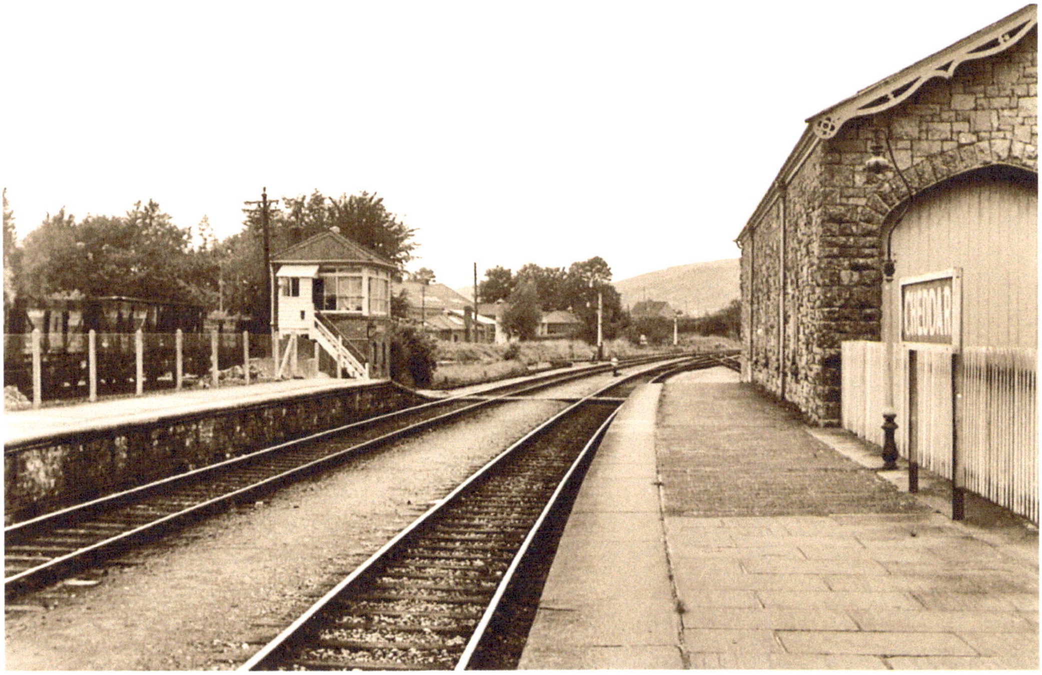

Sustran's Campaign and the Steam Club

The 'Strawberry Line' is the target of a concerted 'Sustrans' campaign to provide an attractive route for walkers and a safe cycling path all the way from Cranmore near Shepton Mallet (where steam trains still run) to Clevedon, via Cheddar. Parts of it are already accessible and a cycle ride or stroll past the reservoir to Axbridge provides a very pleasant excursion on a warm day. Steam locomotion is not altogether a thing of the past in Cheddar – a thriving Steam Club in Sharpham Road, between the station and the reservoir, boasts a 400-yard model railway track in 32mm and 45mm, and a decent sized lake for model steam boats.

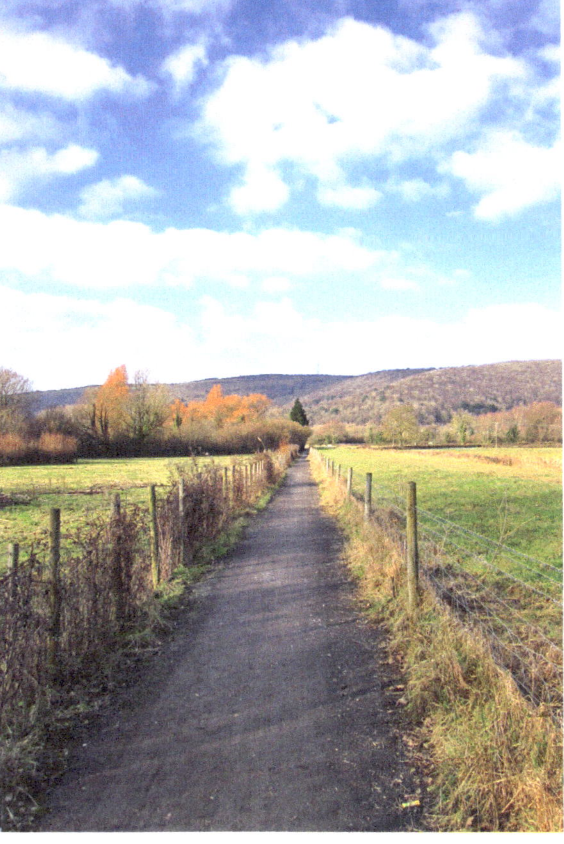

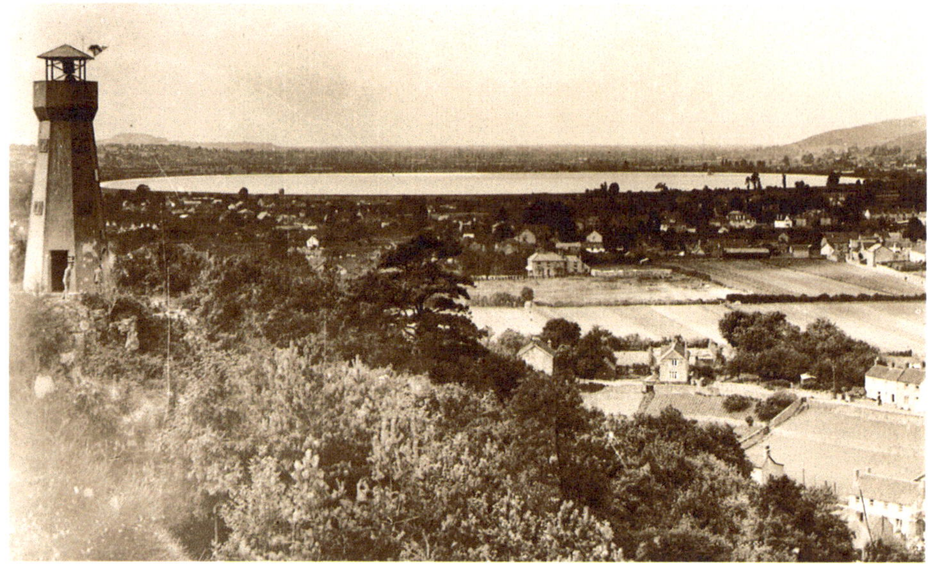

Axbridge Reservoir

A little way along the Cheddar–Axbridge cycleway lies, to the left, Cheddar's great circular reservoir, also known as Axbridge Reservoir. It was opened in 1938 to supply Bristol and remains a significant and important feature in the Cheddar landscape. It is supplied by water from the springs supplying the Yeo River in Cheddar Gorge. Members and guests of the Bristol Corinthian Yacht Club have sailed upon it since 1947 when it became the first water supply reservoir to be used for this form of recreation. It attracts numerous visitors including wind surfers, fishermen, walkers, cyclists, and, as a designated Site of Special Scientific Interest, bird watchers are drawn by its great variety of wildfowl in winter. Discussions are ongoing for the building of an adjacent second reservoir of a similar size. The archive photograph is taken from the ridge at the top of Jacob's Ladder.

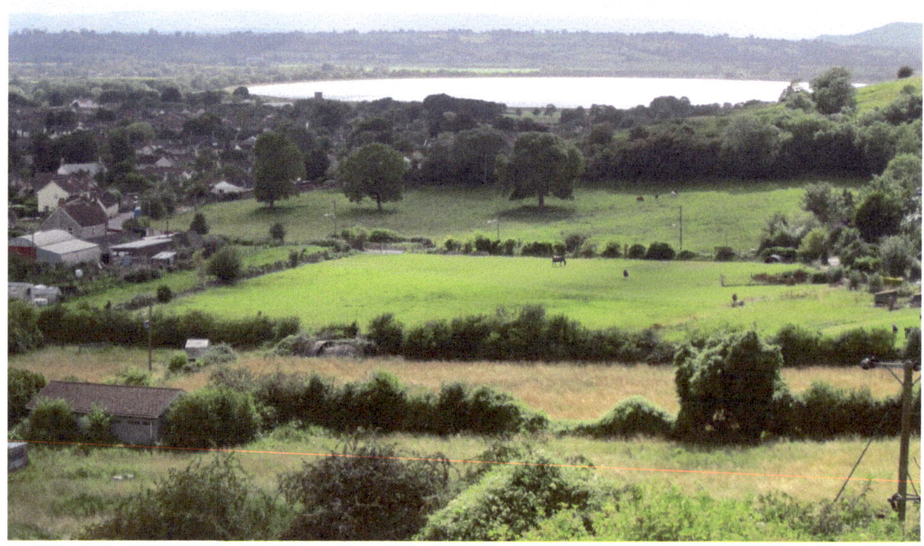

Printed and bound by CPI Group (UK) Ltd, Croydon, CR0 4YY
19/07/2026
02171176-0001